The National Rifle Association and the Media

The National Rifle Association and the Media

The Motivating Force of Negative Coverage

by

Brian Anse Patrick

ARKTOS
LONDON 2013

First printed edition published in 2002 by Peter Lang Publishing.
First electronic edition published in 2011 by Goatpower Publishing.
Second printed edition published in 2013 by Arktos Media Ltd.

Copyright © 2013 by Brian Anse Patrick/Goatpower Publishing.

All rights reserved. No part of this book may be reproduced or utilised in any form or by any means (whether electronic or mechanical), including photocopying, recording or by any information storage and retrieval system, without permission in writing from the publisher.

Printed in the United Kingdom.

ISBN **978-1-907166-98-3**

BIC classification:
Political campaigning and advertising (JPVL)
Communication studies (GTC)
Media, information and communication industries (KNT)

Editor: John Morgan
Cover Design: Andreas Nilsson
Layout: Daniel Friberg

Cover photograph: Tom Osswald
Model: Brooke Wagner

ARKTOS MEDIA LTD
www.arktos.com

Table of Contents

Author's Foreword to the Arktos Edition 7
Introduction: The National Rifle Association in America 15
   The NRA and Public Opinion 15
   Political Paradoxes 18
   Substance of the Book 22
   Mobilization Effects of Negative Coverage. 23
   Social Movement Hybridism 24
   A General Theory of Media Bias 25
   Priests of the Information Age 26
   Caveats 27
   Organization of the Book 28

1. The Media of Social Action 30
   Modes of Social Action 30
   Typology of Social Action Theories 31
   Role of Mass Media in Social Action 42

2. Media Coverage Effects and the National Rifle Association 53
   Views on the Nature of NRA Coverage 53
   Effects of Negative Coverage 55
   The NRA as Social Movement 56
   NRA as Pluralistic-Social Movement Hybrid 57

3. Elite Newspaper Coverage of Interest Groups 61
   Elite Newspapers 62
   Measurement of Coverage 64
   Comparisons of Interest Group Coverage 66
   Non-Findings 115
   Caveats 115

4. Anti-Media Theory and National Rifle Association
Communications 117
   NRA Response to Coverage 117
   NRA Official Publications 118
   NRA Official Journal Content 121
   Social Movement Themes 122
   Media Conflict Themes 124
   General Conflict Themes 127
   Science Conflict Themes 128
   Solidarity Themes 129
   Identity Themes 131

Themes on Journal Covers.. 133
The Ideological Trend 135
Media Bias Communications of NRA Officials...................... 137
Institutionalization of Media Bias.................................. 145

5. The Mobilization Effect 149
Negative Coverage and NRA Mobilization 149
Mobilization of Comparable Groups 154
The Universe of NRA Mobilization 156
American Egalitarianism and Gun Culture 160

6. Media Relations: The National Rifle Association Versus the Journalists... 168
NRA Press Relations... 168
Journalists on the NRA 173
Interview Findings 178
Journalistic Trade Publications..................................... 182

7. Administrative Democracy 184
A General Theory of Media Bias.................................... 184
The Priestly Function of Elite Journalists 190
Mass Administrative Democracy................................... 197
Trends to Suppress Heresy... 200
Social Applications.. 202
Hybridism of Social Action Modes 204

Appendix A: The Interest Groups 207
National Rifle Association of America............................... 208
National Association for the Advancement of Colored People........... 209
American Civil Liberties Union..................................... 210
American Association of Retired Persons............................ 210
Handgun Control, Inc./Brady Campaign to Prevent Gun Violence 211

Appendix B: Methodology 213
Content Analysis of Interest Group Coverage 213
NRA Communication Analyses 219
Interviews with Journalists, NRA Officials, and NRA Members 220
Study Limitations... 221

References... 222

Index... 233

Author's Foreword to the Arktos Edition

This is the second print edition of *The National Rifle Association and the Media: The Motivating Force of Negative Coverage*, which reported the results of my doctoral dissertation research at the University of Michigan. The academic publisher Peter Lang originally released the book in 2002. While I am proud of the fact that the first edition can be found in many university libraries and other collections, my hope in releasing this Arktos edition is to make the book's findings more accessible to people of good sense and independent mind, many of whom wouldn't be found near a university if they could help it.

It took a couple of years to do all the research that informs this book. You will find a great deal of useful information between its covers. The heart of the book is a quantitative content analysis of a decade of elite news media coverage of the National Rifle Association compared to that of similar American citizen-membership voluntary associations/interest groups.

Content analysis research methodology developed after the First World War as a tool for quantifying and measuring propaganda and detecting its sources. It moves beyond the limits of inferences based on mere anecdotal or impressionistic data; content analysis allows for statistical comparisons that are highly reliable. It saw extensive use in the Second World War-era and its aftermath, and was even used as damning evidence in espionage trials of foreign agents that were fronting Nazi propaganda via American newspapers under the guise of news.

Content analysis as applied in this book conclusively shows that major American news media have been fronting anti-gun propaganda under the guise of news. This is done by a variety of standard storytelling and propagandistic techniques that are discussed in the book's third chapter.

I am not comparing American journalists to Nazis, although I once heard a frustrated NRA official refer to a *New York Times* reporter as a "jack-booted journalist." The *Times*, on its part, has regularly demeaned NRA. A recent *Times* editorial, for example, refers to NRA's executive director as "wild-eyed" for his "mendacious, delusional, almost deranged rant." NRA has long been the boogeyman of choice for elite reporters and editors, who, virtually every time some vicious degenerate uses a firearm to kill innocent people, blame this highly respectable citizen association of more than four million members for crimes against humanity. They dehumanize these citizens by calling them a "lobby."

Again, based on a reproducible content analysis that has been tested for reliability, elite American journalism under the guise of news, objective reporting or social responsibility journalism, whether knowingly or for other reasons, in good faith or bad, fronts an ideology of hatred and moral disgust concerning millions of citizen gun owners who have organized themselves into gun rights organizations. These citizens have promoted their rights and values as guaranteed under not only the Second Amendment to the U.S. Constitution, but also the First. The latter includes the rights of association, peacefully petitioning the government, and publishing ideas and values via communication media, the very same practices that *NYT* and other elite news media castigate as "lobbying." For refusing to kowtow to elite interpretations of reality and religious-like beliefs in quasi-scientific sociological theories, NRA and gun culture are denounced as heretics, extremists and deviants.

As is well known, such poisonous language, overt or insidious, accompanies marginalization via deed. Propaganda and hate language help to dehumanize human targets in order to justify actions directed against them. The diagnosis of legitimate civic gun ownership and citizen gun rights as a social problem or disease is a necessary step in the prescription of the quasi-scientific belief system that insists on misidentifying guns and gun ownership as the cause of American violence. Elite journalism routinely sketches gun owners and American gun culture as a moral failing that begs clinical-style administrative treatment. They interpret legitimate gun ownership as a matter for administrative intervention and proscription and, if this cannot be achieved outright, a policy of incremental obstructionism or taxation. Thus more and more barriers, financial and bureaucratic, and an army of officials harass legitimate gun owners, while virtually none of these barriers seriously hamper the murderous few who exist outside of what is right and reasonable.

My analysis compared NRA coverage with newspaper coverage of the American Civil Liberties Union, American Association of Retired Persons, National Association for the Advancement of Colored People, and Handgun Control, Inc., which has since changed its name to the softer-sounding Brady Center to Prevent Gun Violence. Articles came from nationally influential, so-called elite newspapers, the generative media that set the tone, topics and standards for regional and local news across the country: *The New York Times, The Washington Post, Christian Science Monitor, The Wall Street Journal* and *The Los Angeles Times*. More than 1,400 articles were content-analyzed.

Based on personal, impressionistic observations over the years previous to my dissertation project, and a small pilot study, I had expected to find some degree of bias against NRA and gun culture, but nowhere near the extent revealed by the analysis. My findings astonished me.

The first major finding was that statistics revealed a raw and naked bias of large magnitude. NRA was systematically marginalized compared to other groups. Although occasional articles were balanced, in the long run the bias was anything but subtle when measured along a number of objective measures that included use of mockery in headlines, proportions of quotes, use of personalization and dehumanization rhetorical techniques, use of correct or incorrect titles indicating respect (or lack thereof) for organizational spokespersons, the use of organizationally-created events such as press conferences as sources, the use of organizational actors in photographs, whether the group was shown as being opposed to democracy or to science, and even the verbs of attribution that signify credibility of information sources, for example, the use of "said" instead of "claims." In the language of liberal humanists who have studied what has been called *the language oppression*, and who work from the quite reasonable assumption that oppression via language precedes and/or accompanies social oppression via deed, NRA and gun culture people were marginalized into the subhuman category. They became objects of study in a virtually clinical discourse. They were talked about and not allowed to talk. Journalistic treatments of NRA spokespersons commonly read like dark psychological profiles of troubled persons. Treatments of the other groups' representatives often read like hagiographies (biographies of saints) and stopped just short of attributing halos, for example, a description of an anti-gun spokesperson whose smile would "light up a room." Meanwhile an NRA spokesperson might be referred to as "sweaty." Journalists also seemingly preferred their own interpretations of reality to actual political events or trends. For example, throughout the whole ten years of coverage analyzed, *NYT* and other elite newspapers consistently claimed that NRA was divided, defeated and dwindling when in fact NRA membership grew by more than a million persons over that time. Obviously, NRA was anything but divided, defeated and dwindling. Thus it was often not "news" being presented, but a sort of stock melodrama, wishful thinking, hopes and cheerleading for anti-gun ideologies. NRA was treated negatively in all measures when compared to analogous groups. Again, these differences were both statistically significant and large in magnitude. On average journalists disliked NRA and showed it, as was indicated by more than a dozen measures of bias.

The second major finding was, and continues to be, the *mobilization effect* of negative coverage. Negative coverage tangibly and substantially benefited NRA and the new American gun culture in terms of membership. More negative coverage equaled more NRA members in a very strong positive correlation. Negative coverage stimulated more and more people to join NRA. Negative coverage penetrates the national media system and reaches virtually everyone as the smaller and less prestigious media outlets imitate the giants. Such coverage offends and politically mobilizes gun owners. Were it not for the informational heavy-handedness of *The New York Times* and similar news organizations, NRA and American gun culture would not possess the power of numbers they have today. By attacking innocent upstanding gun owners, and in turn mobilizing them, elite media inadvertently helped launch into independent orbit, so to speak, the large-scale social movement that they have dehumanized as "the gun lobby." This new American gun culture exists now as an autonomous, self-directed social movement. It has its own media of communication. It is organized horizontally into local- and state-level groups and associations, online and actual. It is effective. And it continues to grow. Gun rights expand. Elite media diminish. More people read the anti-media of the new gun culture than the *Times*. The informational sociology has changed.

A third finding was that journalists, the people who asked the questions, got very uncomfortable and refused to explain themselves when they were asked questions; they seemed to hold themselves above accountability to mere mortals. With but one exception, when reporters who bylined articles were contacted and asked about how they covered interest groups, they refused to cooperate. They withdrew from the interview, irritated and haughty. Their reactions reminded me of the reactions of the priests and nuns who used to populate my childhood elementary school when I questioned their legitimacy in the divine order of things. The journalists seemed to regard themselves as an essential higher calling, light-shedders, and their work beyond doubt. Who was I, or anyone, to question them and their methods?

My original findings have held up over time. If anything, coverage is worse now than at the time of the original content analysis, as in, for example, coverage spurred by the Sandy Hook elementary school murders. Spurred by this deluge of blameful negativism, NRA membership has increased, as have gun sales. Ammunition is widely unavailable due to unprecedented public demand. In just one day recently, according an NRA insider, more than 19,000 new people joined NRA.

On the basis of their inability to come to grips with social and political realities such as these, one might infer that elite media insiders are not only out of touch with reality, but also that their writings on this subject, and presumably others, reflect more their hopes and dreams than any known relationships between facts. They are essentially spinners of yarns, playing a fantasy game of connect-the-dots, wherein connections are drawn as they would like them to be, rather than according to the pattern of how things really are.

*

Some background. This book flowed out of the fault lines of my character. I am apparently a troublemaker and have seemingly been so for a long time. In elementary school many years ago an aged nun had told me, "Listen buddy, you're going to Hell, but first you're going to prison!" Instead, eventually, I became a Professor of Communication at the University of Toledo, after first earning a Ph.D. in Communication Research at the University of Michigan. If this is Hell, it suits me quite well. I love what I do.

Consistent with my early propensities, however, the dissertation, the book and indeed the whole program of study leading up to it were fraught with trouble. Apparently I say and ask things that some authorities do not want said or asked. The world is up for discussion, in my view, but there are many who demand the final say. And this has caused friction in places where I least expected it. Naively, for example, I had thought and looked forward to graduate school as a place for untrammeled discussion and investigation. It was not.

Thus graduate school for me was something like prison in that it seemed more constraining than liberating. It was in large part a process of socialization into certain ways of thinking. But I became, and usefully so, methodologically informed and acquired skills and habits of inquiry necessary to satisfy modern social-scientific conventions. I have tried to put these skills and habits to good use.

I soon learned, however, that my research interests were academically taboo on the whole. The very idea of a powerful antithetic political mobilization of an increasingly successful American gun culture (as represented by its flagship organization NRA) was anathema, if not unthinkable, to many professors and graduate students, who had imbibed so many of their social opinions from elite media. It's a curious fact, by the way, that the most highly educated people are generally the most susceptible to propaganda, quite contrary to their own beliefs, for they imagine themselves as critical thinkers, and especially as social managers. But they live in streams of information, and hence are exposed to and consume the most propaganda. (For more on this, see my book *The Ten Commandments of Propaganda*.)

I have been professionally associated, in one way or another, with academics for about 20 years. As a very general rule, they often don't like guns, gun culture, shooting sports, gun owners, NRA or the people that they seem to associate with such things—which has sometimes been me. I have often been referred to as a "you people." I have heard outlandish claims made in academic meetings: for example, lumping in the NRA with Nazis and the KKK. I have been told that I am immoral for target shooting.

Especially in graduate school meetings and seminars, academics would often exhibit weird body language when my research topic came up. One senior professor made curdled milk expressions and told me, in high tones, that he had even prevented his children from playing with toy guns. I could go on for some time with anecdotes. Professor Curdled Milk later attempted to rig a dissertation writing fellowship that I was due by changing the guidelines after the fact. I called him on it, and got the fellowship, but he would never talk to me again.

So it seems that I have had a great deal of resistance to my research agenda, much more than colleagues who researched well-worn and politically safe topics. This resistance itself is an interesting secondary finding and indicates something about the manufacture of meaning by our institutions of news and education—namely that they will tell us what things should mean and not the other way around.

Fortunately I have also encountered fair-minded academics, although this sometimes took a bit of searching. Perhaps they are not as rare as I had thought. Maybe some are silent out of fear of attack, or they are just not as aggressive as ideologues and mind their own business (research interests) instead. Quite recently a university committee voted 8-0 to overrule a Dean who tried to bar my promotion to full professor. The Dean, a former Women and Gender Studies faculty member, had argued that she thought I might even be an advocate for gun culture, even though it seemed obvious enough by her comments that she had never actually read any of my books or articles. She also wrote that it was difficult to interpret the meaning of the many answers of "yes" by students to the questions on my teaching evaluations, questions such as, "Did the professor respect students?" and "Did the professor meet the objectives of the class?" and "Was the professor knowledgeable?" and so on. So we have here the phenomenon of the Dean who didn't know the meaning of "yes" when it indicated something she apparently didn't want to hear. An amusing aspect of her comments is that in her discipline, advocacy, often called *praxis* in the Marxist-Leninist sense, in many instances seems to substitute for rigorous intellectual discipline and depth. (A note here: why don't more feminist-gender scholars welcome the idea of armed women? This seems a way of "taking back the night" in a much more efficient way than a candlelight vigil on the library steps.) Often, however, Women and Gender studies and similar "critical studies" approaches in higher education seem merely variants of agitation propaganda undergirded by dreary Marxist-influenced tracts.

The Dean seemed especially indignant regarding a newspaper interview in which I had stated an interest in writing for real people, not just academics. She warned of academic "consequences" for my preference. It was apparently heresy in her worldview. How dare I try to write clearly in a direct style and, worse yet, not particularly care about the (often) lopsided opinions of academics?

On the larger social level, when the topic of gun rights and the NRA comes up, many social elites are also unable to interpret the meaning of "yes," especially when it sounds like it is coming from outside their tiny spheres of reference. With this sort of selective perception, it's no wonder that academics and elite media professionals don't know how to interpret the meaning of the extraordinary rise in gun sales, concealed weapons license applications and licensees (especially for women and professionals), firearm training classes and membership numbers in state and national gun rights associations including NRA. All of these trends are underway despite decades of vertical top-down anti-gun propaganda and anti-NRA editorializing by elite media. These elite professional interpreters of reality like to be the ones who construct what is meaningful—and circumstances have taken this out of their hands.

Thank you, Dear Reader, for taking up this book,

Professor Brian Anse Patrick, B.A., M.A., Ph.D., G.E.D.
University of Toledo, 17 May 2013

Introduction:
THE NATIONAL RIFLE ASSOCIATION IN AMERICA

More is generally believed about the National Rifle Association of America than is really known. Beyond a few truisms that will not stand up to casual inspection, we have at hand virtually no satisfactory explanation of how and why the NRA is able to function as effectively as it does. This book attempts to provide such an explanation. It advances the thesis that NRA effectiveness is attributable in large part to an enormous mobilization effect that it derives from a most unlikely source—negative media coverage. In making this case, the book also has much to say on the nature of modern democratic social action and the role of mass media in its creation.

The NRA and Public Opinion

During his final days in office, President William Jefferson Clinton blamed the National Rifle Association for Vice President Albert Gore's loss of the 2000 presidential election. According to Clinton, the NRA influenced voting outcomes in a number of states, including Gore's home state of Tennessee, thus delivering key electoral votes to Republican candidate George W. Bush (Sisk, 2001). NRA officials were more than happy to accept the blame. NRA Executive Vice President Wayne LaPierre, interpreting a county-by-county breakdown of election results that showed overwhelming rural support for Bush, boasted of "the power of NRA's presence" (LaPierre, 2001).

But exactly when and how did the NRA become so powerful as to sway a national election?

NRA's election-swaying power is especially puzzling considering the climate of public opinion that existed in the United States for at least a decade prior to the election, in which newspapers regularly reported its decline. At various times during this period journalistic accounts described the NRA using terms and phrases such as *vanquished giant, death spiral, atrophying, in virtual shambles, wounded, faltering, steep decline in membership, under the gun,* and as having *alienated its mainstream membership*; all terms taken directly from political reporting and editorials in prestige, standard-setting media that serve as newspapers of record for U.S. political events such as *The New York Times, The Christian Science Monitor, The Washington Post, Los Angeles Times* and *The Wall Street Journal.*

Correspondingly, over the same time frame, these leading newspapers regularly reported on a massive shift in public opinion away from pro-gun, NRA positions. The papers described this shift as a *clamor for gun control, growing momentum* and *coalescing national demand* by an *overwhelming majority of Americans.*

Opinion polls, also reported regularly in the news, would seem to verify the existence of a preponderance of public opinion against pro-gun positions. The General Social Survey — a methodologically sophisticated program of social scientific survey research conducted annually by the National Opinion Research Center — has since about 1960 indicated that somewhere between 67 and 82 percent of Americans would support a law requiring a police permit to purchase a gun. The percentage of respondents favoring more gun control is high even among gun owners. A number of surveys by independent polling firms have shown similar results. A widely reported poll by the EPIC/MRA firm indicated that 55 percent of potential voters support a ban on semiautomatic deer-hunting rifles, while 83 percent favor a total ban on assault weapons (Associated Press, 1995, May 16). The Gallup firm has reported similar results over the years, with between 59 and 78 percent of respondents favoring "more strict" gun control, with up to 90 percent, at various times, supporting a national five-day waiting period for gun purchases. (For an extensive review of such survey results, see Kleck, 1991, pp. 345–349.)

From the point of view of theorists and advocates of mass democracy, this apparent decline of the NRA as a viable social group and the rise of anti-gun opinion constitute a clear political mandate for stricter gun control. But as far back as 1977, public opinion researchers

Schuman and Presser noted the disparity between popular opinion and policy and labeled it the *gun control paradox*.

In general, then and now, there have been few if any strict U.S. gun control measures, and certainly none that remotely rival the restrictions current in virtually all other Western democratic nations. Even in neighboring Canada — a country that shares more than any other country with the United States in terms of culture, economics, demographics, overlapping media markets, geography, and social history — laws severely restrict or prohibit civilian possession and access to firearms and even ammunition. The ban includes many semiautomatic firearms, not only assault-type weapons and handguns but also many shotguns and rifles often used for hunting and sport in the United States (Canadian Firearms Centre, 2002).

Certainly some U.S. federal-level restrictions have been signed into law with great fanfare in the past decade. Upon cold reflection, however, these restrictions are probably best regarded as high on political symbolism but generally low on practical effect. They are cosmetic "solutions" of the sort that sociologist Murray Edelman (1977) dismissed as "words that succeed and policies that fail." For example, a waiting period for handgun purchases, originally established under the Brady Bill in 1991, has since lapsed and been replaced by the instant-check, call-in system for use by federally licensed firearm dealers. The system weeds out known felons attempting to purchase firearms — which was already a violation of federal law — but in a concession to NRA demands, maintains no registry of gun purchases; and private sales in the United States, while subject in theory to federal and local laws, are not monitored. The 1994 Crime Bill outlawed a number of assault-type weapons on the basis of a point system; firearms with a high-capacity magazine *and* a bayonet lug *and* a pistol grip became illegal except for several million "grand-fathered" weapons already in circulation. Assault-type weapons are still manufactured and sold; and millions of high-capacity magazines remain in circulation, without restrictions, since only newly manufactured magazines of more than ten rounds are prohibited. So the assault weapon "ban" of the Crime Bill functionally affects close to nothing in practical terms. Further, no serious ban of any sort seems likely. The same can be said for any proposed scheme of national registration, safety training, or access restriction. Any adult citizen with proper identification who walks into virtually any of the thousands of K-Mart or Wal-Mart retail stores in the United States, after filling out a federal self-disclosure form and satisfying the criminal history instant-check by telephone, can leave with a semiautomatic .22 caliber rifle and 1,000 rounds of ammunition for not much more than $150 cash, check, or charge.

So, given this climate of public opinion, and given also the continuing problems attributed to the availability of firearms, how is it that strict gun control has not happened in the United States?

Political Paradoxes

The standard reply is to blame the NRA, an organization frequently presented in scholarship and mass media accounts as the archetypal example of the special interest "lobby." This term connotes, as mass democracy advocates and journalists often use it, a self-serving political action organization, frequently a trade or professional association, that functions at general social expense, e.g., "the tobacco lobby." Discussions of special interest groups or political campaign reform in American society often begin by citing NRA lobbying activity as a prime negative example of democracy frustrated by the powerful special interest (e.g., Wright, 1995).

The NRA gun lobby, so the tale goes, buys legislative votes with money and intimidation and thereby the will of the people is thwarted. So bad is NRA's public reputation in this regard that in past years NRA has been directly targeted by waves of condemnatory presidential rhetoric apparently grounded on themes derived from focus group research findings (Stengal & Pooley, 1996); and in the 2000 election campaign, presidential candidate George W. Bush, despite enjoying favored son status on the part of the NRA, took pains in public to distance himself from the organization.

Something is obviously wrong with this interpretation, for how does the atrophying, stigmatized lobby described by the national press continually and successfully exert power in the face of massive opposition? How does it sway a national election?

Despite the recurring reports of decline, NRA's power to affect policy appears at no time in the past decade to have been in serious danger of disappearing in clouds of media scorn, presidential censure, or unfavorable public opinion. In fact, judging by current appearances, NRA seems to have won the battle, if not the war. Gun control groups were not making headway by the year 2001 and appeared to be in disarray. In what could be interpreted as an effort to regroup, Handgun Control, Inc., (HCI) the flagship of antigun groups, allied with the defunct Million Moms March organization—acquiring its stock of symbolism but little else in the deal—and also changed its name to the Brady Campaign to Prevent Gun Violence, no doubt to try to recast its public image.

Not so with the NRA. The occasional reverse or failure notwithstanding—as no group in pluralistic U.S. society always gets everything it wants—in recent years NRA has enjoyed a number of fairly spectacular successes. Its political action committee, the Institute for Legislative Action (ILA), has stalled, gutted, or defeated numerous pieces of proposed federal, state and local-level gun control legislation. NRA has influenced the outcome of state, local, and national elections and continues to be a force in this area. In 1994 President Clinton attributed to NRA influence the historic Republican Party takeover of the U.S. House of Representatives. In the 2000 election, NRA members, many of whom are distributed in largely rural, "gun country" states, certainly had much to do with determining the electoral college totals that edged George W. Bush into the presidency; while candidate Al Gore's embarrassing loss of his home state of Tennessee was certainly related to strong pro-gun sentiment in that state as evidenced by NRA rallies and political advertisements on the eve of the election (Cummings & Davis, 2000). So-called grass-roots organizations—all with strong overlapping affiliations with the NRA—have moved state legislators to pass and governors to sign "shall-issue" concealed weapons carry laws so that in more than thirty states, including Florida, Texas, Tennessee and, recently, Michigan, citizens can now legally carry concealed handguns after a permitting process that includes a background check and nominal safety training. NRA-backed lawsuits have challenged and won against key aspects of national gun control law in the federal courts, and NRA continues to be a major force in fighting lawsuits directed against the gun industry by U.S. municipal governments, lawsuits that appear to be vanishing without the active encouragement of the anti-gun Clinton administration. So, once again, if NRA support is melting away, as so often asserted, how does an increasingly isolated lobby achieve, repeat, and maintain such victories? This seems paradoxical indeed.

A *paradox of NRA mobilization* appears also to have been passed over without notice by journalists and mass democracy advocates alike. Given the regular reports of NRA's decline, combined with the massive public opinion in favor of gun control, how can it be that NRA actually increased in terms of membership when looked at over the past thirty years, quadrupling in size, from approximately one million members in 1970 to about 4.2 million by 2001? Only several months previous to the 2000 elections *The Washington Post* and *The New York Times* appeared, perhaps, to finally have discovered that NRA had a large and growing mass membership (Dao, 2000, Edsall, 2000). This long-term increase is all the more remarkable, first, for having occurred in an era reputed for mass political apathy and cynicism, and second for having occurred, until quite recently, beneath the threshold of awareness of major U.S. mass media surveillance. In terms of comparable large-scale social movements, NRA's mass membership must be considered a huge and sustained political mobilization. Even at the height of the civil rights movement, the National Association for the Advancement of Colored People never had more than about one million members. Handgun Control, Inc., despite the public opinion climate favoring gun control, can claim at most only 250-400 thousand members. In contrast, the number of NRA life members alone is more than 500 thousand. How can this sustained level of mass mobilization exist in the inhospitable public opinion climate described above?

The existence of a *paradox of extremism* can also be noted, premised on yet another well-circulated NRA truism. The more-or-less standard variation depicts NRA as a group led by extremist-fanatics who are not representative of a more politically moderate majority of sportsmen who comprise its membership; neither are the extremists representative of gun owners in general, hence, the story often continues, the decline in NRA support. Again looking to national newspapers, this motif pervades coverage, as manifested in the descriptions: *right-wing zealots, irrationality and extremism, Pavlovian opposition, increasingly hard line,* and *strident.*

Again glib explanation runs aground on confounding fact. If NRA leaders are indeed extremists, by definition at the edge of extant social practice, how does NRA function so effectively not only internally but also within the parameters of the U.S. social-political system? Beyond the evidence of the steady increase in membership—which would be most unlikely in the extremist-fearing contemporary U.S. political climate—there is also the internal structure of the NRA to consider. First, the NRA is a highly democratic organization by the standards of national mass membership voluntary associations. Directors are regularly nominated and voted in by life members, with executives serving at the directors' pleasure. Many, if not most, mass membership groups are blatant oligarchies by comparison. The idea that NRA membership is politically divorced from NRA leadership does not stand scrutiny; their connection is fairly direct. Second, NRA-ILA funding derives almost entirely from membership dues and member donations, and not from "the gun industry" as is often supposed. This funding has not declined, as would be expected if membership and leadership were sundered; to the contrary it, too, has steadily increased. Third, those persons who join voluntary associations can, in general, be viewed as more socially committed and/or engaged in many ways than those who do not, the so-called "free riders" who benefit by the actions of the joiners. Consistent with this view, NRA members, like the members of other voluntary associations, would appear on average to be more socially committed than is the norm, expending the considerable energy required for efficacious participation within the extant social system. It is difficult to interpret this profile as a portrait of extremism. It is also relevant that Schuman and Presser (1977) found no relationship between extreme ideology and gun ownership.

Possibly the most important perceptual discrepancy regarding the NRA is the *public information paradox.* How does NRA manage to prosper in an atmosphere of negative public information? Scholars of political communication have long known that modern mass democratic society depends for its coherence upon relatively centralized, omnipresent mass media that carry essential information to citizens concerning the far-flung activities of the society: for the time is long since past when any one citizen could possibly experience directly any but a small portion of events affecting a large, complex society. Mass media connect citizens to the political world. It would be just as correct to say, however, that mass media *are* the political world to many citizens, who have little or no direct experience of the events of which they read, see and hear. Lippmann (1922) pointed out this situation as the existential informational condition of mass democracy.

That said, if one systematically compares so-called elite or prestige U.S. news media coverage concerning the NRA with coverage of similar mass membership associations, it becomes apparent that NRA consistently receives negative coverage compared to other interest groups. I have done this comparison for national newspaper coverage of interest groups for almost a decade, content-analyzing nearly 1,500 articles along a number of objectively defined measures. The results, reported in detail later in this book, are unambiguous: NRA is treated negatively compared to analogous interest groups, and these differences are both systematic and large in magnitude. Thus, persons who depend upon media to inform their political worldview would largely know NRA as it has been cast for them—including, especially, other journalists who tend to look to prestigious newspapers such as *The New York Times* as a professional model. So too would millions of persons who are professionals, managers, academics, students, urban dwellers, administrators or office workers. I have conducted focus groups and survey research among largely urban university students and urban senior citizens and found their opinions generally consistent with elite national media content. Also, I have interviewed academics—in addition to having walked among them for a number of years—and the opinions I have heard also seem generally consistent with this media content: academics are often horrified of NRA and seem, on the basis of my experience, largely content with the "standard" explanations of the NRA phenomenon, variants of which I have heard articulated by different academics. In any case it appears that NRA is losing the public information war on a number of cultural-demographic fronts. So, formally restating the public information paradox, how does the NRA manage to survive and prosper in an atmosphere of negative public information? Why isn't it just swept away by the tides of public opinion for which the editorial writers speak?

Substance of the Book

The purpose of this book is to explain the success of NRA mobilization by unraveling the public information paradox. Along the way the other paradoxes concerning NRA effectiveness will be disentangled—for they are related. For the moment, however, these paradoxes serve as a point of beginning for serious inquiry, namely the admission of a general ignorance. Clearly, as asserted at the beginning of this discussion, and as underscored by the paradoxes, more is generally believed about the NRA than is known in actual fact. Beyond the truisms, we have on hand no good explanation of how and why the NRA is able to function as it does.

The explanations provided by this book derive essentially from a study in political communication concerning the relationship between media coverage of interest groups and social action, as set within the context of modern mass democratic society. These are all topics that have received attention from scholars working in various research areas—e.g., social movements, interest group mobilization, political communication—but up to now have received very little attention as to how they might apply to NRA.

This is unfortunate, for the study of the NRA phenomenon may provide one of the more instructive lessons of past decades on the workings of social action. Despite how one may feel about the organization or the causes it espouses, the fact that NRA appears to thrive in an atmosphere of negative opinion is noteworthy in itself, and should make mass democratic theorists wonder, especially those who would see in the press the voice or forum of public opinion.

To study NRA is to study many of the more dramatic elements of social action, including social cleavage, conflict, ideology, the growth of an apparently indomitable resistance over time and—importantly— the social functions of mass media in modern society. Even should one insist that NRA is somehow an extreme and therefore unrepresentative example of the special interest organization, a doubtful characterization as was asserted above, recollect that William James (1901) argued *for* the study of extreme cases because they most often provide clearly disambiguated examples of complex social or psychological phenomena. Unless one is willing to subscribe to the unlikely notion that NRA is a law unto itself, theory that explains NRA effectiveness will have general applications.

Mobilization Effects of Negative Coverage

In the way of explaining NRA effectiveness, this book advances the thesis that the NRA benefits tangibly and substantially in terms of member mobilization from negative media coverage. In other words, the more negative coverage that the NRA has received, the larger its membership has grown: the correlation is very high. This is a counterintuitive relationship from the viewpoint of theorists who regard mediated public information as informing the political experience of a detached type of citizenship that is several steps removed from the actual experience of political events and processes. Going even further, this book asserts that NRA has been able to institutionalize around this flow of negative coverage, capitalizing on it as if it were a resource, depending on it to power membership mobilization, fund raising, single-issue voting and the other actions-in-solidarity that contribute to its continued success.

Putting the matter as bluntly as possible, if it were not for negative national media coverage, NRA could not possibly be where it is today.

Social Movement Hybridism

I will argue that this mobilization effect is possible because the NRA has fallen into a pattern of political organization-mobilization that is known by sociologists and political scientists under the general rubric of *social movement theory*. This is a Marxist-derived conceptualization of social action that posits direct class or cultural opposition, i.e., conflict or class warfare, as the site of social action and mobilization. The social movement-type organization thus has a distinctive ethos. Typical examples include the feminist movement, gay rights, black power, white power, labor unions, etc., where the class or cultural identity sense goes well beyond the attitudinal measures that are the fodder of survey research on public opinion.

Such movements are thought to arise "naturally" out of social-historical tectonics. It is probably beyond the power of any group to consciously create the class-cultural antagonisms that generate social movement action. But it is certainly possible to recognize, nourish, stimulate, simulate, exploit and attempt to manage such antagonisms: NRA officials, as with all successful social movement leaders, do all these things very well.

What is more, an *anti-media theory* will be shown as a premise in NRA official communications. NRA decodes media content for its members along lines characteristic of social movement mobilization, e.g., allusions to class or cultural media war against gun owners. This suggests an awareness on the part of the NRA of the manifold benefits of interpreting coverage for its members: negative coverage successfully re-interpreted is coverage that mobilizes and reinforces solidarity, a sort of reverse or co-opted form of publicity worth millions measured either in dollars or members.

NRA efficacy will also be attributed in part to hybrid organizational form. While employing a social movement style of mobilization, in many ways NRA retains the institutional structure of the traditional pluralistic special interest group, consistent with its origins under government patronage as an organization to train marksmen for purposes of military preparedness. The NRA is now primarily a political organization. The typical pattern, according to many sociologists, is that social movements tend over time to fall into institutionalization, consequently losing their special intensity in the process. The NRA is an example of the reverse, an institution that has fallen into social movement mobilization, acquiring thereby the intensity of the social movement ethos but also providing a movement with a bureaucratic resource base of the traditional pluralistic interest group so necessary for sustained action, a base that social movements generally lack. The effectiveness of the hybridism is apparent.

The book argues that social efficacy by an interest group is the result of such hybridism, and that the groups that have been most successful in the context of American mass democracy in terms of social action are those that have somehow achieved hybrid mobilization styles.

A General Theory of Media Bias

Returning once again to the issue of media bias, this study also will advance a theory of elite media bias that attempts to move beyond the tiresome variants of bias theory that have been constructed along the *liberal-conservative* continuum. While denying the existence neither of liberal nor conservative bias, nor that these forms of bias undoubtedly affect reporting and news content at times, it will be argued that the intrinsic bias of the elite national media is toward an *administrative control hermeneutic*.

An administrative control hermeneutic interprets the world essentially as a managerial problem to be solved by professional, expert administration. I argue that interest groups or social movements receive coverage in accord to how well they align with this hermeneutic. Thus groups such as the American Civil Liberties Union and NRA both tend to receive negative coverage, despite their being considered by many to be at opposite ends of the left-right political spectrum. They receive negative coverage because of the nature of their agendas: both frequently tend to position themselves athwart the road of administrative design.

I will argue that an important reason why the control hermeneutic so much affects coverage has to do with the distinctive role of media and media professionals in the emergence of a closely related modern approach to mass social management that I will term *administrative democracy*. This is an efficient scientifically managed approach to mass democratic participation, a logical, rational vision of "pure" democracy that is obtainable by means of the accretion of infinitesimal votes. Citizen participation reduces here to that most elemental of possible acts such as voting by pulling a lever. Its administrators rule in the name of public service, legitimated and ensconced within the constitutional apparatus of government, their policies and the length of their tenures warranted by plebiscite or opinion surveys. Political participation affirms the legitimacy of the administrative democratic system; therefore the percentage of people who vote and concepts such as *political cynicism* take on a magnified importance. Political communication research, when informed by this vision, tends toward subject matter such as the quality and effects on the electorate of televised debates by presidential candidates; whether or not people have faith in polls; what citizens learn from political news, etc. The good citizen, in administrative democracy, is an informed participant who, having been made aware of available options, pulls the lever indicating "choice." Mass media do the bulk of aware-making and therefore occupy a position that while perhaps not a monopoly is clearly a dominant position in the information market: they are utterly integral to the operation of the administrative democratic process.

Priests of the Information Age

So important are mass media to administrative democracy that this book will resort to social-historical analogy. The theological rub of the Reformation was a Roman Catholic Church monopoly on Divine Grace. Divine Grace, regarded as a human-spiritual necessity, was dispensed to the masses only through an intermediating clergy in the form of the sacraments. In administrative mass democracy, media professionals occupy a social role similar to the pre-Reformation clergy. Information—regarded as a social democratic necessity that informs the spirit of meaningful citizen participation—is collected, dispensed and interpreted for the public primarily through an intermediating body of journalistic professionals. Journalists, particularly elite journalists, thus occupy a powerful and central social role, a functional monopoly that is charged with the solemn duty of disseminating the administrative word and its symbols unto the public. Elite journalists comprise the informational priesthood of administrative democracy, as it were, without which the mass democratic system would shrivel away or lose its warrant of informed consent.

Curiously, when I investigated possible causes for interest group coverage by attempting to interview journalists who had authored articles used in the content analysis, some reminded me of the priests and nuns who inhabited my parochial school boyhood, who whenever I asked an inconvenient question about their personal role in the divine order of things would either resort to mystification or would fall back on their authority and simply stop talking to me. This is exactly what a number of elite journalists did when I asked about how and why they covered interest groups as they did, withdrawing from interviews by saying things such as, "That's an area that I need to leave quite hazy." In this light *objectivity*, which remains an important news standard albeit a somewhat tarnished one, appears to assume much the same legitimating function as the doctrine of *papal infallibility*.

Caveats

Emphatically, though, this book is not a blame-the-media polemic. There is a great difference between blame and description. Hermeneutics are simply interpretive frameworks that help process complex reality into intellectually manageable bites. Seldom are we able to step back and regard them as interpretive frameworks, per se; we usually regard them simply as reality. If the hermeneutics by which social management is accomplished are working well, seldom will there be call either to notice or inspect them. The pre-Reformation clergy certainly did not regard itself as in the grips of a hermeneutic, but rather as part of the unfolding of the Divine Order. Journalists, similarly, it will be argued, are part of an unfolding vision of a progressively scientific democracy wherein they are charged with weighty public and professional responsibility. Administrative democracy and the role for journalists as a priesthood of mass information are quite natural outgrowths of the spirit of progressively scientific objectivism that informs our age; journalists did not invent the philosophic-epistemic system in which they function.

A final caveat, this book is not in any way opposed to democracy or democratic processes. The study of political communication, however, particularly in the more quantitative sub-fields, has suffered as a useful discipline, I believe, because it has unwittingly become the creature of administrative democracy. Largely this can be attributed to naïve or unexamined assumptions held by researchers on the nature of democracy; in this regard they might well be said to have sinned by omission. Gaining a general understanding of media and its mobilizing role in social action, however, requires not only the explication of such assumptions but also some willingness to try to dispassionately examine modes of democratic social action without treating any particular mode as revealed truth.

Organization of the Book

The first chapter lays a foundation for the book by describing as ideal types the available modes of modern consensual social action along with the characteristic social role of mass media implicit to each mode. The modes are pluralism, social movement theory, and mass democracy.

The second chapter locates the NRA within the social action modes, suggesting that NRA efficacy is achieved by hybridism; the intensity of social movement ethos is complemented by the structure of the pluralistic interest group, with conflict represented by negative media coverage fueling mobilization.

Evidence of negative media coverage of the NRA is presented in chapter 3. Nearly 1,500 articles from five prestigious national newspapers are content-analyzed concerning five mass membership interest groups: The National Rifle Association of America, The American Civil Liberties Union, The American Association of Retired Persons, The National Association for the Advancement of Colored People, and Handgun Control, Inc. This chapter also contains many examples taken from coverage in order to preserve the richness of data that otherwise would be lost through statistical aggregation.

The fourth chapter reports on communications of the NRA, with *anti-media theory* identified as a principal NRA communication tactic. This and other tactics in the social movement style are revealed through an analysis of a decade of official NRA publications and also through interviews with NRA officials.

Chapter 5 sketches a model of the *mobilization effect* of negative coverage. It demonstrates a strong association between negative coverage and NRA membership throughout the past decade. It also suggests—because of a tendency for NRA annual members to enroll, lapse, then re-enroll as members—that the effective membership of the NRA may be considerably higher than its officially reported membership.

NRA press relations are discussed in chapter 6 from the viewpoint of both NRA officials and journalists.

Chapter 7 generalizes the results of this study. It describes the role of the elite media in modern *administrative democracy* and its social ramifications in light of the above findings, including the general theory of media bias. It also looks at *social action hybridism* as an emergent response and blueprint for effective social action by interest groups in the modern era.

Some subjects are reserved for the two short appendices. Appendix A discusses research methods and measures of the study. Appendix B contains backgrounds on the interest groups along with a justification for their comparisons.

I

The Media of Social Action

Modes of Social Action

To arrive at an understanding of how the NRA functions so effectively within American democracy requires first an examination of the available modes of modern democratic social action. These modes each have a respective set of assumptions, implications, and also, especially for the purposes of this book, a characteristic social role that is played by mass media. Without laying this sort of foundation, discussion of the NRA, or any other social group, amounts to little more than a heaping up of anecdotal material, but with it, it becomes possible to factor out causes, effects, trends, and commonalities. The modes provide the framework for comparison.

At the heart of any notion of any modern society that is based on a social contract lies, implicitly or explicitly, a theory of social action. Such theory is concerned with how, why, when, and under what conditions social force apparently arises out of atomistic, individual-microlevel opinion and experience, and then somehow accrues, focuses, and sooner or later comes to affect, or perhaps even constitute, the macro-level movements of social institutions and policies. Owing to the interplay of many variables, organized mass social action remains a force that can be very difficult to comprehend. The problem can be greatly simplified, however through a convenient abstraction.

Social force requires a medium, some sort of vector by which it is carried, for just like any other force it must somehow span the gap between its origin and its effect; in this case between individual affect (emotion or attitude) and social effect. Perhaps, then, the most fundamental feature of any theory of social action is its postulated, abstracted mechanism of transmission, i.e., by what medium and under what condition(s) is social force collected and transmitted from the individual to the larger society?

There are really only a few basic ways of answering this question in the modern world—as we are no longer concerned with the divine right of kings—although many variants, subtle gradations, or intermixtures of theory exist. Stated as pure, so-called ideal types, I propose that a simple typology of theoretical approaches to social action can be formulated on the basis of each theory's approach to this medium for transmission of social force. Looked at in this way, there are only three fundamentally different ways of approaching this problem. I will call these *social action modes*. They are *pluralism, mass democracy theory*, and *social movement theory*. Any serious discussion explaining the actions and effects of the NRA, or any other social group, is unavoidably premised within one or more of these theoretical modes.

Typology of Social Action Theories

Pluralism

Pluralistic theorists say that individual-level *interest* coalesces into groups known as voluntary associations or interest groups, and these groups communicate social action in accord with the magnitude of their constituency, their resource base, their competitors (i.e., other groups in the social ecology) and their ingenuity. Pluralism's medium of transmission for individual-level opinion is the group itself, specifically the *interest group* or *voluntary association* (Adams, 1986), wherein like-minded individuals freely and democratically associate. These individuals need not be like-minded in all ways, or even in important ways; they just need to share some particular interest(s).

These groups in themselves are thought to constitute "publics" by some social theorists (e.g., Blumer, 1946), and individual opinion or interest does not, by definition, become "public opinion" until it is thus focused. Obviously, there can be as many such groups as there are interests, and involvement in any one group does not necessarily rule out involvement in others.

The net sum of group efforts at the macro-political level is a negotiated compromise, which de facto or by design, creates, constitutes, and/or modifies the general social order, along with its social institutions and policies. The classic political idea of checks and balances is virtually characteristic of pluralism.

Pluralism, like the other ideal types discussed below, can in its purer forms be regarded as both an ideology and a normative worldview of a participatory paradise on earth, as it purports to provide the individual with meaningful avenues and methods with which to democratically influence social change (e.g., Adams, 1986). By *meaningful* it is meant that the individual vote by itself amounts to very little when cast against the backdrop of a mass society; only by means of association can the individual realistically hope to exert influence. Neither the importance nor the right of the individual to vote is discounted in this view—far from it—but rather the interest group as the most effective medium available for communicating individual opinion is the central and characteristic emphasis of pluralistic theory.

Social theorists such as Bentley (1908), Adams (1986), Blumer (1946) and Wright (1995), among others, view United States society as a tapestry made up of such interest groups. Such groups—that have been variously parsed by theorists into categories such as *citizens groups, lobbies, special interest groups, voluntary associations, issue groups, professional associations,* etc.—compete and interact to produce a fluid, ever-changing social order. Bentley, whose theoretical perspective could perhaps be regarded as constituting the far horizon of pluralistic theory, thought that understanding a society was a matter of gaining an understanding of these groups and their interactions.

At the societal level, the system of interest group action is highly dynamic and ongoing. The formal structures of the groups assure sustained action over time, which is important for continued social efficacy, although old groups decay or evolve to serve new purposes, and new groups constantly appear. An ecological model would therefore well describe this teeming social landscape.

Many attempts have been made to extend pluralistic theory to account for how interest groups are able to mobilize their members. The influential Mancur Olson posits *incentives*, i.e., member services, as attracting members, who under a rational economic choice model would otherwise remain free riders, enjoying the social benefits wrought by the group but not having to pay the costs of belonging

(1965). In Olson's explanation, groups bribe membership by providing incentives. Walker (1983, 1991) posits different sorts of mobilization: occupational-professional mobilization based on economic self-interest; a mass public opinion, reform type of mobilization originating from the "educated middle class," which is distinct from the social movement theory of Marxist origins that will be discussed below and throughout this study; and lastly an advocacy-type mobilization organized from above by professionals usually for the benefit of those thought to be unable to mobilize on their own. In all of Walker's forms, *patronage* is the leaven of mobilization, where the group is subsidized in effect by some powerful financial backer such as government, industry, or philanthropy, although professional associations are most able to pay their own start-up and maintenance costs based on member contributions. (The modern NRA does not seem to fit well into any of Walker's types, although its beginnings in the nineteenth century were clearly the result of government patronage.) Clark and Wilson (1961) offer what amounts to a typology of mobilization wherein the *purposive group* fulfills some ideological impulse of joiners; the *material group* offers economic benefits; and the *solidary group* has some general social benefit. Adams (1986) sees mobilization as individuals in voluntary association working pragmatically together in the act of social creation or construction, ideally for the social good; these associations arise out of the Protestant-Judaic religious traditions of "loyal dissent" within a larger society. Adam's view, similar to Bentley's, is of a dynamic social order based on these voluntary associations: "By their groups, their associational fruits, shall ye know them," writes Adams, for humans are "associational beings" (1986, p. 10). Mobilization thus proceeds from a sort of associational psychology on the part of human beings. Adams, never naïve, also notes what he calls "pathologies" of voluntary associations, namely groups that work at social expense.

Whatever motivates group membership, a distinct conceptualization of social action follows from the pluralistic view. It differs fundamentally from social action as conceived under mass democracy theory or social movement theory, both soon to be discussed below. The fundamental difference is that the groups themselves rather than atomistic individuals or a simple mass majority of individuals are thought to embody public opinion; again, individual opinion and/or attitude transmutes into public opinion *only* when focused by the actual behavior of group membership.

Pluralism is a behavioral concept. The fundamental pluralistic assumption is that if an individual actually had an opinion on some matter, he or she would align with or attempt to form a group. Thus the orthodox pluralist would regard as ridiculous the notion of public opinion as the aggregated responses of random individuals to questions asked by means of a randomly dialed telephone interview; the pluralist would point out that the responses that are elevated into "public opinion" by pollsters in many cases did not independently exist in the respondent's mind until the instant that the interviewer poised the question. It is no more than a "response" to a stimulus, and by no means an "opinion." This distinction is important because pluralistic public opinion is viewed essentially as a *behavior*, i.e. group involvement, rather than merely a latent *attitude* held to at no personal cost and therefore at a very doubtful level of intensity.

Some regard pluralism as a debunked notion. It is not even mentioned in the indexes of some recent books on political mobilization, where mobilization is seen as the creature—here used in its literal meaning, *the creation*—of patrons or of political choices offered by politicians (e.g., Rosenstone & Hansen, 1993; Walker, 1991). Or else pluralism is disdainfully viewed as "inclusive," in reference to the relatively small proportions of the total population that become interest group members, hence the democratic warrant of the pluralistic social order becomes suspect (e.g., Dahl, 1982). E. E. Schattschneider perhaps puts the matter best: "The flaw in the pluralist heaven is that the heavenly chorus sings with a strong upper-class accent" (1960, p. 35).

Mass Democracy Theory

Mass democracy theory says that social action is the will of the majority as expressed by the aggregation of individual votes, or, as some would have it, by attitudinal preferences given in response to public opinion polls.

The medium for translating individual opinion into social action is the constitutional or bureaucratic apparatus of government officialdom and/or elected representatives who—existing by social contract and/or the will of the people—translate individual opinion as measured by votes for leaders, representatives, or referenda into social action policy.

The conceptualization of social action under mass democracy is an outgrowth of Enlightenment age rationalism, rooted in the humanistic celebration of individual worth. Historically, mass democratic social action has often come about as a reaction to absolutism. Egalitarianism, equality, freedom, political enfranchisement, sufferance—all are its bywords; while opposed to it are all forms of social force exerted nonconsensually by economic or physical means, by coercion or by virtue of superior social position. It is a noble undertaking at heart. The importance of the individual vote is virtually fetishized in extreme or naïve forms of the conceptualization, for the individual's vote in local or national elections is viewed as the most meaningful form of political participation, with the possible exception of running for or holding office. The point that matters in the mass democracy conceptualization is that social action is legitimate only with the explicit consent of the governed, obtained additively, and this consent is ultimately obtained at the individual level. The machinery of constitutional government, and no other conduit, legitimately translates individual opinion or attitude into social action.

When someone talks of submitting some controversial matter to "the court of public opinion," mass democracy is implied as an ultimate normative social standard. The concepts of *public service* and *public servant*, as commonly used, express mass democratic ideals: e.g., the career politician must serve the public and not him- or herself. Likewise, it is the vision implied or assumed in a great deal of populist political oratory and commentary, for it lends itself well to bombastic flights of rhetoric justifying policy in the name of the common person; in this it is unlike pluralism, which is a more difficult concept to "get across" in mass address, as the latter requires either a considerable degree of audience sophistication or unwieldy explanations by the speaker. The topics of "government by special interests" and "campaign reform" arise generally from social criticism premised on mass democratic ideals. So too is talk of a "public mandate."

As political scientist Harold Lasswell (1936) pointed out, social elites also tend to speak in terms of the common destiny. The problem of representativeness is always chronic in mass democracy, i.e., do the vocalizations of political representatives or advocates *really* represent the voice of the people? Or are representatives and advocates more self-serving than public serving? The voice of the people is only articulated by their choosing between yeses or nos, or between limited numbers of candidates on a ballot, while the policies and problems of government are complex, myriad, and ever-changing. Disjunction to some degree is inevitable: resolving it to the extent possible is considered to be the art of good government under the mass democratic system.

Mass democracy must also exist at a level that is many orders of magnitude above the more immediately participatory forms of democracy represented by town hall-style meetings, committees, university department faculties, or by the exclusive conditions of citizenship that existed in the ancient Greek *polis*. The sheer scale of modern nationhood precludes any such intimacy, except ersatz intimacy via television or radio. Professional advocates or representatives carry on civic discourse at a level that is relatively remote from the common person, most often; and nationally televised "town hall meetings" are now scripted media events lacking the spontaneity and lively debate (along with the incessant, mind-numbing caviling) of more immediate forms of democracy. Thus a truly representative mass democracy, while exceedingly easy to proclaim, is by no means an easy thing to achieve or maintain.

Since the arrival of methodologically sound techniques of inferential statistics in the mid-twentieth century, e.g., random sampling and probabilistic confidence intervals for accurately estimating population parameters, public opinion polling has been held forth as a new scientific tool for obtaining a more perfect democracy (e.g., Gallup & Rae, 1940). Hence a good indicator of the mass democracy ethos at work is a constant reliance for justification on polls and survey data as if they were some higher form of revealed truth.

Another indicator is the mass democratic theorists' uneasiness with pluralism's influential groups, which they see as impediments likely to unfairly thwart the popular will and promote an unhealthy social situation that has become known as Madisonian factionalism (e.g., Berry, 1997; Lowi, 1969). Madison had worried that U.S. democracy would degenerate into a condition in which groups or factions blindly pursued their self-interests with no thought to the common good.

Pure mass democracy has been much feared traditionally, for at some uncertain point it turns into mob rule. The *tyranny of the majority* is a classic problem for the framers of democratic constitutions, who build safeguards into constitutional governments in order to impede the too hurried implementation (or stampeding) of the popular will. These safeguards amount to the institutionalization of at least some degree of pluralism as a remedy; bicameral legislative houses and separate judicial, legislative and executive branches serve as checks not only to the excesses of other branches of government, but also to excesses by voters.

Mass democracy regularizes and sustains social action by periodically collecting individual opinion/attitude and channeling it along constitutional lines. It espouses a highly rationalized, reductionist social system much unlike the pragmatic, ad hoc blend of pluralism.

Social Movement Theory

Social movement theory regards the world from within the materialistic confines of a Marxist political-economic-sociology wherein class and cultural structures are situated oppositionally. A well-organized, elite, resource-rich class controls the means of production, and thus dominates the disorganized, resource-poor masses. Social action for the resource-less individual is accomplished through organized mass action leading to direct class conflict. Class boundaries are seen as more or less fixed fortifications that must be broken down, undermined or assailed, unlike in pluralism or mass democracy, where boundaries are seen as more permeable or less important. Strictly speaking, no medium for social force is required in social movement theory because oppositional bodies come in direct contact, i.e., *conflict*. Class identity and solidarity are thought to directly communicate individual affect; in a sense, individual affect becomes collective affect through *solidarity*.

The term "grievances" is sometimes applied to polarizing events that lead to social movement-type action, e.g., an environmental movement responds to corporate manufacturing waste that threatens the quality of life for an urban minority community. Although grievances are thought to be not so distinct an organizing principle as social class (Johnston, Larana, & Gusfield, 1994), which provides perhaps the best launching point for action-in-solidarity, unionism being an excellent example. There is also thought to be a "new" social movement ethos or theoretical formulation, wherein social movements are said to rise "in defense of identity" (Melluci, 1980, as cited in Johnston et al., p. 10). Examples of these pure *identity* type movements are provided by groups pivoting about various identity-axes such as gay rights, black power, white power, and some of the more militant forms of feminism. The concepts of victimization and culture when used as mobilizing tools can be construed as social movement–type mobilization and also, recently, what appears to be an emerging "gun culture." More will be said of this gun culture later in the book.

In any case, what is definitely required for mobilization to occur under either the "old" or "new" social movement theory is the creation or harnessing of class, racial, gender, or cultural consciousness, i.e., *identity*. This is often done with the assistance of propagandas of agitation and consciousness-raising (Arendt, 1948; Ellul, 1965). The individual is awakened from social unconsciousness or an ideologically inspired dream state fostered by the dominant class, a "false consciousness," and then impressed into an organized, irresistibly massive and united force, a counter-class phenomenon described as *solidarity*. Of solidarity Tarrow states, "This involves mounting collective challenges, drawing on common purposes, building solidarity and sustaining collective action—the basic properties of social movements" (1994, p. 3). Movements offer meaningful avenues of participation for the individual, whose aggrieved identity is manifested in direct action and reaction.

The essential, distinctive features of social movement force (i.e., mobilization), in summary, are *conflict, solidarity* and *identity*. Johnston and his coauthors—who discuss the analogous concepts of *grievances, collective identity,* and *ideology*—caution that even though such terms may be "analytically separate, there is a strong relationship between them" (1994, p. 22). Nevertheless, the three concepts usefully distinguish the mobilization style of groups such as labor unions and gay rights organizations from that of quilting clubs and bowling leagues.

A series of three concentric spheres, all contained within the largest sphere, could be used to illustrate the social movement's psychocosmology. At the center, the smallest sphere is identity, the individual alone and potentially unprotected. The outermost sphere is that of conflict, the hostile and threatening world. The intermediate sphere is solidarity—the bulwark between identity and conflict. Undoubtedly an orthodox social movement advocate who favored a collectivist rights approach would object at this point and say that there really should be only two spheres: the outer sphere of world conflict and an inner sphere of merged, collectivist-class identity. I don't disagree, and from a practical point of view there is little difference, for in either case maintaining the sense of identity depends totally on keeping intact the bulwark of solidarity. The two-sphere dichotomous worldview, us versus them, is an excellent representation of the individual who has been successfully mobilized in the social movement.

In social movement conceptualizations, the mobilization process is often represented as a historically inevitable process of development, the outgrowth of systemic social injustice. Thus the mobilized individual becomes aligned with the supposedly nomothetic forces of Hegelian dialectic that Arendt has half mockingly called the "train of history." Historically, both Hitlerean and Stalinist totalitarianism, she concluded, had the same general type of unfolding historical explanation at their cores, despite the apparent differences on their political surfaces. Because of the primacy of these "unfolding of history" notions in social movements, Schumpeter has identified the social movement approach as sharing utopian pretensions of millennialist religions (1943). The revolution will lead us to the Promised Land. At any rate, many scholars have noted a religious-like fervor peculiar to social movements. Sometimes romanticized notions of a glorious past substitute for grand nomothetic philosophies; e.g., the tendentious "histories" of extreme white and black power movements that view more or less mythic past racial achievements as standards for the unfolding future; or the imaginings of certain environmental activists about getting back to a "natural" state where, presumably, insects would eat neither them nor their organic gardens. The ideologies of all such groups allows individuals to perceive themselves as warriors or pioneers engaged in the struggle for a heroic cause, and it makes little difference that the cause might be restorative or remedial in its scope. In every case, though, individual opinion and/or affect channels through a collective social action that is focused at some perceived establishment that is an ongoing source of injustice or aggravation.

The identity-sense that fuels action-in-solidarity goes well beyond the "agree or disagree" variety of attitudinal measures used for survey research that crop up so often under the mass democracy ethos. To give an example of the distinct difference, many if not most persons will identify themselves as "environmentalists" when responding to surveys, answering "agree" or "strongly agree" to questions on whether economic growth should be sacrificed when environmental matters are at stake. This is an armchair response in most cases, for no action follows or is seriously intended, but the person whose *identity* is that of an environmental activist—who, by the way, would also respond with "strongly agree" on such surveys—does something tangible to defend or advance this sense of identity, i.e., action-in-solidarity, and he may demonstrate, get thrown in jail, or perhaps even sabotage logging operations.

Social movement leaders and would-be leaders tend to speak of "mass movements," and mass mobilizations are often implied in social movement rhetoric, as a class is more than a few people; but many movement/identity type organizations do not appear to be all that massive, e.g., movement type organizations on university campuses where a "mass meeting" may only draw a dozen participants. Or at the very least it is unclear just how large many of these groups might be. Nevertheless the injustice type grievance that provides the organizing germ for the social movement is often treated as a warrant by group spokespersons to advocate on behalf of "the masses" or for whole classes of persons who are absent from meetings and who are perhaps not even aware of the grievance. Much of this has to do, no doubt, with the distinct identity sense found in movements, where the case is perhaps as Aristotle observed, most people think that others think in the same way as themselves (Roberts, 1954); but also contributing to this sense of license are the "train of history" explanatory tendencies of movements, so that advocates are speaking, as it were, on behalf of inevitable historical forces. Some social movement groups can turn out many thousands of persons for contentious demonstrations, as has been shown, and obviously do represent some sort of true "mass" movement. Mass organizer Vladimir Lenin talked of collecting all the "drops and streamlets" of mass excitement over social outrages and combining them into a "single gigantic flood," a task that he and his fellow revolutionaries ably accomplished (Lenin, 1929/1966, p. 111).

Social movement theorists regard interest groups with suspicion, for they do not as a rule see individual-level "interest" as a legitimate or just social-organizational principle and normatively opt instead for the collective approaches based on shared class, race, or cultural identity. In a seminar once on social movements, remarkable primarily for the normative intensity with which many of the participants approached the topic of social movement mobilization, I heard one of the participants try to explain away the apparent existence of right-wing social movements that were based on "individual rights and interest," which was "bad," as opposed to "good social movements" that were instead based on "collective rights." For this reason, in that participant's view, any individual-interest-based movement could not possibly be a "real" social movement.

My own observation, too, has been that social movement advocates tend more to proselytize than converse in their interactions with nonaligned others, i.e., others find them argumentative, while the pluralist is more able to accord validity to another's interests.

Also troubling to social movement advocates is the multiple interest aspect of pluralism, where a person exerts influence perhaps by joining several groups that are disparate in purpose; this is troubling because a person cannot normally hold multiple collective identities with any level of intensity. A collectively held "class" identity is regarded as a more just warrant for political action.

Pluralistic type interest groups are also suspect to many social movement theorists because they are quite reasonably viewed as a private conversation between bourgeois or upper class sub-elements. McAdam (1982) puts it in this way:

> There may exist a political arena in America, but it is not the teeming convention hall depicted by the pluralists. Only those groups with sufficient political capital need apply. Lacking such capital, most groups in American society have virtually no bargaining power with which to advance their collective interests. Instead, by virtue of their disproportionate control over the political arena, powerful groups are generally able to exclude the powerless with little fear of political reprisal. (p. 20)

Social movement theory and mass democracy theory thus would agree that pluralistic interest groups are insiders who manipulate the political system at social expense.

Sustaining social action over time is a serious problem in social movement theory, as the stimulating grievance may vary in intensity over time, or the opportunities for successful collective action may not often present themselves. Prosperity, to use the well-known example, kills unions. Similarly, people may take to the streets under extreme conditions, but at some point they must go home to sleep. Whenever movements institutionalize to solve the problem of sustained action, they become subject to the same laws of oligarchy as any other organization and can loose touch with their constituents and origins. Social activism quickly degenerates into featherbedding.

Of course, the three modes of social action intermix in political theory and in real life. Many observers and political commentators carry with them unexamined assumptions that fit, more or less, into one of the modes; others seem to exist in more than one mode at a time; but others are quite consciously dogmatic regarding their views on consensual social action. Politicians, in my experience, preach mass democracy while practicing a vigorous and pragmatic pluralism behind closed doors, while at times it is impossible to discern where social movement theory leaves off and mass democracy begins. For purposes of this discussion, however, the modes are now sufficiently outlined so that the reader can recognize them as general types.

Now, very important for the purpose of understanding NRA effectiveness, each of the three modes of social action is accompanied by fairly specific views on the role/function of mass media in society and in social action. Once again these views can be summarized according to the three ideal types.

Role of Mass Media in Social Action

Pluralistic Media

Pluralistic approaches to the social role of mass media have traditionally been dominant in the context of American representative democracy. Since approximately the beginning of the twentieth century, scholars, propagandists, and public relations practitioners have produced numerous accounts from the pluralistic vantage point of how mass media are affected by press strategies by various organizations, including interest groups. The most basic structural assumption of the pluralistic approach is that of message competition in an open system, an arrangement that Lasswell (1934) once referred to as a free market place of competing propagandas. Dahl's well-known studies of pluralistic influence fit this mold, where society is seen as the net result of its contributing groups (1963, 1982).

Always, in the pluralistic view, messages and media are assumed to serve special interests, with media organizations and journalists themselves simply constituting additional sets of interests. There is no such thing as "pure" information. As was the case with the early American newspapers researched by Schudson (1978), partisanship and special interest, if not baldly explicit, are regarded as implicitly informing virtually all mass-mediated messages. The pluralistic theorist would wonder why anyone would reasonably expect otherwise, unless that person, as a consumer of information, were willing to pay the considerable price of gathering information instead of relying on mass-mediated information that is provided and/or subsidized (in effect) by advertisers, patrons and other self-interested organizational sources.

An *instrumental* social role for mass media is embodied in pluralistic-style press relations, public information, and communication strategies. Such strategies, or techniques, on the whole, are aimed at designing, packaging, and targeting of advertising or publicity-type messages in such a way that messages will simultaneously, to some degree, suit the needs of journalists, the publics for which they are intended, and, most importantly, the originators of the messages. Pluralistically informed media research aims at understanding these techniques and their effects under various conditions. Much of the huge literature in this area can be grouped interchangeably under the paradigms of either *public relations* or *propaganda*. The principal idea is that press coverage — and by extension, mass public opinion — is simulated, manipulated, exploited, or created outright in a number of ways by voluntary associations business, special interests, or governments, sometimes at the expense of the public (see J. M. Sproule's historical reviews; 1989, 1996), but often for the public good as well. The latter is the unifying idea behind the works and careers of seminal pioneer practitioner-theorists such as Edward Bernays (1928, 1929) and Ivy Lee (see Cutlip, 1994). Propaganda or public relations is seen as promoting the general well being by propagating new services and social programs.

Public relations theorists and practitioners generally take pluralism as a matter of course, not even bothering to think about it, for the idea of mobilizing or communicating with various *publics* underlies and defines, virtually, current public relations theory (e.g., Cutlip, Center & Broom, 2000).

It is significant, however, that under the pluralistic approach even though interest groups utilize mass media news sources (just as mass media professionals symbiotically utilize interest groups for information), interest groups do not rely exclusively on mass media for their communication needs — far from it, in fact.

Wright suggests a vital communication function of interest groups in his work on interest group effects on public policy. He maintains that an *informational model* explains the influence of interest groups because, in an almost monopolistic fashion, interest groups excel at the "acquisition and strategic transmission of information that legislators need to make good public policy and to get reelected" (Wright, 1995, p. 2).

Obviously, too, many special interest organizations excel at specialized communication with their membership and also with mass media to the point that, from a functional viewpoint, such organizations could be regarded as nodal information systems distributed throughout society. The system of American voluntary associations, looked at in this way, becomes a system of overlapping information networks that operates within and without the mass media system. Regarding interest groups or associations as nodal information centers is possibly one of the best ways of understanding how they operate, for in this aspect media and everyone else depend heavily on them as sources. It should then come as no surprise that pluralistically informed theorists and practitioners who work for such groups tend to regard mass media as supplemental instruments, although often as extremely important supplements, helpful in achieving special interest goals, i.e., instruments.

Those having no professional experience with this side of the information world often have little understanding of the high degree of artificiality of the mass-mediated world manifested by news. Most American news, despite the independent pretensions of journalists, comes ultimately from organizational sources such as press releases and special events. This was as true in the 1920s as it is today, with the current proportion of such "synthetic" news estimated at 50 to 80 percent (Jackall & Hirota, 2000). Partly because investigative reporting is a budget-straining rarity, although practiced at times by the larger news organizations, news comes largely from centralized sources, e.g., the White House, large corporations, Beltway interest groups, and state universities. Journalists, by no means passive receptacles, freely modify information, sometimes in ways nearly unrecognizable to the frustrated practitioners who have staged media events and provided the information, but the fact remains that the media coverage initiative lies mostly with public relations or media-relations practitioners. Even in the case of natural events like floods and earthquakes, practitioners have become so adept over the years at garnering coverage that these events are often virtually co-opted by various organizations: the natural disaster story instead becomes the story of organizational response or White House empathy as formulated by staff speechwriters in time for evening news production deadlines.

Journalists, more or less, are seen as hacks or even as obstacles in the more cynical versions of pluralistic media theory. At best, the pluralistic theorist or practitioners views journalists as "information workers" who process, repackage, and redistribute material that has most often been manufactured by others. If one has ever had the experience of writing a press release and subsequently seeing it published virtually intact, or as a major portion of a news story, but under the byline of a journalist, then one is familiar with this aspect of journalism. Many public relations practitioners regard journalists as autonomous fellow professionals (the converse may not be so often true) and attempt to pursue accommodative strategies, hoping to simultaneously advance the agendas of their organizations by meeting journalists' needs for timely information.

It is especially important for purposes of this discussion that, in general, the pluralistic model regards interest group communication strategies as causing media coverage. Events occur, of course, independent of any organizational plan, e.g., accidents and scandals, but even here the pluralistic goal is to resume the informational initiative through damage control and the credibility-enhancing release of "appropriate" factual information to news media. Good coverage is controlling how stories are cast so as to legitimate the organization and further its goals.

Mass Democratic Media

American journalists and normative conceptualizations of journalism such as the "social responsibility" theory of mass media, progressive era "reform-style" journalism, and "public journalism," appear, on the whole, to be anchored within the mass democracy framework for social action. These conceptualizations regard mass media as an integral part of the structure of social action because they serve to connect the individual voter with policy makers, thus providing individuals with information required for responsibly exercising the right (or as some would say, the obligation) to vote rationally. In the most pure and possibly naïve form of this approach, the mass democratic theorist views media as the glue that holds together modern mass democratic systems. In this formulation, mass media link individual voters to their representatives in government; to current ideas; to their political parties; to events; and hence, collectively, media can be viewed as a medium of social action that complements the formal structure of constitutional government.

Special interests are seen as a threat, unless they are duly elected or appointed interests clearly working for the general social good. Journalists, accordingly, should regard information with suspicion until it is properly checked out—and it is paramount that journalists are not taken advantage of by special interests or self-serving political actors who are seen as eagerly attempting to manipulate the news. Thus is justified the growing journalistic style of *interpretative journalism*, documented by Patterson (1994), wherein journalists tend to point out the intentions of would-be public opinion manipulators. Here, reporters discuss the public relations strategies of newsmakers such as politicians, analyzing each move as if reporting a championship game of football. Mass media are seen as duty bound in this conceptualization: they must report accurately, objectively and substantively on "the facts," and/or their meanings as interpreted by journalists, so that the citizen can optimally and rationally arrive at well-informed decisions about how to best spend his only vote. Journalists themselves often become political experts, and this is expected from the best journalists. Lippmann (1922) regarded this sort of expertise as the solution to the inherent mass democratic problem of the relatively uniformed electorate with no direct experience of political events, and many journalists seem more than willing to take on this burden. The proliferation of news programming on which journalists interview other journalists concerning political events is an excellent example.

Mass media professionals like to regard themselves in the reflection of the mass democracy model because it elevates them from mere functionaries, hacks and/or talking heads to the status of expert social guardians. The notion of "media standing as a watchdog over government is one of the cherished images of U.S. journalism" (McLeod, Kosicki, & McLeod, 1994, p. 153). Journalists have an integral role, an important role. In effect, mass media professionals become a priesthood charged with informational augury reading; they examine convoluted raw information and issue simplified interpretations of its meanings. The doctrine of a free press takes on religious overtones as well. Adversarial and watchdog models for the role of media are also well regarded under this approach—as long as there is illumination without too much accompanying cynicism, wanton destruction, or sensationalism—while lapdog tendencies are censured because they impede truly democratic discussion of ideas by not properly scrutinizing ideas and their sources. The press are charged with social responsibility and above all must not serve to legitimate special interest needs.

The valence of press coverage over the long term is thought to be extremely important, as press coverage is virtually equated with the development of public opinion and agendas that eventually lead, via the mechanics of representative democracy, to policy agendas. Rephrased, if the press are the interpretive experts, what they say matters. Coverage here is seen as the outcome of the application of a set of journalistic and social norms to objectively occurring events; the social norms concern the public's right to know while the journalistic norms concern obligation and methods to reveal relevant truth. The metaphor often encountered is of media constituting the public forum where ideas are tested by debate and judged by all in the clear light of day. This differs from the "competing propaganda" view of pluralism because journalists are here thought to be the guardians of the system, the providers of illumination and balance, while the pluralistic view downplays the journalist's role by attributing the responsibility for information more or less directly to organizational sources; where balance, if any, is provided by competing organizations. In mass democracy's media practices, the journalists provide balance and fairness based on professional routines, or upon their own or their editors' judgment of what constitutes fairness or balance. Although the mass democratic media system can go wrong in a number of ways that require ongoing media self-criticism and self-correction, overall, coverage is regarded as vitally important in that it legitimates or delegitimates persons, groups and the ideas promulgated by groups and persons.

Again, an important distinction, coverage in this model ideally is thought to be controlled or caused by objective events as interpreted by the journalists — acting in their professional roles as expert guardians to democracy — and if the trend is otherwise, the system is viewed as having miscarried.

Social Movements and Mass Media

Consistent with the notion of class conflict that underlies Marxist sociology, social movement theorists see mass media in the Western democracies as more or less overt instruments of social control or class-cultural dominance. Herman and Chomsky's (1988) model of propaganda "filters" for news exemplifies this kind of analysis: ownership concentration, huge start-up costs, centralization, structural bias, ideological bias, and elite class interests all intersect, and the net result is to keep the news free of inconvenient truths that might seriously threaten ruling/owning class control.

The basic idea behind social movement press relations, such as they are, seems to be collectivist protest or confrontation, "to turn news into contested terrain" (Ryan, 1991): if a group can garner coverage through challenge or disruption of an established hegemonic social order, it is achieving its goal. Ryan, in her guidebook for social movement media activists, describes this strategy in terms of the "challenger message." A repertoire of collective action techniques is available too within the culture, which under the right conditions, i.e., the proper "opportunity structure," can be used to demonstrate against the establishment (Tarrow, 1994; Tilly, 1978). The recent World Trade Organization protests in Seattle, Washington, provide an example of an opportunity structure and use of collective action techniques by environmentalists, apparently organized along social movement lines, to disruptively challenge and thereby earn considerable media attention.

For the most part, large-scale challenger accomplishments such as Seattle are difficult to accomplish due to an imbalance of power and resources. Therefore, a closely related goal of social movement activists—and of many social movement theorists who are influenced by the doctrine of praxis—is to raise consciousness on the part of oppressed classes on how to properly "decode" dominant media messages (see Hall, 1980; Streeter, 1978).

For an example of decoding at work, Herman and Chomsky (1988), with their propaganda model, offer what is in effect a decoding key that reveals the "true" content of media messages as opposed to "preferred" decodings that support what they see as a dominant American imperialist ideology. According to their model, news passes through a number of ideological and structural "filters" such that the final product shows "deserving" and" undeserving" victims in such a way as to justify U.S. military-economic imperialistic tendencies.

More generally, if a person can somehow be convincingly shown that mass media constitute a capitalist engine of socialization, economic exploitation and/or placation, rather than a "marketplace of ideas," then through living with the omnipresent mass-mediated messages of modern life, that person henceforth perceives what is in effect a different world, the subterranean mechanics of which have been succinctly explained. I prefer the term *disambiguated*. Many people prefer this sort of easy-to-understand explanation to everyday, baffling reality, as has been noted by Arendt in her study of social movement totalitarianism (1948); by Jung in his investigations of myth (1956); and by Ellul in his reflections on the religious-like needs fulfilled by propaganda in mass society (1965). To successfully provide a potential mass media audience member with just such a decoding key is a major accomplishment, and hence a goal, of virtually any social movement organization—for henceforth mass media exposure becomes a constant provider of proofs and perceptual reinforcements that confirm the existence of the basic conflict or injustice that necessitates collective action. Moreover, messages thus decoded affirm and reinforce the identity of the decoder as the object of systematic oppression or distortion, thereby inciting the in-group solidarity necessary for mass action.

I will term this process of decoding and reinforcement as *antimedia theory*, while the solidarity benefits that negative coverage confers upon organizational membership will be referred to as the *mobilization effect*. By these means it is possible that even the most negative sort of media coverage concerning the social movement group can build member solidarity and lead to more effective organizing, a situation that is quite the reverse of the more conventional notion that negative press will impede both organizational effectiveness and influence.

Several caveats need to be made at this point concerning social movements. Many an organization that has been described either by itself or by journalists as a "movement" is probably no such thing. To begin with, social movements can be fashionable, so an imitation factor exists; anyone can claim to represent a social movement, and often does. More, social movements are often perceived as responsive to social injustice, i.e., the grievance; movements consequently often have a high moral tone about them. It is no accident that the civil rights movement sprang in large part from American churches. So for an organization or group to succeed in labeling itself as a social movement can be an excellent public relations device. It shows an organization that is innately "good" in comparison to some rejected social standard.

What is more, the repertoire of collective action techniques described by Tarrow is nearly as available to pluralistic public relations practitioners as it is to social movement activists. A protest demonstration and a media event are much the same; some protest demonstrations have been known to pay "protesters" by the hour; many well-paid professionals represent themselves as social activists; and some organizations that represent themselves as mass social movements are in all probability staff-run advocacy groups whose constituency is a mailing list and whose popular warrant is based on the interpretation of public opinion polls. The line is blurred, and becomes increasingly blurred as public relations practitioners—doing what they do best—pseudomorphically adapt their clients, strategies, and tactics to new social trends.

Also, *identity* is a well-harnessed concept in advertising, but just because a consumer is described, for example, as a "Pepper," referring to product users in certain television soft drink advertisements, this does not mean they are involved in serious social-economic conflict with the class of non-Peppers. This very common sort of commercial use of identity usually falls far short of the entrenched sense of identity at the core of social movements. A great deal of money has been made, though, by mass marketing counter-culture type products (e.g., music) to adolescents and young adults, encouraging or taking advantage of what might be construed as an entrenched collective sense of identity. So once again the line blurs, with the difference hinging in large part on the ultimate goal in evoking the identity sense, namely economic exploitation in marketing versus political mobilization in social movements.

Finally, the term *social movement* itself does not necessarily mean the same thing in everyday language, or the language of journalism, as it does in social science and as it is used in this book. In the vernacular, it could variously refer to a fad, a short- or long-term trend in public opinion polls, a coordinated communication campaign on some issue or another by an organization, or it could merely be a term that a journalist has picked up from a press release that promoters have used as a label for their special event or program. In-depth case studies would be required to judge accurately in many instances.

Turning finally to the basic relationship between media coverage and social movements, in this mode of social action, extant coverage patterns essentially predetermine social movement strategies. This is necessarily true because the genuine social movement is by definition outside, i.e., in conflict with, the dominant structures of society, which would include of course major mass media. A true social movement does not, it cannot, control media coverage in the same fraternal manner as the pluralistic type interest group that happens to be a subcomponent of the dominant classes. As an underclass the movement has matters to address that the dominant classes would prefer to leave off their civic agenda. Therefore the movement generally finds itself responding to, or maneuvering around, coverage patterns that are outside of the movement's control.

Again, it is important to remember that the foregoing typology of social action modes is based on ideal types that appear to be prevalent in the modern democracies. So, too, with the corresponding ideas presented regarding the respective roles of mass media. Everyday examples will often present a mixture of types, sometimes muddled beyond hope of clarity.

Likewise many who speak of political-social action appear to have no clear idea whatsoever of what they really mean; or that they may be confined by an unexamined set of assumptions concerning the nature of social action; or else they may hold to some normative bias based within one of the social action modes to the point of perceptual distortion.

Much discussion of the NRA has been conducted under such conditions. Hence, in part, the existence of the apparent paradoxes outlined in the introduction, for what is paradox other than the point of intersection at which unexamined assumptions have collided?

By using these abstracted types of social action as a theoretical foundation, it becomes possible to show more clearly how the NRA—long considered a more or less conventional pluralistic interest group—has been able to utilize negative press coverage in accord with social movement principles to organize and mobilize its members, thus vastly increasing its organizational effectiveness. In fact, I put forward and will later support the claim that NRA has not only benefited from the existence of negative press, but also has come to rely upon its presence as an important strategic tool in its communications.

2

Media Coverage Effects and the National Rifle Association

Views on the Nature of NRA Coverage

In accord with pluralistic media theory, because the NRA is a well funded, well-organized interest group, we would expect on the whole that its media strategies and techniques would result in favorable media coverage. The pluralistic model in this case would be the model taken from public relations where, in the most general and simplified form:

Group Communication Strategy → Media Coverage

The arrows are not meant to suggest an absolute causal relationship, merely the general pattern of events resulting in media coverage; and the diagram could be complicated with the addition of all sorts of contributing factors, but these additions would not alter the central idea that, under the pluralistic arrangement, groups create coverage.

But this has not been the case with the NRA, at least not according to NRA officials. Through means of its publications and spokespersons NRA has frequently charged the national news media with a systematic negative reporting bias against the NRA, firearms, firearm owners, and the very idea of the individual right to own firearms. NRA's official journal, *The American Rifleman*, for a typical example, has denounced "the American media's anti-gun agenda" as a national media "vendetta against the Second Amendment" (National Rifle Association, January 1994, p. 49).

Similarly, Etten (1991) examined 117 stories from state and local newspaper, concluding that pro-gun control bias occurred four times more often than anti-gun control bias, a finding that would certainly carry over into NRA coverage. NRA also received negative coverage in small-scale studies that I have conducted preliminary to this research (Patrick, 1997, 1999). What is more, content analysis findings of U.S. elite newspapers that will be presented in the next chapter show that press coverage on NRA tends very much toward the negative as compared to analogous mass membership interest groups.

In accord with role expectations for the press under the mass democracy role of media, many mass democracy theorists and journalists would explain that if NRA coverage is indeed negative, it is because the coverage reflects the nature of reality: coverage simply mirrors reality. As a journalist asked during a recent interview concerning my findings on NRA coverage, "What else can you say about an organization that says and does such outrageous things?" The claim that is being advanced here is that generally, in its most simplified form:

$$\text{Reality} \rightarrow \text{Media Coverage}$$

Of course the claim is untenable in this pure form, as everyone knows, as this would be a model not of journalism, but of revelation. Journalists themselves cannot possibly be without influence in the coverage that they write, thus the more reasonable model is

$$\text{Reality} \rightarrow \text{(Journalists)} \rightarrow \text{Media Coverage}$$

Wherein journalists act as an intermediating professional body that processes reality according to a set of established routines and standards before passing on what is judged to be relevant information to their publics. Once again, the central relationship could be complicated with other contributing factors, but once again this would still not alter the nature or general direction of the basic arrangement. Here, it is thought that if the NRA does or represents negative things it will receive negative coverage as the indirect result.

If actual barriers exist to fair NRA coverage, then the social movement model comes into play. The social movement model reverses the direction of the pluralistic model — since structural and ideological factors assure that media coverage will be generally unfavorable or inaccessible, and the group will be stigmatized in fairly systematic ways. NRA communication strategy must then necessarily follow from the type of coverage that will be received. Shorn of all complicating factors, the general social movement model schematic is

> Media Coverage → Group Communication Strategy

It is through the application of this latter model that NRA success can be explained, for it is the model that best fits the evidence of successful NRA mobilization in the face of negative coverage. The existence of both mobilization and negative coverage can be demonstrated, and they are correlated, as must indeed be the case if the model is true. The evidence is presented concretely in chapters that follow.

Effects of Negative Coverage

If the social movement model has explanatory value, we would expect to find a number of confirming indicators, the initial indicator being the existence of a broad pattern of negative media coverage of NRA, verifiable and measurable via a systematic content analysis.

Next, this negative coverage would predetermine to a large extent NRA communication strategies, which would be based upon the social movement mobilizing principles of identity, solidarity and conflict. We would expect also that the NRA would go to considerable lengths to co-opt this omnipresent negative coverage by providing an anti-media theory that would decode and disambiguate coverage for its members and potential members, thereby promoting in-group action-in-solidarity.

Last, we would expect NRA mobilization to be assisted by negative coverage, i.e., a mobilization effect. This is so because social movement- type organization as it is conducted in defense of identity springs from oppositional forces that operate at the societal level. The differences that spur the true movement exist a priori, although they can be aggravated or managed artificially once present. In the case of the existence of widespread negative coverage, individuals would be reached virtually everywhere in the United States, but with the message most intrusive to those whose sense of identity was most at stake. Every such message would be proof and reinforcement not only of the existence of a basic conflict but would also act as a goad to mobilize.

Even apparently bland messages on a grievance topic would likely be construed as threatening to someone with a besieged sense of identity.

It is not my intention to construct a comprehensive psychology of social movement organization, as this would be a serious undertaking in itself (although well worth doing). A few words seem necessary, though. Psychoanalysts have long known that clients whose sense of self-identity is somehow at stake can show an incredible hypersensitivity to events, interpreting the impersonal as highly personal, projecting their insecurities on others, and otherwise making even the most insignificant of external occurrences loom large psychologically. Psychoanalyst Karen Horney (1950) discussed these tendencies at length, as did Harold Lasswell (1934) in his early treatment of politics and individual insecurity. But perhaps above everything else in considering these matters we should not forget that media coverage *is* the perceived political world for many persons who do not otherwise experience the activities of macro-level politics; grievances are thus conveyed and made salient.

A characteristic sensitivity to media coverage appears to exist among NRA members and potential supporters. I have been a guest on call-in radio talk shows several times during the past year to discuss NRA media coverage. Some of these shows were on public radio stations where the producers assured me that their call-in audience tended to be reflective of "liberal" university communities served by these stations. Despite the producers' predictions, in all cases, public stations and others, the ratio of pro-gun or pro-NRA callers to anti-gun or anti-NRA callers was approximately ten to one.

A more systematic proof of the existence of this media sensitivity (detailed in the content analysis findings presented in the next chapter) is that NRA officials and supporters are more than six times as likely to complain of bias in coverage than are other interest groups. Based on personal observation and research, this media sensitivity is widespread if not virtually universal among NRA supporters.

The NRA as Social Movement

Edward Leddy (1987) appears to have originally suggested that the NRA be treated as a social movement. According to Leddy, over time the NRA turned from a narrowly focused sporting and conservation club into a politically charged mass membership organization. In 1977, in a bitter coup that has come to be known as the Cincinnati Revolt—after the site of that year's annual NRA meeting—the organizational by-laws were changed so that members rather than NRA's president could nominate directors. As a direct result, the membership voted out the old conservationist leadership and firearms-rights activists took over (see Tartaro, 1981, for a history of the revolt).

To support his social movement hypothesis, Leddy content-analyzed NRA's official publication *The American Rifleman* from 1926 to 1983 and was able to show the emergence of political themes as opposed to hobby and technical themes that had dominated the earlier publications. But the political themes, despite the value of Leddy's study, do not in themselves constitute a social movement; they are necessary but not sufficient. The emergence of the political themes, according to Leddy (pp. 29-54), were the result of "gun culture" mobilizing in response to an "adversarial culture," a "new class," or "managerial culture" that sought to manage out of existence traditional values of the sort epitomized by gun ownership. A number of similar class-cultural explanations of mobilization are beginning to converge about the politics of gun control, with a collection of such papers published as *The Gun Culture and its Enemies* (Tonso, 1989). Nisbett has explicated a "culture of honor" concept derived from herdsman traditions with which he has attempted to explain southern U.S. propensities for gun ownership and settling of disputes by use of firearms (Nisbett, 1996). So a convergent set of findings points to the NRA phenomenon as being intertwined with an emerging social movement that is based on a class-cultural identity.

NRA as Pluralistic-Social Movement Hybrid

Despite its relatively recent acquisition of social movement characteristics, the NRA since its beginnings in 1871 has a long history as a fairly conventional pluralistic interest group, with the help along the way of considerable government patronage. The original purpose was to encourage marksmanship in an age of infantry, a need that had been convincingly demonstrated by the abysmal shooting skills of Union soldiers in the Civil War. In this sense it was originally entirely consistent with Walker's patronage model of interest group mobilization.

Thus NRA chronicler O. Davidson has commented on the irony of this patronage, vis a vis NRA's current reputation as a bastion of fierce individualism, stating, "For much of its long history, the NRA's fortunes would rise and fall according to the largess of public institutions" (1993, p. 22). For many decades as well NRA offered powerful incentives to members—a member could buy a U.S. military surplus bolt action rifle in excellent condition in the 1920s for as little as two or three dollars—so that for a long period of time concurrent with government patronage, Olson's incentives explanation of mobilization also fit the organization well. But NRA membership and political influence have continued to grow well after both patronage and significant incentives have almost entirely disappeared. The exertion of NRA political influence has resulted in the withdrawal of the last traces of patronage from the NRA such as government support of national championship rifle and pistol matches along with Director of Civilian Marksmanship ammunition for service weapon competitions. And a major reason behind the Cincinnati Revolt was that the former conservationist directors of the NRA were considering re-positioning the NRA as a recreational-environmental group that would be more attractive for grant-making patronage organizations such as private foundations and corporate sponsors (see Leddy, 1987, pp. 93-102). When the membership did not respond favorably to this proposal it in effect rejected patronage along with the incentive-giving power that would have resulted from patronage.

Because of its current mode of organization the NRA could be considered from the pluralistic point of view quite possibly a model of the ideal mass membership special interest group. This is a type of group that Wright has called a *citizens group* because of its large membership base and democratic methods of operation; opposed would be *staff groups* that are essentially small professional staffs in charge of a "membership" that can at times amount to little more than a mailing list, a membership with little or no control over the direction of the organization (Wright, 1995).

Further, in harmony with Wright's previously mentioned "informational model" for the strategic acquisition and transmission of information to policy makers, the NRA functions as an expert source and advisor to legislators and regulators, a practice for which the dysphemism is "lobbying."

If the NRA behaves indeed as a "model" pluralistic special interest organization, despite the recent acquisition of a social movement mobilization pattern, one would still expect to find the typical pluralistic battery of communication strategies and techniques installed and practiced in the NRA organization, especially including the standard accommodative media strategies associated with modern public relations. Although there appears to exist no systematic description of NRA communication strategies, it is apparent that the NRA does attempt to conduct fairly standard press relations of a sort, even hiring the occasional communication undergraduate as an intern. I have talked with journalists who have described faxes and press releases sent out by NRA media relations personnel. These same journalists report having also interviewed NRA spokespersons representing the media relations office. NRA also operates at least two large-distribution (i.e., available to the public or journalists) e-mail groups; the first covers legislative matters, the other contains press releases. It also hosts a sophisticated web site (NRALIVE) that features video feeds, transcripts of speeches, and other relevant news to persons interested in firearms issues. It also appears that NRA has of late begun to encourage, or at least make use of, "pro-gun" research, thus implementing the indirect technique of having "scientific" evidence produced by supposedly disinterested third parties. Taken altogether, these are the signs of a fairly serious effort at pluralistic type public relations; whether the effort is successful or not is another matter, although I believe the NRA to have been successful in this regard when they have been able to bypass national media.

The NRA also excels in direct communication to its members; in this sense it appears to be an extremely effective nodal informational network. Each month it publishes and mails approximately four million copies of each of its three major publications, *The American Rifleman, The American Hunter,* and *America's First Freedom* (formerly *The American Guardian);* the former two serve sportsmen and hobbyists, the latter is a relatively new publication for persons who are not particularly interested in the sporting aspects of firearms ownership. All three contain essentially the same political and organizing information each month. Only the NRA's *Shooting Sports* magazine contains little political content, being directed mainly at the formal competitive shooters who constitute only a very small percentage of members. NRA also sends out numerous fundraising letters and appeals—members may receive a dozen or more such appeals annually—and like many other organizations, appears on the basis of impressionistic evidence to be partial to the practice of fund-raising through survey-type direct mail approaches. It also has a highly sophisticated capability to customize its magazines and mailings with inserts directing key voting information by states and congressional districts, thus leveraging local and national elections by helping members cast their votes for NRA-approved candidates and referenda.

The NRA, for all of the foregoing reasons and examples, appears to be a hybrid type of social action organization, a pluralistic interest group organizational structure that has acquired a social movement mobilization style. The modern NRA does not mobilize members through patronage, as there is none left to speak of, nor from incentives, as these are insignificant compared to the cost of membership. Social movement theory remains therefore as the most plausible mobilization alternative. This hybridism largely solves the problem of sustained collective action that is chronic to social movements. NRA efficacy is achieved additively; the intensity of the social movement ethos combines with the proven machinery of the pluralistic interest group.

I contend that the route to group effectiveness is social action hybridism of one sort or another. This is one of the major conclusions of this book. But we will revisit these matters more in later chapters. It is time now to present evidence.

3

Elite Newspaper Coverage of Interest Groups

If NRA press coverage is on the whole negative, if barriers prevent fair coverage or access, then the social movement model of mass social action applies. Under this model, structural and/or ideological factors assure that media coverage will be generally unfavorable or inaccessible: the group will not be able to control coverage valence nor create issue-agendas through the standard battery of pluralistic media relations techniques. Group communication strategy must then follow from the type of coverage that will be received; the general situation of the group is described by the social movement schematic of media coverage:

Media Coverage → Group Communication Strategy

This chapter looks systematically at the first half of this schematic, at media coverage patterns of interest groups in what have been termed *elite* U.S. newspapers. Analysis of coverage patterns in elite newspapers is particularly useful because these newspapers serve as models for U.S. media, both in form and content. This chapter contains discussions of (1) the definition and social functions of elite newspapers; (2) methods and measures of quantifying media coverage of interest groups; and (3) evidence of systematic unfavorable NRA coverage in the form of the comparative results of content analysis over a period of nearly a decade, 1990-98. This last discussion item, with numerous examples, comprises the major portion of the chapter.

Elite Newspapers

Definition of Elite Press

A number of newspapers and magazines can be considered as comprising an elite or prestige press in America. The definition is not exact, although it is an attempt to set apart an elite press from the *mainstream press*, the latter being a broader and more inexact concept, and also from the *local press*, many of which are fairly large municipal dailies, but some of which function as little more than community bulletin boards and advertising circulars. The elite press comprise the serious papers and/or magazines of political-social reporting and analysis that enjoy national (or at least regional) and sometimes international status, reputations and circulations. They are regarded as setting national standards for reporting in terms of style and content and also as having considerable influence on administrative and political elites.

Included in the elite or prestige press would be a fair number of publications: *The New York Times, The Wall Street Journal, The Boston Globe, The Washington Post, The Chicago Tribune, Time, Newsweek,* and *U.S. News and World Report,* among others. Not included would be national newspapers or magazines such as *USA Today* or *People,* which appear to be designed more for mass-entertainment markets.

Influence of the Elite Press

In matters of form and content the elite press set the standards of journalistic style and aspiration. Journalists themselves frequently read them. Wilhoit and Weaver (1986) found that 33 percent of the journalists they surveyed regularly read *The New York Times,* 25 percent read *The Wall Street Journal,* and approximately 50 percent read *Time* and/or *Newsweek* magazines. Elite media set news agendas to a large degree. If *The New York Times* covers an event or issue, coverage is likely to follow in other media, particularly broadcast news. Geography factors in also, as most elite media are concentrated in the East, closest to the traditional centers of political power, such that they cover news at the source. While using news from wire services and other elite newspapers as they see fit, elite newspapers maintain sufficient reportorial staff to independently cover presidential events and the doings of government and private organizations in the Washington, D.C., Beltway area, New York, and elsewhere. They cover these centralized sources of power to a far greater extent and depth than is possible for the smaller local papers, which must rely heavily on wire services or stories taken from elite papers for national content. Graber uses the terms "generative media" and "pace setter media" to contrast elite newspapers with local, more "derivative media," also noting, "The heavy reliance of newspeople on these eastern elite media is one reason why patterns of American news coverage are so broadly similar throughout the country" (Graber, 1989, p. 66).

The elite press function as newspapers of the managerial-administrative and middle classes, serving as papers of record for U.S. political events, and of world events as interpreted from the U.S. perspective. They are thought to directly influence managerial and administrative elites, perhaps more so than the "average" person, a phenomenon noted by both Lippmann (1922) and Graber (1989), and which can be interpreted as an essentially pluralistic function whereby political-social managerial elites representing different publics and organizations are communicating with and monitoring each another via the elite news. Merrill has assigned the elite newspapers a global function in this regard, stating, "They are the well-informed, articulate papers that thoughtful people the world over take seriously" (1990, p. 93). The term "managerial elites" refers of course to those professional administrators who are charged with responsibility for navigating their organizations, private or government, rather than merely working within them in as technicians in sharply delimited roles. A social movement–inspired activist could at this point raise the objection that these seemingly disparate managerial elites are but sub-components of a single dominant class. This objection carries some weight.

Elite Newspapers Studied

The discussion of interest group coverage presented in this chapter is based upon 1,474 articles that appeared from 1990-98 in five of the elite newspapers: *The New York Times* (*NYT*), *The Washington Post* (*WP*), *The Christian Science Monitor* (*CSM*), *The Wall Street Journal* (*WSJ*) and, *Los Angeles Times* (*LAT*). These papers were selected because they are important and broadly influential, well representing what informed persons would regard as the elite dailies.

NYT has long been recognized as *the* standard for journalistic writing, and functions virtually as an archival reference work and paper of record for political events. Also a world and national standard is *WSJ* that, like *NYT*, appears daily as if by magic on the desks of managerial-administrative elites across the country. *WP* is widely read because of its proximity to federal sources and the legion of interest groups headquartered in the Beltway; for this reason it serves as a generative source of political reporting for many other news organizations. *CSM* is known for its detailed and well-reputed reportorial contributions on national and global social-political issues. The selection of *LAT* balances geographically the preponderance of East Coast newspapers; however, in its own right it too is a large and well-staffed paper that well signifies the emergence of California as a social model for the nation and the world; *LAT* at the very least is a regional standard, and with the other papers above can be found in libraries, reading rooms, and bookstores across the country.

Measurement of Coverage

Content analysis is used to examine and compare patterns of interest group coverage in the elite newspapers, a research method that has been used since before World War II in the humanities, social sciences, public relations, and propaganda analysis to quantify mass communication according to explicitly defined categories of content (Holsti, 1969).

Content Measurement

Content category measures presented in this chapter are selected for their apparent face validity and consistent reliability over repeated measures. By face validity it is meant that measures represent the most basic properties of news articles from the point of view of the interest group covered: how much the group is allowed to speak in articles; whether the coverage is based on an event staged by the group or by others; whether or not the coverage includes photographs of the group's officers or events, or of non-group persons and events; whether or not group officers or spokespersons pictured or quoted are identified by their proper organizational titles; whether information is attributed to the group by using attributive verbs having positive, negative, or neutral semantic connotations; and whether or not the coverage is headlined by a joking or punning headlines and how the group fares in terms of any satire, humor, or mockery that might be directed at the group (or by the group at others). Few would argue that measures such as these are not valid indicators of how a group fares in coverage.

Valences of articles are measured on scales for content themes that represent fundamentally important cultural themes or values often reported and discussed in the news: e.g., whether the group is shown negatively, neutrally, or positively in regard to themes such as democracy or democratic processes, progress-science, and extremism-dedication. Valence measures can also quantify the semantic tone of editorials concerning the respective interest groups. Also included is a content category that indicates whether the concept of media bias is mentioned in the coverage.

Methodological details concerning the content analysis can be found in Appendix A.

The Interest Groups

Coverage of five mass-membership interest groups provides the basis for comparison: The National Rifle Association, The American Civil Liberties Union, The American Association for Retired Persons, The National Association for the Advancement of Colored Persons, and Handgun Control, Inc. Although differing in their major purposes, these groups are functionally analogous. They are all large citizens groups that offer numerous services to members and the community. They represent *publics* in the pluralistic sense, in voluntary association, and function also as nodal information centers for the strategic collection and dissemination of specialized information (Wright, 1995) that is directed inwardly, to members and sympathizers, and outwardly to other publics and decision makers. To a greater or lesser extent, all of these organizations recruit, lobby, provide services and incentives to members (and others), publish magazines and newsletters, raise and expend funds for strategic purposes, and carry out special events, in addition to other functions that make up the standard battery of public and government relations practices. Taken together, these functions are how interest groups carry out their business in the context of consensual democracy, for even though group purposes may vary, the overall battery of pluralistic techniques is fairly standardized.

Comparison between groups is essential because it is insufficient to show only that a single group (or issue) receives generally negative coverage. The important question is, of course, *negative compared to what?* For the case could well be that a more or less uniformly adversarial press treats all groups and issues negatively.

Appendix B justifies the comparisons of the interest groups, additionally providing background information on the groups and a catalog of their main functions and concerns.

Comparisons of Interest Group Coverage

Content analysis reveals large systematic differences in the treatment of the interest groups by elite newspapers across virtually all of the content measures. These differences, whether measured as mean scores or proportions on the different content categories, are highly significant, most often at levels of statistical confidence exceeding 99 percent.

Compared to coverage of AARP, ACLU, NAACP, and HCI, those articles discussing the NRA tend on average toward fewer paragraphs with direct quotations or attributed viewpoints, less utilization of group pseudo-events, less favorable use of personalization techniques, and more use of joking or punning headlines. They also have higher levels of satire or mockery directed at the group, more negative use of verbs of attribution, less use of appropriate titles of organizational spokespersons or actors, and lower means scores for measures of pro- or anti-democracy themes, extremism themes and science-progress themes. There is also a much greater likelihood of the NRA being the subject of editorial commentary and less use of photographs of NRA actors and events than for the non-NRA groups. Tone and semantics also tend more toward the negative for the NRA in editorial and op-ed coverage than for other groups. Lastly, NRA coverage is much more likely to include themes of media bias than that of other groups. The only measures on which all the groups fare much alike are those for cohesion/dissension within the group and malfeasance vs. orthopraxy on the part of group officials.

With few exceptions that will be noted, the differences hold whether the non-NRA groups are considered in aggregate and then compared with NRA coverage, i.e., NRA versus non-NRA, or if the comparisons are made on a group-by-group basis, i.e., NRA versus NAACP, NRA versus AARP, etc. The differences persist across article types and across different newspapers. What is more, again with relatively few exceptions to be discussed in turn, the non-NRA groups generally do not differ significantly from each other, just from NRA. For the most part, the non-NRA groups fare much alike over the long term, while NRA fares badly. These differences are neither subtle nor ambiguous.

Although these quantitative findings speak for themselves, and should be regarded as core findings of this study, numerous examples from the newspaper articles are also presented. My intentions here are first to preserve in part the richness of data that otherwise would be lost though statistical aggregation, and second to place the reader in a better position to independently judge the validity of the content measures. Observations of patterns of coverage related to the measures are also included wherever such patterns became apparent during the course of the analysis.

All else being equal, these data strongly support a conclusion of systematic marginalization of the NRA in elite newspaper coverage, as compared with other interest groups. NRA is treated as an object much more than as a participant in social discourse. None of the other interest groups receives similar long-term treatment, so it is difficult to plausibly dismiss such large differences in manifest content. Possible reasons for (and effects of) these differing coverage patterns are beyond the ken of the content analysis method per se—which can only tell us what is and not how it came to be—and will be discussed in later chapters.

Amount and Proportion of Quotations

How much an organization is able to put its view across in coverage is perhaps the most important aspect of coverage; it is the point of coverage, in so far as pluralistic interest groups are concerned. It is an important matter also according to the mass democratic role for mass media, wherein fair, balanced, and impartial coverage of events and the principals behind the events fuels the engines of rational citizen participation. Social movement theorists would, of course, assume that the social movement group is largely shut out in this regard.

In this vital aspect, both the number and proportion of quotes or attributed viewpoints are less for NRA than for ACLU, NAACP, AARP, or HCI.

In raw numbers of quotes per article, NRA receives on average only approximately one-third, M (mean) = 1.14 paragraphs per article, of the amount allotted to NAACP (M = 3.44), and not quite half the amount allotted to each of the remaining groups (AARP, M = 2.75; ACLU, M = 2.5; HCI, M = 2.9). See Figure 3.1a.

In proportions of quotes, NRA averages only one-half the proportion that goes to HCI and only approximately one-third the proportion going to the other groups. So while NRA averages about 8 percent of paragraphs of quotes per article, NAACP, ACLU and AARP all average about 25 percent, with HCI at 17 percent, still somewhat more than twice the NRA level. These are large differences in representational space, especially considering they exist throughout nearly a decade of coverage (Figure 3.1b).

When article type is controlled for by looking at straight news instead of general coverage, the difference not only persists, it becomes even more distinct. In straight news, possibly the most important source of information for the rational citizen, M = 1.4 of paragraphs of quotes per article for NRA, an increase that would be expected in straight news that is based on attributed information; but with means of 2.8 for ACLU and AARP; 3.1 for HCI and 4.0 for NAACP. This large difference is statistically significant at high levels of confidence between NRA and each of the other groups but the small differences between NAACP, AARP, ACLU, and HCI are not statistically significant. What this means is that the non-NRA groups are being treated alike, more or less, while NRA is consistently allotted less space for its views. Any difference between the groups disappears in editorials, as would be expected, owing to reliance on commentary in editorial writing rather than on attributed quotes or viewpoints.

So in straight news and in general coverage NRA speaks less on average than do the other interest groups, while the other groups are treated similarly to the point that no significant differences exists between them. The only exception among the non-NRA groups is

NAACP, whose advantage in quotes over ACLU is also large enough to be significant. But this does not change the rankings: NRA is at the bottom and quite some distance up the scale in ascending order are ACLU, AARP, HCI and NAACP. We will see this ranking pattern repeated or approximated a number of times on other measures of coverage.

When the groups are looked at in aggregate, i.e., NRA versus the combined other groups, the mean differences between number and proportions of quotes are also large and significant at confidence levels exceeding 99 percent, where $M = 2.9$ paragraphs per article for the non-NRA groups compared to $M = 1.14$ for NRA (Figure 3.1a).

Figure 3.1a: Average Number of Paragraphs of Quotes in Elite News Articles on Interest Groups, 1990-98

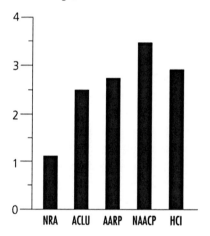

Note: Differences are significant between NRA and the other groups combined at $p < .001$: $F(4,1472) = 30.5$. On multiple comparison tests between the specific groups, differences between all groups and NRA are significant, as is the difference between ACLU and NAACP, where NAACP holds the advantage. The other non-NRA groups do not differ significantly from each other.

Figure 3.1b: Proportions of Paragraphs of Quotes in Elite News Articles on Interest Groups, 1990-98

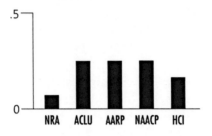

Note: Differences between NRA and the Non-NRA groups are significant at $p < .001$: $F(4, 1472) = 56.1$.

The measures count only paragraphs with direct quotes from organizational officials and/or paragraphs with paraphrased, explicitly attributed information. If an interest group succeeded in providing unattributed background information to articles, as many interest groups in fact manage to do, then content analysis measures could not possibly be sensitive to it.

An interesting pattern was noted concerning the journalistic standards of *balance* and *fairness*. In specific articles on NRA, it was sometimes true that the number of paragraphs of quotes from each source appeared to be scrupulously balanced: e.g., three paragraphs of quotes from NRA opposed three paragraphs of quotes from HCI. But in the long run, articles on all of the non-NRA groups contained more quotes from the respective groups than did articles concerning NRA.

Pseudo-Event Coverage

Perhaps even more than quotes, the proportional treatment of the pseudo-events staged by interest groups predetermines group representation. Pseudo-events are events staged or released mainly for media consumption such as press conferences, special events, demonstrations, polls, reports/studies, scripted committee proceedings, press releases, and any other artificial device or spectacle designed or intended to procure news coverage for the organization. Boorstin (1961) introduced the term, although pseudo-events have been the staple of public and media relations technique throughout the last century, if not longer. Through pseudo-events, groups set or influence news agendas, with a major portion of all national news originating from organizational sources by means of such contrivances.

Proportions of coverage of pseudo-events for the groups differ strongly, with pseudo-events of non-NRA groups covered at much higher rates than NRA events. Only 6.6 percent of NRA coverage consists of NRA pseudo-events, while a whopping 43 percent of AARP coverage is based on such events. The NRA pseudo-event coverage rate is less than one-fourth the proportion of pseudo-event coverage received by the least well favored of the non-NRA groups, ACLU, whose events comprise 28.6 percent of its coverage. This pattern holds strong whether the groups are considered individually or in aggregate, i.e., NRA versus the non-NRA groups together (Figure 3.2).

Even more interestingly, unlike all the other groups, NRA receives more coverage as a result of *other* organizations' pseudo-events (21.6 percent) than it does from its own events (6.6 percent). This is not true for *any* of the other groups. So in other words, not only does NRA receive less pseudo-event coverage, discussions of NRA at pseudo-events other than those staged by NRA carry over strongly into the news.

If news is to be considered as a public forum, such large differences in use of media events for coverage suggest the NRA as an object of discourse more often than a contributor.

Pseudo-Event Examples

Typical NRA-generated pseudo-events include the NRA annual conventions. All of the NRA conventions during the course of the study were covered by elite dailies.

Also found in pseudo-event coverage are occasional letters or op-ed pieces written by NRA officials, e.g., a seven-paragraph letter by NRA research coordinator Paul Blackman headlined "Guns and Responsibility." Other such letters concern NRA's interpretation of the Second Amendment and its views on assault weapons and so-called cop-killer bullets. One such letter by an NRA official published in *LAT* protests the lack of recognition of the role of NRA in the passage of "three strikes" legislation to permanently imprison repeat criminal offenders (LaPierre, 1994).

Figure 3.2: Proportions of Pseudo-Event Coverage in Elite News Articles on Interest Groups, 1990-98

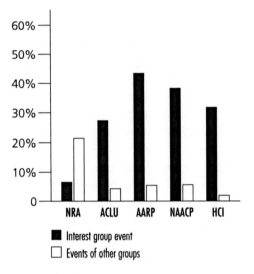

Note: Differences are highly significant in cross tables for NRA versus Non-NRA groups in aggregate, X^2 (2, 1472) = 242.8. The strength of association Φ = .406.

As can be seen in Figure 3.2, NRA is more often mentioned in coverage of pseudo-events generated by other organizations. In this it is unique among the interest groups who are all able to showcase themselves in pseudo-event venues of their own choosing. Typical examples of NRA coverage generated by other groups' events include an announcement of indictments for traffic in illegal guns by the U.S. Attorney General's Office, a Citizens Against Gun Violence event about gun rationing in Virginia (covered, oddly, as a *WP* editorial rather than in straight news, as one would expect), and a 1993 *LAT* article, "Protesters Against Gun Violence Target NRA Office," which appears to be taken more or less directly from a press release put out over the Religious Wire Services.

Another unique aspect of coverage of NRA pseudo-events is that, totally unlike event coverage of other groups, reporters tend sometimes to interpret and analyze the event itself as a pseudo-event, calling attention to it as an attempt at media manipulation. Such is the case in "Journalists Take Their Best Shots: NRA Hopes to prove its Point of Gun Bill" (Tapscott, 1991), which covers an event where NRA attempted to show journalists the differences—or the lack of differences from the NRA point of view—between so-called assault weapons and so-called sporting weapons. In the article reporters interview each other instead of the NRA officials, and report that they felt they were being "wooed" by NRA. The article sums up the NRA event in these words: "Today NRA took its turn at media relations." The purpose behind the pseudo-event is said to be "an effort to back away from rhetoric." Again, there is nothing like this in any of the other articles of interest group coverage, despite the fact that other groups' events are covered at much higher rates. It should be noted that organizational events are often identified as press conferences, or accompanying photographs make this obvious, but there is no attempt to show events by other groups as manipulative, even though such is indeed the nature of all pseudo-events.

Much of the 43 percent of AARP coverage based on pseudo-events reads as if it were taken more or less directly, virtually without editing in many cases, from AARP press releases. Letters by AARP officials are also common. A representative example is a four-paragraph letter written by Louise Crooks, AARP president, on the need for legislation to protect the jobs of caregivers for the elderly. Many straight news AARP pseudo-event articles concern the availability of AARP member services, e.g., insurance, hotel discounts and driving classes for the elderly. Another set of AARP-generated articles concerns consumer fraud of the elderly and its prevention. One such portrays the activities of an AARP volunteer working with federal law enforcement officers to entrap criminals who defraud the elderly by means of spurious telephone offers. Often these member service articles end with the name and telephone number of an AARP contact person. There is no comparable coverage of NRA member services.

AARP pseudo-events are often tandem in nature, two groups piggy-backing to generate coverage. Examples include a coalition of Democratic senators and AARP officials who combine to attack a Republican health care proposal. Another features a town-hall-type event where students (representing the new generation) discuss the future of Social Security, an event staged jointly under the auspices of the White House and AARP. The Clinton presidential administration and AARP also co-produce a White House brunch for the discussion of the future of Medicare.

AARP-generated studies also appear regularly, apparently intact, just as the press relations office might have issued them. Some typical articles on AARP-sponsored studies are headlined: *Grandparents Lack Child Care; Job Applicants Face Age Bias, Study Finds; AARP Study Finds Job Applicants Face Age Bias,* etc. The latter article contains five out of six paragraphs total of direct quotes from AARP officials, with other such articles generally containing similarly high proportions of direct quotes. Once again, there appears to be no comparable NRA coverage.

NAACP events, also covered more extensively than NRA events, include annual conventions, announcements of the election of new officers, and letters on various topics by officials. NAACP pseudo-event articles tend to contain many paragraphs of direct quotes by officials, the most out of all the interest groups.

ACLU pseudo-events include frequent letters from ACLU officials. The executive director of the ACLU, Ira Glasser, appears perhaps to have possessed the ability to have letters published in the *NYT* at will, judging by the series of such letters. These usually address traditional ACLU concerns such as freedom of speech, freedom of religion, and matters pertaining to unreasonable search and seizure by police powers.

HCI pseudo-event coverage includes articles such as an eight-paragraph op-ed piece jointly written by the director of the HCI affiliate organization Center to Prevent Handgun Violence and the director of the Center's Legal Action project (Lautman & Henigan, 1990). Tandem events are also common in HCI coverage, e.g., a press conference staged by HCI and a California politician who survived a recall attempt financed in substantial part by the NRA. The politician is referred to in the article as "an NRA survivor" (Schwada, 1994). HCI also conducts events in tandem with the White House and with political figures such as congressional representatives.

Use of Photographs

When compared to coverage of non-NRA groups, NRA coverage tends toward significantly less use of photographs of organizational actors or events. Only 6.0 percent of NRA coverage uses photographs of NRA actors or events, compared to 27.1 percent for the non-NRA groups, another large difference. Another distinction is that unlike all the other groups, articles on NRA are more likely to be accompanied by a photograph of some non-interest group event or person(s): the proportions are 30.2 percent of NRA articles have non-NRA event photographs compared to 20.5 percent for all the non-NRA groups in aggregate (Figure 3.3).

The contrast becomes more visible when looked at on a group-by-group basis. Compared to the 6.0 percent NRA proportion, photographs of NAACP officials or events appear with 41.2 percent of NAACP news articles; while the least well depicted of the other groups, ACLU at 11.8 percent, is still nearly twice the NRA proportion.

Controlling for article type, the association between photographic subject and interest group disappears or becomes statistically insignificant for all other article types except straight news, as would be expected considering the general absence of photographs in editorial coverage. Once again, though, the difference becomes more distinct in straight news, where 8.6 percent of NRA articles feature photographs of NRA officials and/or events, while 30.7 percent of the other interest groups' coverage contains photographs or graphics of officials or events of the respective interest groups. This situation is again complemented negatively in NRA straight news coverage by the 34 percent proportion of NRA articles bearing non-NRA group pictorials, while only 19.7 percent of the articles on the other groups show non-group pictorials.

Figure 3.3: Proportions of Interest Group Versus Non-Interest Group Photographs in Elite News Coverage of Interest Groups, 1990-98

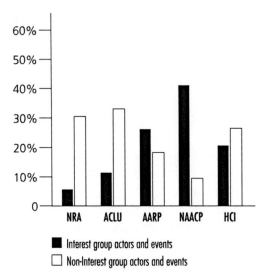

Note: The differences are significant. For NRA versus Non-NRA groups in aggregate, $X^2 (2, 670) = 58.64$, $p < .001$, $\Phi = .291$.

The higher proportion of pseudo-events for the non-NRA groups corresponds to their higher proportions for group-related photographs. Simply put, pseudo-events generate photographic opportunities (just as they generate opportunities for group representatives to be quoted). Many pseudo-events amount to little more than a photographic or symbolic visual event around which quotable rhetoric is assembled, e.g., "the sound bite."

Also present in NRA coverage is an apparent pattern of a photo-association technique that is not often present in articles on the other interest groups, where photographs situated directly next to an NRA article, although not explicitly linked to the article, depict scenes of violence or crime. The technique implies causality. One such *WP* article (Isikoff, 1990) on assault weapon importations cites heavy pressure from the NRA as a reason why no remedial action has been taken. It is paired with a photograph captioned "A Massacre Remembered" (Associated Press, 1990). The photograph shows a mother embracing her crying seven-year-old daughter as they walk away from a schoolyard in Stockton, California where five children had been murdered a year earlier. It is unclear from the caption if the photograph was taken at the time of the shootings or at an event commemorating the massacre (the latter seems more likely judging by the headline) but the emotional message is quite powerful. Other pieces of NRA coverage appear side by side with photographs of convicted Oklahoma City federal building bomber Timothy McVeigh.

A more typical use of photographs in NRA coverage is a *WP* article with three photographs of handgun victims, including a three-year-old wounded by his father's gun and a fifteen-year-old killed by his cousin. The latter is a photograph of a photograph, and shows a mother and sister holding a picture of the dead teenager (Pressley, 1991). Another NRA *WP* article shows two photographs: James Brady, giving the thumbs-up sign, alongside a photograph of Sarah Brady. Yet another front-page photograph shows Sarah Brady in neck-up profile, looking uncannily like the cameo of Queen Elizabeth on Canadian and British currency.

As said already, many photographs in NRA articles depict pseudo-events of other organizations, e.g., former New Jersey governor Jim Florio is shown together with the state attorney general and James Brady examining "an assault-type rifle" at a pseudo-event staged in the governor's office (King, 1993).

NAACP photographs occur most frequently of all the groups and tend to favor organizational officials at organizational events. Guests sometimes appear alongside officials. A typical NAACP photograph shows the Rev. Jesse Jackson onstage at the podium of the 1995 convention handing what the caption identifies as a donation check to an usher (Terry, July 13, 1995). Of course on some occasions NAACP photographs have been of NAACP officials accused of malfeasance, but these are exceptional instances.

ACLU shots often depict persons or organizational places affected or involved in legal challenges.

Other non-NRA interest group photographs also tend more to be straightforward shots of organizational officials or actors.

Titles of Organizational Actors

The use of titles is undoubtedly one of the most basic ways of showing respect by according or denying legitimate social status to others. In this aspect, yet another large difference exists contingent on which interest group is being covered. Only 19.6 percent of NRA coverage identifies NRA spokespersons or organizational actors with their proper titles (or with some reasonable approximation). For NAACP, however, the proportion of articles using appropriate titles goes up to 72.7 percent. Proportions for ACLU, AARP and HCI are more than twice that of NRA (Figure 3.4).

By far the most frequent label applied by journalists to NRA officials is *lobbyist* or *chief lobbyist*. Tanya Metaksa, executive director of the NRA Institute for Legislative Action during most of the course of the content analysis, is almost always identified in news articles as "chief lobbyist" or some slight variation on this theme. The same is true for her predecessor, James Baker—later reappointed to the position, thus becoming her successor in 1999. The term *lobbyist* is on a few occasions applied to AARP officials and, occasionally, to HCI staff persons. The term *spokesperson* is also occasionally applied to NRA officials and, to a lesser extent, to officials from other organizations, including AARP, ACLU and HCI.

Some articles are unbalanced in their application of titles. An article on the election of Wayne LaPierre, NRA's executive vice president, does not explicitly link his title to his name, but does provide the proper title of Josh Sugarman, an anti-gun activist working for the Violence Policy Center, who is quoted concerning NRA. Weirdly, a *WP* article identifies a man alleged to be a high-ranking militia member by his appropriate militia title, "communications director" for the Gadsen Minutemen, even though neither man nor militia appear to have resources or significant organization associated with them, and the man is interviewed in a hotel room. This same article, however, identifies the NRA source only as an "NRA spokesperson." A *WP* news article quotes "HCI president Sarah Brady" along side of NRA's "chief lobbyist" Tanya Metaksa. Another quotes Robert Walker, "legislative director for HCI," while NRA officials in the articles are simply "spokespersons." Sometimes the titles are vague. A *WP* straight news article identifies LaPierre as "the NRA's national leader," while "NRA lobbyist Wayne LaPierre" is cited in another article. The trend is clear enough.

NRA officials tend to get a promotion, so to speak, when covered in articles concerning the actions of coalitions formed by NRA with other interest groups. When NRA, ACLU, and NAACP are all involved in an event, e.g., a coalition to oppose the expansion of federal police powers, then all officials from all of the organizations—including NRA—are appropriately identified. This is true for all such "coalition" articles encountered in the analysis.

Figure 3.4 also calls attention to another important aspect of the use of titles in coverage, namely, a systematic absence of titles. No titles whatsoever in journalistic-style coverage indicate, on the whole, that no one from a group is speaking, i.e., the interest group has no voice. Note that 55.9 percent of the NRA articles fall into this no-voice category, while only 24.6 percent of the other groups (in aggregate) do so.

Personalization

Compelling personalized stories can be written in ways that are sympathetic or unsympathetic toward a group being covered. Personalization is probably one of the more important aspects of news coverage and can be regarded as manifestation of a general need for disambiguation provided by dramatic accounts involving heroes and villains. In illustration, a human interest or feature story thus could melodramatically frame a welfare mother sympathetically, as a woman struggling for a better life for her children against social and economic inequality, or unsympathetically, as a slattern who is chronically lazy and irresponsible; or a story on welfare or welfare mothers can be objective and neutral in the style of a scientific or business report, but the latter are not so easily digested. This is why personalization techniques, e.g., the caricature, the stereotype, the human-interest "angle" and the atrocity story, have long been mainstays of propaganda, advertising, news, and public relations practice (Lasswell, 1927, 1936). Thus, in 1917 American news Uncle Sam is a virtuous patriarchal figure, the Kaiser a ravenous beast. Likewise Herman and Chomsky (1988) see the U.S. news system as a drama of policy justification that shows sympathetic and unsympathetic "victims" that must be helped or left to their well-deserved fates in accord with American imperialistic values.

Figure 3.4: Proportions of Appropriate Title Use for Organizational Actors in Elite News Coverage of Interest Groups, 1990-98

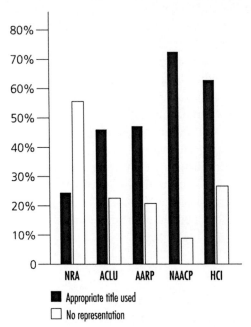

■ Appropriate title used
☐ No representation

Notes: The association in cross-tables between the interest group and title use is significant, X^2 (8, 1473) = 270.77, $p < .001$, and strong, Φ (Phi) = .429. When cross-tabulated on the basis of NRA coverage as opposed to the other combined groups, the associational measure Φ remains strong at .394, with X^2 (2, 1473) = 228.77, $p < .001$.

Average personalization valences are distinctly different between groups, with negative NRA portrayals outweighing positive portrayals. In other words, accounts of dramatic personal events are included in the articles in ways that show NRA or NRA positions in an unfavorable light. In ascending order, mean scores on personalization are NRA, 2.73; ACLU, 3.02; AARP, 3.19; NAACP, 3.23; and HCI, 3.61. The mean of the aggregated non-NRA groups is 3.19 (Figure 3.5). So again, NRA anchors the low end of the scale.

These differences persist in both straight news and op-ed coverage. Statistically, ACLU, AARP, and NAACP are treated so similarly as to be indistinguishable from each other, but NRA and HCI stand distinctly apart at opposite ends of what can be thought of a personalization continuum.

In way of interpretation, personalization is a valence type measure on a five-point scale, where a score of 1 = very negative, 2 = negative, 3 = neutral, 4 = positive, and 5 = very positive. Thus the 2.73 mean score for NRA indicates that on average, NRA coverage is negative. This is not to say there is no neutral-objective coverage in so far as personalization themes are concerned, far from it, there is a great deal; but NRA is the villain in personalization dramas to the extent that it is the only one of the groups that averages out in the negative. The other groups are all treated more positively on the whole.

Personalization Examples

Negative personalization themes toward NRA appear in numerous articles. Handgun victims are a theme common to many straight news, editorial, feature, and cartoon articles. A *WP* article, "When Tragedy Lurks an Error Away" shows a photograph of a yawning child held by a man identified as the father. The father is quoted in the article, "If this bill saves the life of one child," [he] said, choking back tears, "It's worth it" (Pressley, 1991). Pseudo-event based articles about political figures such as congressional representatives discussing NRA also carry negative-coded themes, e.g., testifying mothers and gunshot victims. One describes a grieving mother clutching a photograph of her dead child. "Mothers Protest Effort to Appeal Assault Gun Ban" is an HCI pseudo-event featuring a gigantic mock up of a mother's day card festooned with photographs of dead children, letters and poems (Associated Press, May 16, 1995). An account of U.S. House of Representatives subcommittee hearings quotes a mother as asking, "Was it a well-regulated militia that killed my son?"

Figure 3.5: Average Personalization Theme Valence Scores of Interest Group Coverage in Elite Newspapers, 1990-98

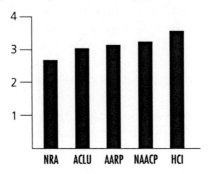

Notes: The mean difference is significant between NRA and the other groups taken individually, $F(4, 1378) = 42.37$, $p < .001$, and in aggregate, $F(1, 1381) = 137.1$, $p < .001$. Bonferroni multiple comparison tests show NRA as significantly different from all other groups, also ACLU, AARP, and NAACP do not differ significantly from one another. HCI also differs significantly from the other groups, representing the high end of the personalization scale measure.

Short, almost gratuitous accounts of the wounding of former presidential press secretary James Brady, whose wife, Sarah Brady, is currently chair of HCI, seem to be inserted in literally dozens of NRA articles that are otherwise impersonal, objective-voiced, factual accounts of proposed legislation and counter-legislation. Many of these accounts appear as if they might have been taken directly from HCI press releases, for the wording in different accounts is often similar. The frequency of these sympathetic Brady accounts explains in part the high average score of HCI on the personalization measure and the low score of NRA; for in an NRA article the presence of a personalized, sympathetic account of the Bradys is coded as negative toward NRA. The Bradys, together and individually, are also the subjects of many feature articles and political cartoons, as well as participants—quoted, noted, or photographed—in numerous non-NRA pseudo-events.

Many articles describe the Bradys in very flattering terms. Occasionally journalists seem even to gush. Phrases in such articles deal with James Brady and his *indefatigable wife, Sarah*, who *are effective, courteous, proponents of gun control*. Others phrases are *bravely lobbying*, and *power and wit* [of James Brady]. "Tasteful hardball" is how they are said to play the political game (Isikoff, 1991). A 100-paragraph *NYT* human interest story from 1990 contains 37 paragraphs with direct quotes: Sarah Brady is shown as a working woman who crusades uncomplainingly at her husband's side. A great deal of charming personal banter between the couple is included. Their motivations are accepted at face value. The Bradys are described with terms such as *characteristic zeal, effective advocate, consuming mission, driven by consuming passion,* and *relentless good humor and vitality.* They function as a powerful personalization symbols. Consider this sympathetic portrayal:

> Although she is married to a man who will remain largely paralyzed and in constant pain for the rest of his life, there is nothing about Sarah Brady that spells martyr. Driven by a consuming mission, she is not some one who attracts or accepts the slightest hint of pity. She does not lecture, she does not plead, she does not seem angry. She is rail thin, green-eyed and blond. Her smile is a tad horsy, but it will light up a room. She is very funny. A bit of Imogene Coca, if you go back that far; Candice Bergen, if you don't. (King, 1990)

A David and Goliath framing approach is common to articles, with the Bradys and others gun control activists shown as courageous human adversaries to the monster mega-lobby NRA. An *NYT* column (Winerip, 1992) is headlined, "Gun Juggernaut vs. a Gentleman named Kean," and uses terms "fair man", "gentleman," and "independent thinker" to describe former New Jersey governor Thomas Kean, whose "voice retains a human quality" and whose "words seemed to have more firepower than the National Rifle Association lobbyists."

A typical cartoon example of the recurring man-versus-the-NRA-machine motif shows a fragile Mr. Brady in a wheelchair facing a gigantic and heavily armored tank labeled "NRA" that is bristling with grotesque weapons.

Or personal themes are framed in wrenching atrocity stories. An *LAT* editorial, accompanied by a photograph of a smiling and handsome rookie deputy killed in the line of duty, links NRA with "The Death of a Brave Deputy" [headline]. It says, "The National Rifle Association argues that only law-abiding citizens are hurt by limitations on the manufacture, importation and sale of handguns. Tell that to the family of Nelson Yamamoto."

Personalization themes applied to NRA organizational actors tend not to be flattering—quite the reverse. Marion Hammer, the first woman to be elected NRA president, is described in *NYT* as being "tough as a day-old biscuit." Thomas L. Washington, NRA president who died while in office and was succeeded by Marion Hammer, is described in a 1995 *WP* article as "the portly president" of NRA. A 1995 human interest story on NRA executive vice president Wayne LaPierre, is entitled "On the Defensive." It depicts LaPierre as ambivalent and conflicted, a burned-out bureaucratic functionary who says that politics turns the stomach. He thinks about buying an ice cream shop. And his friends say he doesn't even like guns all that much. Only eleven paragraphs out of 49 (22 percent) in the article contain LaPierre quotes. Terms applied to LaPierre are *squinting, sweaty session, husk of his old self,* and *sense of malaise.* The legislative director of HCI, of all people, is quoted on the subject of LaPierre, saying, "I've never really regarded him as being terribly effective" (Zoroya, 1995).

A cluster of *LAT* articles on NRA also shows how personalization is employed in distinctly different ways for NRA and non-NRA actors. In an *LAT* interview (Terry, 1994) then-congressman Charles Schumer refers to NRA as a "monster." The article, bylined by an *LAT* editorial writer, is largely in the question-and-answer format and presents a broad portrait of Schumer, who has many paragraphs of apparently unedited quotes, preceded by a resume¢-like biography. The headline describes him as "Vanquishing the NRA," and the underlying theme is a celebration of Congressman Schumer as NRA/dragon slayer. Schumer is described with eulogistic terms such as *pragmatic, family man, ambitious, precocious,* and *political acumen.* His voice monopolizes the article.

Ten days later appears another *LAT* article with a punning headline, "The Straight Shooter," a human interest story on Bob Corbin, former president of NRA (Dean, 1994). Corbin is said to "put a spin on his arguments." His "fever" is over the Lost Dutchman mines, and this hobby/fascination is mocked with a comment in pseudo-vernacular, "Corbin may not know where that th'ar [sic] gold is hiding." The article quotes Corbin's daughter, who is described as "estranged." It also quotes a politician who was indicted when Corbin was Arizona's attorney general, who says that Corbin is "fascist at heart." It is ambiguous, ambivalent, heavily edited and interpreted, a dark psychological picture of a strange man, a man who is shown looking backward in time and would appear to have a personality problem such that he can neither compromise nor get along with anyone. Corbin is described with terms such as *shoving ways, little big man, banty rooster,* and *sees only blacks and whites.*

This same nearly clinical dissection of the subject appears throughout other pieces of NRA coverage. A 1994 *NYT Magazine* article says of NRA-ILA director Tanya Metaksa:

> Metaksa appeared in the doorway. She is an intimidating presence. Square shouldered, large-breasted, handsome. She has a withering stare that she says comes from her late father. . . . Metaksa, 57, seems like a character out of Ayn Rand. Later, in her office, I saw a dog-eared copy of "Atlas Shrugged" in a bookcase.
>
> Our conversation rapidly became disputatious, which didn't seem to bother Metaksa all that much. (Weiss, p. 70)

After dismissing Metaksa's "libertarian patter" and the "backwoods dandies" who are said to "stereotype the NRA activist," the same article formulates a psychological theory of personality for NRA members and gun owners in its attempt to explain the "personal dimension" and the "fervor of the absolutist" found in the "gunnies":

> But they wanted to avoid reality at all costs. A real encounter would be both uglier and richer than the fantasy. . . . The gunny's dream about subduing endless enemies was like a pornographic illusion. . . . Asking a gunny to go back to a less sophisticated firearm was like asking a devotee of pornography to go from videos back to still photographs: the degree to which the thing stimulates a primal experience, was greatly diminished. (Weiss, p. 100)

There are no attempts in the coverage of groups other than NRA to establish theories of personality to explain either group or personal actions. Nor are the breasts of other organizational actors ever discussed.

NAACP news personalization often flatters. For example, the ascension of Kweisi Mfume to the presidency and chief executive office of the NAACP is marked with glowing descriptions in a 1995 *NYT* news article (NAACP's New Hope). The article states:

With his handsome looks, smooth manner and current girlfriend—an actress...who won an Emmy Award in 1991 for her portrayal of Josephine Baker in an (sic) cable television movie—he brings a measure of glamour to an organization sometimes seen as frumpy.

A retired federal judge is quoted in the same piece as saying of Mfume, "In our new president we have the brilliance of DuBois, the eloquence of Martin Luther King, the toughness of Thurgood Marshall, the caring of Ms. Bethune and Harriet Tubman and Sojourner Truth." Other terms used to describe Mfume are *savior, grabbed hold of life, political acumen, credibility,* and *personal responsibility.*

A 1998 *NYT* article on the NAACP's choice of Julian Bond as board chairman refers to Bond as a "reluctant savior" and states, "While the years have turned his soft curly hair gray, Mr. Bond still retains the looks, deep voice and telegenic quality of his youth" (Bumiller, 1997). Editorials describe Bond with terms such as *solid charismatic figure.* Once again the style is eulogistic.

AARP and ACLU actors are not so often described in personal terms, either negative or positive. Some exceptions are sympathetic portraits of AARP volunteers and members and "gadfly" type characterizations of ACLU officials where an official is depicted as working tirelessly, albeit in an abrasive, Socratic manner, toward the common good. Terms applied to an ACLU official in one such article are *principled purist, a quintessential quotable thorn in mayoral sides,* and *passion for constitutional freedoms.*

Derisive Headlines

A headline can indicate a great deal. Serious events receive serious headlines (e.g., major earthquakes) and the seriousness of headline treatment received over the long term by a group is a reasonable indicator of how it is regarded by journalists. In any case, it is easy to convey derision with headlines, and certainly at times it would be difficult not to considering the notorious foibles of political personalities and organizations.

In the matter of derisive headlines, 26.8 percent of NRA coverage uses some sort of joking or punning headline, while articles on the other groups are much less likely to do so. Proportions of joke headlines for the other groups are 5.9 percent for NAACP; 10.8 percent, AARP; 12.6 percent, ACLU; and 13.5 percent HCI (Figure 3.6). The latter appears to be as high as it is because HCI is often mentioned in articles that also discuss NRA; the humorous headlines seem for the most part to be directed at NRA, e.g., "Faltering NRA Finds Itself Under the Gun."

In editorial coverage the association disappears. Overall, there is a rough equality in editorial headlines. If an interest group happens to be the subject of an editorial or op-ed piece, it will likely be treated in headlines the same as any other group subjected to editorializing, i.e., derisively. In editorial/op-ed coverage the proportion for NRA, 27.8 percent, remains relatively unchanged from the overall coverage proportion, but ACLU, at 38.7 percent joke headlines, is the proportional butt of more headline/op-ed humor than any of the other interest groups. In part this is attributable to the treatment ACLU receives from the editors of *The Wall Street Journal* and *The New York Times*, who seem to have had some difficulties in past years in accepting ACLU's positions on publicly financed displays of religious symbolism during the holiday season and also in schools. But ACLU is much less often the subject of editorials than NRA.

Also, unlike the other groups, a strong tendency for joke headlines carries over into straight news NRA coverage; only 4.8 percent of non-NRA groups are captioned with joke headlines, compared to the NRA percentage of 21.3.

Contributing of course to NRA's overall higher proportion of joke headlines is its tendency to receive proportionally more editorial coverage than the other groups. NRA's percentage for editorial coverage is 24.1, nearly double the 13.6 percent for non-NRA groups, a relationship which is also significant, $X^2 (1, 1473) = 24.34$ ($p < .001$).

Many of the NRA joke headlines must be regarded as no more than feeble or stupid puns, but this same sort of punning—feeble or otherwise—does not carry over into the general coverage of the other groups at anywhere near the same rate.

Figure 3.6: Proportions of Derisive-Joke Headlines on Interest Group Coverage in Elite Newspapers, 1990-98

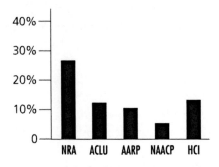

Note: The cross-table relationship between NRA and the non-NRA groups in aggregate for the presence of derisive/joke headlines is significant X^2 (8, 1468) = 71.50, $p < .001$, $\Phi = .221$.

Some are very funny, others merely crude. Examples of NRA joke-derisive headlines are:

> *The Guns of Testosterone. Moses Leads the NRA off the Slippery Slope. The Gun Lobby, Over a Barrel. In Fight Over Assault Weapons, Everyone Gets to Take a Shot. NRA Flips on the Safety in New Pitch to Women. Did NRA Shoot Itself in the Foot? Judgement at Newtburg. Heston Bites the Hand. NRA's Moses gets a Dousing. NRA Must put its Guns on the Table Before Discussing Crime, Clark says. NRA Way Off Target. Dodging Bullets. Wayne LaPierre, on the Ropes. Gunning for his Enemies: Neal Knox, the Real Power at NRA, Sees Diabolical Plots Everywhere. NRA Cartoon Missed the Bullseye. NRA, in Crosshairs of Critics, Fires Fresh Volley of Words. Aiding and Abetting a Bad Aim. Have Gun Will Shoot. Roberti Recall Bid Backfires on NRA. The Gun Lobby, Loaded for Bear. Shootout at the AK Chorale. Faltering NRA Finds Itself Under the Gun. Small Arms Industry Comes on to Women. Gunning for Research. An NRA Potshot at Science. Connecticut Can K.O. the NRA. Missing the Target. NRA Woos the World.*

Joke headlines from NAACP articles are relatively rare. Only eleven instances are present in 187 content-analyzed NAACP articles. Examples are:

> *Saving the NAACP's Soul. Don't Mess With History. After the March, a Marriage. The NAACP, Lost in Yonkers.*

AARP articles with joke headlines are also relatively scarce, with only 17 of 159 articles falling into this category. Examples are:

> *AARP is Adding Some Spice to its Menu. For the Boomer in Chief, it's the AARP birthday, Speaking of Business. The Senior Promenade: At the AARP Convention the Retired Never Tier. More than Grand. AARP, for Grannies or Gold? AARP Hands Members a Poison Pill.*

Exactly 22 of 175 ACLU articles samples bear joke headlines:

> *A Zero for Jesus in Public Schools, Affirmative Reaction, Deadly Assault Books. Two Cheers for the ACLU. ACLU Still Finding Success in the Courts, But Not in the Court of Public Opinion. ACLJ VS. ACLU: Battling Acronyms* [ACLJ = American Center for Law and Justice]. *A Klan Christmas. ACLU Doesn't Have a Prayer. Et Tu, ACLU?*

As mentioned, HCI articles are sometimes headed with joke-pun headlines apparently directed at NRA. For example, a human interest story in the *NYT Magazine* is headlined, "Sarah and James Brady" and "Target: The Gun Lobby." However, in no instance does a derisive headline appear to be directed at HCI, although one could well argue that the direction of humor is irrelevant or ambiguous in such instances.

Satire-Mockery Themes

Mockery and satire are basic to communication. Sometimes their application amounts to little more than crude name-calling, but on the whole how a group is thus treated indicates much. Mockery can be directed against a group, i.e. the group can be treated negatively, or a group can direct mockery at others, i.e., a positive use of mockery/satire from the perspective of the group (and this study). Or an article can be neutral. Once again this is matter of valence.

On the measure for satire/mockery the NRA mean (2.63) differs significantly from the means of all the other groups except ACLU, $M = 2.74$. Means for the other groups in ascending order are AARP, 2.91; NAACP, 2.94; and HCI, 3.25. The positive 3.25 mean for HCI shows that coverage often makes use of satirical quotes or otherwise attributes mockery from this group directed at other groups or sources. In other words, a mean greater than 3.0 indicates a group that tends to be an originator of mockery instead of its subject. NAACP, AARP, ACLU, and, especially, NRA all tend more than HCI to be subjected to satire or mockery that originates from other sources or groups in the articles.

All groups are the object of satire or mockery on occasion, even HCI, despite its high mean score, and which usually directs mockery at NRA, but has none directed at it or its positions excepting for a few instances where pro-gun actors are speaking (not journalists).

One of the most distinct features of NRA coverage noted during this study was a persistent mocking tone regarding NRA, present especially in editorials, a tone that is rarely present in coverage of the other groups.

A few of the many instances of mockery or satire against NRA include:

> *National Redneck Association. Membership numbers of the NRA are dropping like ducks in a shooting gallery. The Glasnost Gun Lobby... National Russian Roulette Cooperative (the equivalent of our National Rifle Association). Congress despite strong lobbying efforts by the NRA, bans private ownership of aircraft carriers. Bagged Bambi with an Uzi. The mayhem market. Not for Bambi. True to bad form, officials of the NRA. Years of semi-automatic victories. Fred Carbuncle, a lobbyist for NRA . . . in his bedroom pistol range. [NRA] drew a bead on 24 Congressmen and gubernatorial candidates. Anybody who thinks about it longer than the crack of an AK-47. The NRA, of course, is outraged. A sacred cow of the NRA. Heston and Co. Rattlesnake in a closet. Intentionally obscuring the issue. Protect ducks more than human beings. Screw loose. Charlton Holster. Crazed law-abiding gun owners. Certifiably kook position. NRA prophesized the end of the world as we know it. Scrambling to recruit among the fearful. Flush with predictable outrage. The attack missed but NRA reloaded. Increasing the available firepower in Bubbaland. The hearings had an odor about them...and it's clear that NRA is the skunk. The NRA has reared its ugly head. Buying a gun takes about as long as a quart of milk. You're going to shoot a duck with an Uzi?—If he was going to break into your house, wouldn't you? Rushing lemming-like. An organization that goes to war every time a meddler tries to interpose an obstacle between a gun and a would-be owner. NRA bigshots. Stuck in the NRA's craw. NRA and its semi-automatic water carriers in the Senate. Vintage NRA hysteria. Holster*

Heaven. Semi-automatic mouthpieces. One-note political tune of the NRA any-gun-is-great lobby. Semi-automatic assault mouth.

Figure 3.7: Average Satire-Mockery Theme Valence Scores of Interest Group Coverage in Elite Newspapers, 1990-98

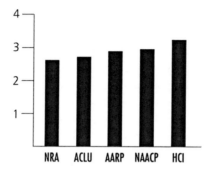

Note: Multiple comparison tests show NRA differs significantly ($p <$ .001) from all other groups except ACLU. ACLU does not differ from AARP significantly. HCI differs from all other groups at $p < .05$ levels.

NRA representatives sometimes direct mockery at others, although these positive-coded (for NRA) instances are few. They are sometimes found in letters to the editor written by NRA officials. An example is an NRA official who, commenting on an IRS audit of the NRA remarks that a person would have to believe in "the tooth fairy" to think that the audit wasn't politically motivated. Another example is an official of the NRA discussing the urban-versus-rural dimension of the cultural war over gun control in the state of Virginia. He states, "It's Biff and Muffy that want to show their contempt for Bubba and Donna Jean because they eat chili and have to shop at K-Mart."

Examples of mockery or satire involving AARP include:

> Gray-haired lobbying gorilla. I knew I was getting old when I realized that my children belonged to the AARP. The 800-pound gorilla of American politics. Biggest old folks club in the world.

An example of positive satire, where an interest groups is quoted directing satire against its foes, in an ACLU article is a mention of parts of the country where the First Amendment is an "unverified rumor."

HCI is not mocked in editorials or straight news coverage.

Verbs of Attribution

Verbs of attribution substitute for the word *said*. Journalistic style requires such verbs when crediting sources for quotes or information. But verbs of attribution can also qualify information or positions through semantic shading. Examples with positive connotations would include *shown, proved,* etc.; negatives are *alleged, claimed, asserted,* etc.; and neutral uses would be *stated, said, reported, says,* etc. A very positive or very negative usage would have an adverb attached or some other modifier or qualifier that would function to raise or lower the level of certainty implied by the verb, e.g., *shrilly claimed,* or *resoundingly demonstrated.* Or a fanciful word coinage could be scored as very negative or very positive depending on its connotations, e.g., the connotation is very negative when William F. Buckley "vapors on" in an *NYT* article (Goodman, 1993).

In rank order on the verb of attribution measure, once again we see NRA at the bottom, with the remaining groups situated as they have been on other measures. Means scores are NRA, 2.80; ACLU, 2.86; AARP, 3.09; NAACP, 3.09; and HCI, 3.12.

Figure 3.8: Average Verbs of Attribution Valence Scores for Interest Group Coverage in Elite Newspapers, 1990-98

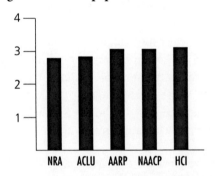

Note: Multiple comparisons show no statistical difference between NRA and ACLU, but with NRA differing from the remaining groups at $p < .001$ statistical level. HCI, NAACP, and AARP do not differ statistically.

NRA and ACLU are virtually paired, as there is no statistical difference between them. But a reason exists for the low ACLU score that does not explain NRA's score. Much ACLU coverage is concerned with ongoing litigation or threats of litigation. The associated legalistic language and its peculiar verbs of attribution are coded negatively in accord with the content analysis scheme, e.g., *contends, argues, alleges,* etc. This is the sort of language that is used when legal matters are discussed. But only a small minority of the NRA coverage concerns litigation, so it would seem that the journalistic use of verbs of attribution in the legalistic context does not explain the treatment of NRA. The journalists appear simply to be underscoring NRA positions as tentative claims.

The AARP, NAACP, and HCI mean scores above neutral are explainable in part due to the higher rates of coverage of pseudo-events put on by these groups. They are all treated essentially alike, as there is no statistical difference between them. Coverage is frequently based on interest-group-generated reports, studies, and polls using positive, "scientific" attribution verbs such as *found, showed, demonstrated,* etc. And the low mean of the NRA coverage is due in part by its lower rate of pseudo-event coverage and higher rates of op-ed type coverage wherein NRA positions are described by using negative verbs such as *claims, asserts, whines, would like us to believe,* etc.

Other examples of NRA verbs of attribution follow, presented in and out of context:

> *NRA lobbyists bleat the usual big brother government. NRA chief lobbyist asserts a net gain* . . . *but Sarah Brady, chairman of Handgun Control, says. Whine. Weasel-wording his way.* [HCI study] *finds.* [NRA] *alleging* [CDC studies flawed]. [NRA] *likes to argue. Gun lobbyists would have everyone believe,* [while police officers] *speak from front line experience.* [NRA] *researcher asserts. Made more of a fuss about this legislation.* [NRA] *claimed victory. According to. Likes to portray. Boasts. In often shrill language the NRA touted. Pitching. Asking unctuously* [while] *Mr. Bush has spoken truly. NRA contended. NRA crowed* [while CDC issued] *rigorous, unbiased studies. Insists. Chortled. Officials of the NRA have dredged up objections, claiming. NRA maintains. NRA officials contend* [while D.C. officials] *predict. NRA ridiculed* [positive-coded]. [Tanya Metaksa] *miffed. Or so they said. Claim to believe. An assertion by the NRA. Conceded. Shouted. As if to prove their point. Acknowledged. Conceded. Admits. In a statement that is disputed by gun control activists he added. NRA says* [while] *HCI has.*

An interesting aspect of the use of verbs of attribution noticed during the course of the analysis was that many articles used verbs of attribution for NRA sources and opinions while using variants of the verb "to be" for other sources and opinions. Note the very last example in the above set: NRA *says* and HCI *has*. Functionally this qualifies NRA positions as tentative while representing the opinions of other sources as undisputed fact or absolute state of existence. Unfortunately the content analysis measures are not sensitive to this practice, so little can be concluded at this time about how extensive it may be, nor about how it would affect mean scores on the verb of attribution measure, although it would be reasonable to code such usages negatively, and consistent application would of course place the mean score of NRA even lower on this measure. Journalists also attach more negative qualifiers and modifiers to NRA positions than to other groups (see the second-to-last example immediately above).

Negative verbs of attribution occasionally carry over into headlines for NRA articles, unlike the other groups, e.g., "Heston Asserts Gun Ownership is Nation's Highest Right" (Seeyle, 1997).

Examples from AARP articles include: *reported, indicated, shows, concludes, documents, found,* and *AARP blasted*. Again, the generally positive tone of the AARP verbs is consistent with the high proportion of AARP pseudo-event coverage, in which AARP officials proudly announce AARP programs to the community.

NAACP coverage contains verbs of attribution such as *NAACP spoke out, leveled a blast, promise, vowed, reminded, declared, pledged, persuaded, hinted, alleges, announced, endorsed, plans,* and *made their case*. Notice the power of the last phrase; there is nothing like it in NRA coverage.

Verbs of attribution from ACLU articles include: *cited, dithers, articulated,* and *vow*. As mentioned, ACLU positions tend to be legalistic and therefore are qualified accordingly, but occasional editorial bashes include some very strong language, e.g., *dithers*.

HCI verbs of attribution examples include: *argues sensibly, points out, exulted, noted, testifying,* and *speaks out*. When HCI officials appear by themselves in an article, then positive-coded verbs of attribution are often used, but when they are side-by-side with NRA spokespersons, then information from both groups is more likely to be qualified with negative verbs such as *claimed* or *alleged*. The rigid application of the professional journalistic standards of fairness or balance for story construction would explain this practice.

It should be emphasized that verbs of attribution are generally neutral for all groups, as expected of coverage written by the premier journalists of the elite newspapers. But negative verbs of attribution are directed at NRA more often and more systematically than at the other groups. It requires some searching in the coverage to find examples of negative verbs of attribution used for the non-NRA interest groups (excepting ACLU). Once again this is in part related to NRA's greater likelihood of being the subject of editorial coverage, where language is less restrained. But whether NRA is the subject of straight news or editorial coverage, it still tends to score lower on the verb of attribution scale than do the other groups.

Democracy Themes

Sociologist Herbert Gans identified *altruistic democracy* as among the most enduring and commonplace of American news values (Gans, 1979). American journalism admonishes those who would oppose democracy and celebrates those who would further it, for America is mythologized, perhaps above all else, as the place where the "little guy has his say." It is a paramount cultural value. Thus it matters if, in the long run, a group or person is shown negatively, as opposed to democracy (or its synonym, *public opinion*) or positively, as supporting or otherwise representing democracy or democratic processes. Or a group may be portrayed neutrally, meaning being treated with balance or with silence, concerning democratic themes.

NRA is the only group whose overall mean score is negative for democratic themes. It is frequently shown as opposed to public opinion or democracy, while the other groups are more often shown as aligned, and in some more extreme cases, as the virtual embodiments or representatives of public opinion or democracy. Scores in ascending order for the groups are NRA, 2.62; AARP, 3.14; ACLU, 3.23; NAACP, 3.30; and HCI, 3.38.

The non-NRA groups all receive essentially the same treatment while NRA is portrayed frequently as a special interest that is frustrating democracy through lobbying and financial incentives to elected representatives. The gap separating NRA from the other groups is larger for this measure than for any other.

Much of the language on democratic themes is very strong, underscoring perhaps the importance of this news value to journalists.

Typical instances of anti- or pro-democracy themes involving NRA include:

Figure 3.9: Average Democracy Theme Valence Scores for Interest Group Coverage in Elite Newspapers, 1990-98

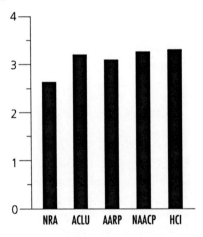

Note: multiple comparison tests show NRA as significantly different from each of the other groups at $p < .001$. Mean differences between AARP, ACLU, NAACP, and HCI are not significant.

National Rifle Association may feel that it has to continue to veto democracy. Government by those who scream the loudest. Pseudo-grass roots campaign. NRA is the Rasputin of American politics. [NRA opposed to] *overwhelming majority of Americans, including gun owners, law enforcement and presidents. Obstructionist. Filibuster. He promised to vote with us* [NRA] *then sold out to the electorate* [from satire]. *Buried Under NRA Money* [headline]. *He must kiss the ring of the NRA* [said of speaker of the U.S. House of Representatives]. *Public taken in by special interests. Polls show a majority of the public drifting from its views. Manchurian candidates the NRA ran in the last election. Backroom political tactics. Stranglehold over national legislation.* [Congress] *should heed demand of 95 percent of the people. The police add their voices to the clamor for gun control. Coalescing national demand* [NRA opposed to].

Many articles focus on NRA political activities and how they frustrate democratic processes but make no mention of similar activities by other groups that are also attempting to influence political outcomes by similar or identical means, e.g., *WP* runs a story on campaign support from the NRA, detailing political contributions by NRA to members of Congress (Babcock, 1996). The story is somewhat balanced within itself; a Common Cause "president" describes the NRA's actions as "a classical example of how political money influences congressional elections"; while the "NRA's chief lobbyist" said "she did not agree." But there appears in the long run to be no comparable story on the sizeable political donations that are made by HCI or many other groups.

A cartoon with an anti-democracy theme shows a congressman on the steps of the Capitol receiving a check from a man at a desk labeled "Vote with the NRA Gun Lobby." Horrified citizens look on, one saying to the other, "Now I see where the 'instant check' comes in," a reference to NRA-backed legislation mandating instant computer checks for gun buyers (Herblock, 1991).

NAACP coverage tends toward the positive on Democracy and Public Opinion themes, although there is some fluctuation. A piece of 1995 convention coverage in *NYT* describes a "squabble" concerning the organization's "road to the future." While the article describes considerable disruption and infighting among factions at the convention, a Harvard Law School professor is quoted as saying of the debate, "It's pure democracy" (Terry, 1995).

Negative anti-democracy themes applied to AARP are limited generally to editorial commentary on self-interested AARP actions at the expense of society, e.g. senior citizens grabbing too much of the pie in the form of social benefits. These seldom appear, however.

ACLU is sometimes shown as frustrating democracy in its pursuit of its absolutist visions of constitutional rights. The will of the majority is ignored because ACLU has insisted on some arcane, occasionally absurd, point of law.

For HCI, democracy themes are often put in grandiose positive terms such as *groundswell of popular opinion*, where HCI is shown as championing democracy and public opinion, at times as its embodiment. The contrast between NRA coverage and HCI coverage is striking in this regard.

Group Intensity Themes

Intensity refers to the strength with which opinions are held or manifested. Euphemisms or dysphemisms can connotatively shade a group's intensity levels; thus, *dedication* indicates a generally positive property in that we all admire the dedicated; while *fixation* does not, for we avoid the fixated, sometimes by institutionalizing them; and either term could be applied in many cases to the exact same action or person, for the terms convey value judgments. Pejoratives thus are *zealotry* or *fanaticism*, while euphemisms would include terms such as *activist, dedication,* or *commitment.* Neutrality is also a possibility, with either group intensity not mentioned or in instances where positives and negatives cancel.

NRA and ACLU are coupled once again on this measure, with mean group intensity scores in the negative. In ascending order, mean scores are NRA, 2.71; ACLU, 2.89; AARP, 3.04; NAACP, 3.11; and HCI, 3.21.

One of the most extreme examples is the linking of Oklahoma City bomber Timothy McVeigh with the phrase "I'm the NRA," the theme of a long-standing NRA promotional campaign. A rare example of a positive NRA intensity term is *passionate*.

Negative terms very frequently designate group intensity in the NRA coverage. Just a few examples are:

> *An old extremist message. Pavlovian opposition of the National Rifle Association. Desperate campaign. Radical NRA Tactics Backfire* [headline]. *Extreme right. Increasingly hardline. Assault weapon extremists. Intransigent. No compromise. Strident. Fanatical perch. Irrationality and extremism. Gun zealots. Irresponsible obsessions Right wing zealots. Defiant. Extreme religious devotion...absolutist. Mantra (Second Amendment). Bellicose rhetoric. An almost religious battle. Characteristically feisty and furious. As uncompromising and ornery as ever. Not changed their tune one iota. Irrationality and extremism. NRA leaders have done their best to stoke the siege mentalities of members.*

Figure 3.10: Average Group Intensity Theme Valence Scores for Interest Group Coverage in Elite Newspapers, 1990-98

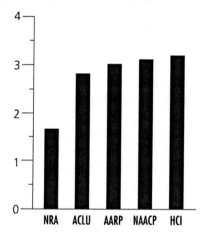

Note: NRA differs significantly from all of the other groups, $F(4, 1468) = 60.74$, $p < .001$. Multiple comparisons show no non-NRA group as significantly different from one another.

NAACP intensity, when discussed, is most often discussed with positive terms such as *outspoken, commitment, crusade, ambitious, energy,* and *personal odyssey.*

ACLU is treated more ambivalently than NAACP, with terms such as *discrimination crazed, zealously, near absolutist, absolutist–First Amendment,* and *principled.*

AARP coverage includes a number of descriptions of *volunteers* who are said to be *dedicated.*

HCI coverage often includes euphemistic descriptions such as *a personal cause* and similar phases with positive connotations. We might also revisit the examples given earlier of personalization themes that showed the Bradys—certainly the most well-known representatives for HCI—as models of dedication, conveyed by positive terms such as *characteristic zeal* and *vitality.* On the whole in elite news coverage HCI organizational actors have zeal while NRA actors are merely zealots.

Growth–Dwindle Themes

The "who's ahead" aspect of coverage is important as well. Patterson (1994) studied coverage of political contests and discovered that it reflected not so much as substantive issues, but rather who is perceived to be winning or moving ahead. He called this *game schema* journalism. Reports of the waxing or waning of power (or the relative power of groups) may have little to do with actual events. Lippmann and Mertz (1920) studied coverage of the Russian Revolution in elite American news and concluded that news reflected more the wishes and dreams of the men writing the news articles than it did actual political events in Russia. News in this sense can resemble cheerleading, exhortation, or the narrowest parochialism.

NRA has the lowest score on the growth–dwindle measure, reflecting persistent themes in coverage of defeat, membership decline and resignations of prominent and not-so-prominent members. The groups rank: NRA, 2.72; NAACP, 2.95; ACLU, 3.01; AARP, 3.13; and HCI, 3.35.

HCI once again has the highest mean score, and again this is related largely to its frequent opposition to NRA in conflict-style coverage in which NRA is described as defeated or having lost momentum, allies, or supporters while HCI is associated with victory, momentum, and accrued support. For the first and only time on any of the measures, NAACP joins NRA on the negative side of the scale, reflecting periods of coverage that associate NAACP with irrelevance, and hence its decay as a viable organization, or with a fall from past glories due to infighting, malfeasance, or misfeasance of officials. Interestingly, some articles conveying themes of NRA diminishment appear at times of peak NRA membership or membership growth.

Typical growth–dwindle themes from NRA coverage include:

> *NRA's Lost Clout. NRA Must Decide Whether to Refocus its Aim as its Membership Shrinks to Smaller Caliber* [Headline, note puns]. *Once ranked among the most powerful lobbies...[suffers] unprecedented setback. Another Loss for NRA* [headline]. *NRA no longer seen as invulnerable...we're beating them back. Membership numbers are dropping and its credibility strained as it fights even reasonable gun control measures. Growing momentum* [against NRA]. *As its influence in Washington wanes. Debilitating defeat. Marked as second defeat in as many months*

for the powerful National Rifle Association. *Big Lobbies Appear to be Losing Their Grip* [headline]. *People who hate guns are the majority now. Steep decline in membership. Woe at the NRA* [headline]. *In virtual shambles. Atrophying. Chain of recent defeats. Stinging defeat for the NRA. Alienated its mainstream membership. Faltering NRA Finds itself Under the Gun* [headline]. *Important symbolic defeat for the influential gun lobby. The NRA wounded. Death spiral. Like Rearranging Deck Chairs on the Titanic* [said of NRA reorganization].

Positive growth themes concerning NRA can be found in the coverage on occasion, but not often. A *WSJ* article headlined "An NRA Victory That's Not Fit to Print" describes a major come-from-behind win by the NRA in a gun control referendum in the state of Washington. Significantly, the article notes that the win has been almost entirely ignored by major news media. NRA defeats and possible indicators of decline, however, are frequently celebrated in editorials, e.g., *NRA was sent home to lick its wounds* and *rub the arrogant lobby's nose in the dirt*.

Two patterns emerge. First, a substantial number of NRA articles appear to be based in large part on articles that preceded them. It appears that journalists are reworking previous stories or story frames ("angles") from their newspapers' article files instead of thinking up new approaches. Therefore these frames appear sometimes to outlast the events they initially tried to describe. So if early articles reported that NRA was in serious decline, later articles echoed this theme, whether accurate or not. I believe this is a major reason behind the general elite media failure to notice NRA mobilization until quite recently; the journalists are playing follow-the-leader. More so, this perhaps classically manifests Lippmann's old observation on stereotyping—first we define, then we see, and not so often the other way around.

Figure 3.11: Average Growth/Dwindle Theme Valence Scores for Interest Group Coverage in Elite Newspapers, 1990-98

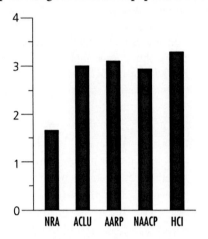

Note: Multiple comparison tests show the NRA as significantly different from all other groups, $F(4, 1468) = 25.89$, $p < .001$. NAACP, ACLU, and AARP do not differ significantly from each other. HCI stands significantly apart from all other groups.

Second, articles also seem to celebrate downturns in NRA membership that in the long run could only reasonably be viewed as minor fluctuations in an upward trend that has been underway since about 1970. No article ever celebrates an upward NRA trend; and it was not until after the period covered by the content analysis, in late 2000, that such growth was even noted.

Some frames are force-fits, to say the least. "Ideological War Pits NRA Hard-Liners Against More Moderate Staff" (Mintz, 1995) relies on quotes from a disgruntled former NRA financial official to paint a picture of internal struggle and imminent collapse (at a time of near-peak membership, apparently unbeknownst to the reporter). In order to fit this frame to the facts, the article links former NRA president Harlon Carter to gun control moderatism. This notion is ridiculous to anyone who has tracked the evolution of NRA: Carter had emerged as a central figure in the Cincinnati Revolt, which politically charged the entire organization, and he was also the first director of the NRA's Institute for Legislative Action, its lobbying arm. The disgruntled former NRA official quoted in this article appears in a number of other articles around this time before finally disappearing from coverage. The article also discounts the quality of new NRA members, of whom it says, "Few new members are the kind of well-to-do, well educated hunters and gun enthusiasts who make up the group's main membership base."

NAACP growth descriptions are much more balanced in tone than NRA's. While NAACP is sometimes described as fading, much of the coverage has a cheerleader-like quality to it. Consider, for example, a set of *NYT* editorials titled, "New Directions at NAACP" and "Moving Forward at the NAACP." NRA, by comparison, is never said to be moving forward.

Reflecting this tonal balance, NAACP is variously described:

> *Socially energized; old, wounded, deeply in debt; hobbled; the old warrior for social justice may soon wither and die; a still vital organization poised for rejuvenation; black support wanes* and *relevancy questioned.*

NAACP's continued existence is a cause for journalistic and social concern. Possible indicators of its decline are gravely examined, rather than celebrated, as is the case with NRA.

Editorial Tone and Semantics

Looking only at editorial and op-ed article coverage on the five-point scale for the tone of editorial and op-ed articles, NRA once again anchors the set of interest groups. Here "tone" means essentially positive, neutral, or negative assessment on the same type of five-interval scale used in previous measures. Group means in ascending order are NRA, 1.68; ACLU, 2.35; AARP, 2.73; NAACP, 3.00; and HCI, 4.20.

These differences in tone can be directly attributed to avowed editorial policy. The editors of *The Washington Post, The New York Times* and *Los Angeles Times* have all at various times stated on their editorial pages their newspapers' support of British-style systems of gun control with no or very few guns in the possession of civilians. The papers are admittedly partisan in this regard. NRA is denounced as an obstacle to such schemes. Consider the following passage taken from a 1991 *WP* editorial:

The struggle to get the right legislation controlling firearms has been long and frustrating—this paper has been involved in it for decades and we know whereof we speak. It is incredible that so many people who know better yield to the threats and blandishments of the National Rifle Association [and refuse to] end the mayhem gun proliferation has caused.

A similar *LAT* editorial opinion is expressed in "Taming the Monster: The Guns Among Us," where it is stated:

The Times supports a near total ban on the manufacture and private ownership of handguns and assault weapons.

Semantics found in the editorial treatments of NRA flow directly out of such positions, for NRA editorials contain a great deal of unrestrained language, the likes of which are seldom directed at the non-NRA groups.

In ascending order the means for semantic treatment of interest groups in editorials are NRA, 1.78; ACLU, 2.61; AARP, 2.90; NAACP, 3.0; and HCI, 4.20. Once again NRA anchors the scale, although it is significantly lower than the next highest group, ACLU; and once again ACLU also tends toward negative treatment.

To say that NRA editorials contain unrestrained language is an understatement. Ad hominem attacks are not uncommon. None of the other groups are systematically treated in this way, and only ACLU and AARP on infrequent occasion are subjected to strong verbal abuse.

Examples of some of the many instances of negative semantics applied to NRA are:

Figure 3.12: Tone of Editorials on Interest Groups in Elite Newspapers, 1990-98

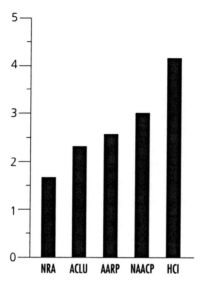

Note: Difference of means test is significant, $F(4, 290) = 19.31$, $p < .001$. Multiple comparison tests show NRA as different from all other groups at levels of $p < .015$ or better. NAACP, AARP, ACLU, and HCI do not differ significantly from one another.

Wayne LaPierre, Executive VP in charge of defamatory blather. Arrogant obstinance of the gun lobby. Disingenuous sophistries of the NRA. Pet NRA boondoogle. The mendacious interpretation . . . urged by the National Rifle Association. Paranoid fantasies. Money-bearing lobbyists for the NRA. Fans lunatic flames. Frantic. Ludicrously inconsistent. NRA/GOP pogrom against federal agents. [NRA] puts money from gun sales first, public safety last. Exceeds the limits of principled advocacy. Hard core. We have the NRA to thank for this...often murderous business of selling guns. Lunacy. See the mayhem. NRA smoke screen. NRA's disinformation campaign. Venomous assault. Social insanity. NRA's paranoid stance. The twisted line of the NRA. NRA lie. Wacky. Cynical and disingenuous effort to undermine sensible firearms regulation. Carnage. NRA wants to confuse people, not debate the issue. [NRA's] diversionary advertisements. The thugs who run the NRA. Knee-jerk opposition. NRA's broad brush propaganda campaign against all Federal law enforcement agencies. Disgraceful stealth. NRA likes weak laws. The blood of a Houston Family is on the head of the National

Rifle Association. Pernicious influence and conduct. Criminals, terrorists, fanatics and unstable people might begin each day by giving thanks to the NRA.

Such editorializing language is not always confined to editorials. A straight news *WP* article (Kovaleski, 1996) contains an unattributed, apparently gratuitous comment on the part of the journalist that describes NRA as, "a recreational organization that has instead become a strident, monomaniacal lobbying group."

NAACP semantics have generally approving connotations such as *solid, charismatic, fine job, steady compass, transformation, stunningly, renaissance approach,* and *illustrious history,* although it is by no means immune from the occasional burst of negative commentary such as *a disoriented and at times paranoid quality about the organization.*

AARP, too, is beaten up on occasion by editors who describe organizational actions with phrases such as *the taint of financial self-interest.* A small set of *WSJ* editorials admonishes AARP in eloquent and fiery terms for being more of a business than a member service group for senior citizens. But these sorts of denunciation stand out as exceptional instances rather than the mode, as is the case for NRA coverage.

HCI is not abused in any editorial coverage except for a very few op-ed pieces written by gun activists. In this regard it appears uniquely privileged among the groups.

Figure 3.13: Semantics of Editorials on Interest Groups in Elite Newspapers, 1990-98

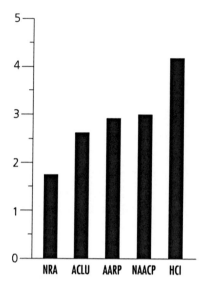

Note: Differences are significant, $F(4, 289) = 19.87, p < .001$. On multiple comparison tests NRA differs from all other groups at levels of $p > .005$; ACLU, AARP, and NAACP do not differ; and HCI differs from NRA and ACLU, but not from NAACP and AARP.

Labeling of Interest Groups

Journalists typically attach descriptive labels to the groups they cover. Inevitably such labels have connotations, e.g., consider the difference implied by *citizens group* versus *special interest group*, even though either might apply equally well to the same group. Sometimes it is the group that succeeds in labeling itself, through apt public relations strategies, and sometimes journalists or others label the group, thereby indicating value judgment. As suggested by the above example, labels can also convey positive or negative information on how the group stands in relationship to democracy and democratic processes. The foregoing description of a "strident, monomaniacal lobbying group" does not evoke the image of good citizenship in a civil society.

The labeling of interest groups in the coverage is systematically different. NRA is more than five times as likely as the other groups to be described as a lobby or special interest group—terms having negative connotations in a democracy. For if the groups are considered as comparable voluntary associations, which they certainly are along many dimensions, there is no good reason why one should be consistently labeled positively as a citizens group and another negatively as a lobby. And yet this is indeed the case.

Of the NRA articles, 28.8 percent label NRA as some variant of *lobby* or *special interest* group, but only 5.5 percent of articles on the other groups apply such labels. The proper name of the organization (or neutral labels such as *organization, association,* or *group*) is used in 70.7 percent of NRA articles but increases to 84.4 percent for the other groups. Only 0.6 percent of the NRA coverage uses labels with positive connotations such as *citizen group, advocacy group,* or *civil rights group,* while more than 10 percent of articles on the other groups attach these or similar positive labels to the group. Examples of variations of labels applied to the NRA are:

> *Semi-automatic caucus. Lobbying juggernaut. Gun lobby. The powerful gun lobby. Eastern lobbyists. Gun organization. Powerful interest group. Radical gun lobby. Single interest. The classic Washington super lobby. Private grass roots organization. Special interest gun lobby. Arrogant lobby. The gun lobby consisting of everything from neo-nazis to nature-loving hunters. Most feared lobby in the country. Strident lobby for nation's gun manufacturers. Gun man-ufacturer's lobby. Evil Empire. Intimidating lobby of weapons peddlers. The evil and lavishly funded gun lobby. The Beltway's loudest lobby. The NRA, a rich and paranoid organization. Impermeably strong lobby. Vicious lobby. Vested interest. A fanatical organization that is awash in the blood of homicide and suicide victims.*

Figure 3.14: Labeling of Interest Groups in Elite Newspaper Coverage, 1990-98

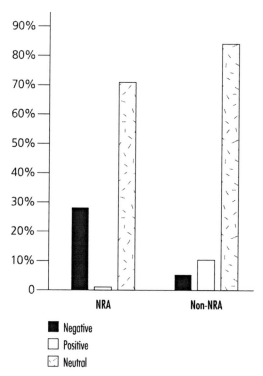

Note: Cross tables test significant at: X^2 (2, 1403) = 168.78, $p < .001$, $\Phi = .347$.

Certainly the most frequent label applied to NRA other than its proper name is *the gun lobby*.

NAACP is never described as a *lobby* or *special interest group* in any of the sampled coverage despite the fact that it is indeed a special interest group that lobbies. Without exception in 182 articles NAACP is identified either by its proper name or as some variant of *civil rights group* or *advocacy* group.

A particular NAACP label that frequently recurred verbatim was *the nation's oldest and largest civil rights organization*. This label recurred so frequently that it was assigned its own acronym, NOLCRO, in the content analysis. Its source is probably NAACP press releases and other NAACP handouts (and web sites) from which journalists are working.

Labels identifying NAACP include:

National civil rights group, venerable civil rights organization, oldest and most respected civil rights organization, black organization, the leading civil rights organization in the United States, the nation's oldest and best known organization that advocates for blacks, and *the storied civil rights group.*

AARP is variously labeled, and like NRA is at times referred to as a lobby or special interest but at nowhere near the same rate (only 15.1 percent for AARP versus 28.8 percent for NRA). Labels applied to AARP include:

The powerful AARP. Influential organization. Consumer group. Retirees' group. Nation's largest lobbying organization. Lobbying behemoth and service organization for the elderly. Advocate for the elderly. Non-profit group. Powerful lobby group. Membership group. Non-profit group. Influential group. The 33-million member association best known as a lobbying group for the elderly. Powerful organization that represents many elderly people. Influential lobbying group.

ACLU is also variously described, but only 1.2 percent of the articles label it as a special interest or lobby. Typical label examples are:

Civil liberties group. Nation's most controversial private organization. Liberal group. Abortion rights group. Leading liberal champion of defending and expanding minority rights.

HCI is referred to as a lobby or special interest in 15.1 percent of its coverage, almost equaling the AARP percentage but still only about one half the percentage for NRA. When HCI is thus labeled, though, it is almost invariably in an article that also identifies NRA as lobby. Journalistic fairness and balance standards would account for this practice, for if the one group is called a lobby it is only fair to apply the same term to its counterpart organization within the same piece of conflict-style journalism. Not to do so would stand out. But HCI is called a citizen group or other positive label in 7.7 percent of coverage, contrasted to NRA's negligible 0.6 percent. HCI is labeled as:

Citizens' lobby, advocates, movement, HCI lobby, non-profit organization, Washington-based non-profit group that lobbies for gun control, public interest group, a citizen's group based in Washington, and *citizen members of Handgun Control, Inc.*

NRA, it should be pointed out, is never referred to as a *citizen's lobby*, despite its four million members compared to HCI's relatively meager membership of 400,000 at most, and the most frequent single label applied to NRA is *gun lobby*. HCI labels generally imply a level of representation of the popular will that is lacking in the NRA labels, e.g., so even when HCI is referred to as an interest group—which it certainly is—it becomes a *public interest group*. It is also worth pointing out that HCI describes itself as, "a nonprofit citizens' organization" in its own communications (Handgun Control, Inc., 1999), so HCI appears to be somewhat successful in floating its preferred image of itself in media coverage.

Science-Progress Themes

Scientific progressivism stands as one of the principal values of modern times. It distinguishes, in substantial part, modernity from supposed and actual unenlightened times that went before. It would not be at all hyperbolic to say that Scientism has largely replaced Religion as universal explanation. Interest groups often attempt to drape themselves with the mantle of scientific respectability (or inevitability) by having scientific and social-scientific studies manufactured by front organizations and think tanks. Or the groups borrow "scientific" materials as they please. Of course "science" as thus defined always somehow seems to forward the agenda of the group. To be unscientific, opposed to science or its progress, is virtually an impossible position to uphold. Science is countered with more science.

Too, if interest groups are regarded as nodal information centers distributed throughout society, one of their chief informational functions is to bring to bear scientific-technical information upon problems with the view of affecting policy. This matter lies at the heart of how interest groups function in U.S. society. So how a group fares in terms of science-progress themes in national media coverage is no small matter.

Rankings for the Science-Progress measure show NRA and ACLU in the negative, opposed to science, with NRA once again at the bottom. The rankings are NRA, 2.92; ACLU, 2.97; AARP, 3.09: HCI, 3.15; and NAACP, 3.17. The means differences are significant, one-way ANOVA tests, $F (4, 1464) = 15.45$, $p < .001$, while on multiple comparison tests NRA differs at $p > .005$ levels from all of the other groups except ACLU. NAACP, while HCI and AARP do not significantly differ. At the high end of the Science-Progress scale are HCI, AARP, and NAACP, with no significant difference between them; their scores are essentially identical from a statistical point of view.

For examples of how negative Science-Progress themes are often applied to NRA, NRA is criticized in editorials and op-ed pieces for attacking U.S. Center for Disease Control (and other) studies related to gun violence. NRA is also criticized for opposing so-called taggant technology for marking explosives in an *LAT* article "Lobbyists Stymie Effort to Trace Explosives' (Meyer & Feldman, 1995). There seems to be an editorial sense of indignation that NRA disagrees with "science"; in these cases headlines appear such as *Gunning for Research: In the NRA Attack on Firearms Studies, Scientific Truth is the Most Important Casualty,* and *An NRA Potshot at Science.*

The low ACLU score is due mainly to articles on public education in which ACLU legal challenges have apparently disrupted school systems and educational access programs such as Schools of Choice. (The science measure includes educational themes.)

HCI is linked approvingly with U.S. Justice Department studies on guns and violence and with social science studies by other groups, hence its high group mean.

NAACP is frequently linked positively with educational issues and social progress. One of very few instances of a negative science theme for NAACP concerns NAACP dragging its feet in allowing historians access to its files on the civil rights movement.

Media Bias Themes

At times groups may complain of bad or unfair coverage. Letters to the editor may protest treatment in specific articles or editorials, or group representatives may assail journalists or the media in general when interviewed by journalists or at group events that are covered in articles. All articles fit into one of two possible categories. Either the article mentions bias in some way by quoting or attributing a claim of media bias made by the interest group, this could take the form of criticizing coverage in particular or general, lack of coverage, and so forth; or else the article does not mention bias.

Yet another very sharp distinction emerges here. NRA coverage is more than five times as likely to mention media bias than is that of the combined other groups, with 7.8 percent of NRA coverage containing media bias themes compared to only 1.3 percent for the non-NRA groups.

Controlling for article type reveals what I perceive as a characteristic media sensitivity of NRA supporters. Considering only letters to the editor, the proportion of media bias themes for NRA increases to 30.6 percent of coverage compared to only 5.3 percent for the other combined groups. Apparently the NRA members and officials who write these letters are much more responsive to the perceived fairness of media coverage than are the members and officials of the other organizations. A possible alternative explanation for the lower non-NRA rate is implausible; it would be difficult to believe that editors are refusing to publish media bias letters from people representing other groups. The NRA–media bias relationship is also stronger for feature-type articles than for coverage in general, because feature articles usually contain more NRA quotes than straight news or editorials, allowing NRA officials to more freely speak their minds. Thus in the case of feature articles, 15.6 percent of the NRA coverage contains media bias themes while no feature article for any of the other groups does so.

Figure 3.15: Media Bias Themes in Interest Group Coverage in Elite Newspapers, 1990-98

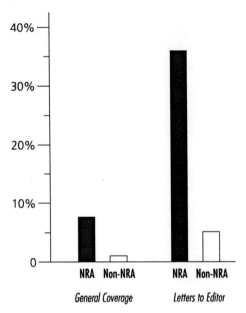

Note: The cross table test for dependence in General Coverage is significant, X^2 (1, 1138) = 25.99, $p < .001$, $\Phi = .151$. For letters to the editor the relationship is also significant, X^2 (1, 147) = 16.05, $p < .001$, $\Phi = .330$.

An *LAT* letter to the editor, "George Bush," expresses a typical NRA media bias theme; the writer refers to media treatment of former president Bush's resignation from the NRA in 1995 as "just one more facet to a well-orchestrated media effort to vilify and discredit the NRA, gun ownership and the Second Amendment" (Pacer, 1995). Another such letter responds to an editorial cited earlier in the discussion of personalization themes, where *LAT* editors in as many words blame NRA for the murder of a deputy sheriff. In response the letter writer states, "[The deputy's] death is simply used as fodder for *The Times* political agenda. *The Times* made him a victim twice!" (Keirsey, 1992).

On the few occasions when non-NRA group representatives complain of bias in coverage it is in reaction to an alleged inaccuracy or misrepresentation in a particular article or on an issue, rather than a blanket indictment of the newspaper or mass media.

Non-Findings

Contrary to expectations raised during a pilot study (Patrick, 1997), a measure for in-group cohesion-dissension shows no significant difference between groups, although dissension is frequently reported between a group's members or its leaders. NAACP has received considerable coverage of its internal struggles, e.g., arguments over whether to modify or discontinue NAACP's traditional integrationist stance in education; these are often framed as debates. Likewise, the warring of internal NRA factions over finance and policy are covered at various times, generally framed as a struggle of extremists versus moderates for control of the organization. AARP coverage during the first year of the Clinton presidency contained dissenting opinions of AARP members who unequivocally expressed displeasure at the organization's direction on health care policy.

Group differences for coverage of malfeasance-orthopraxy by the group or its officials are also insignificant. All of the groups or their officials except HCI are portrayed on occasion as malfeasant or irresponsible, either in matters of finance, scandal, bad management, social irresponsibility or poor business practices—but none significantly more or less more than any other. NAACP's embarrassing problems with officials misspending organizational funds on limousines and for the settlement of personal sexual harassment lawsuits received prominent coverage in articles during the mid-1990s. In some NRA coverage former employees bitterly denounce NRA officials for misspending and driving the organization to the brink of financial ruin. Once again, HCI alone appears to be above reproach. This, coupled with the other instances of positive HCI treatment, says something about the sympathies of the news people.

Caveats

As shown by the foregoing evidence, NRA beyond any reasonable doubt tends to be treated negatively compared to other interest groups. This negativity is systematic, meaning it persists over time, across newspapers, and across content and article types.

All this is not to say there is no fair coverage of NRA, or even that fair coverage is rare. Although elite newspaper editorial content is consistently and strongly slanted against NRA, straight news content is often objective and balanced. Some articles on NRA could be used as models for teaching accurate, objective journalism in accord with the highest professional-academic standards. What is more, the NRA side of issues is sometimes presented with apparent conscientiousness. Editors at times publish responses to their anti-NRA stances in the form of letters to the editor or op-ed pieces written by NRA members and officials, although we should not forget that the editors are the ones choosing which rebuttals and counter-claims they print, and also that letters to the editor are frequently edited extensively, sometimes beyond their author's recognition, before they see print.

Also the inclusion of criticism has an important function relating to credibility: it allows editors and reporters to conspicuously demonstrate fairness and magnanimity, even though the numbers reported above suggest they are neither in regard to NRA.

So on the whole, NRA is systematically marginalized in the elite newspapers that set the national standards. As the comparisons show, it is an object of discourse rather than a participant; it is shown in opposition to important cultural values such as Democracy and Science; it is derogatorily labeled and mocked; its representatives are not accorded the same level of titular dignity as the representatives of other organizations; and when its representatives or positions are quoted, they tend to be qualified as tentative. The statistical probability of such large differences being attributable to chance approaches zero on virtually all of the measures.

A condition of negative coverage indeed exists, as postulated by the model of social movement media coverage laid out at the beginning of this chapter. We now turn to an examination of communication strategies on the part of the NRA.

4

ANTI-MEDIA THEORY AND NATIONAL RIFLE ASSOCIATION COMMUNICATIONS

NRA Response to Coverage

The social movement viewpoint regards group communication strategy as following generally from the type of media coverage that will be received under a media system that is unsympathetic or somehow closed to the group:

Media Coverage → Group Communication Strategy

The first half of this schematic—media coverage of interest groups—was examined in the previous chapter. This chapter turns now to an examination of the second half: NRA communication strategies as they are revealed by NRA official communications and through interviews with NRA officials.

The quantitative foundation of this chapter is a content analysis of the 99 issues of NRA's official journal, *The American Rifleman*, published between January 1990 and July 1998. But the chapter also draws examples from latter issues of official journals and from communications of NRA officials up to and past the 2000 elections.

The analysis focuses on communication themes that define and characterize the social movement style of mobilization: *identity, solidarity,* and *conflict*. And while it examines conflict themes in general, major sub-themes of conflict are also looked at, particularly *media conflict*, for it is this latter sub-theme that acts as a major goad to NRA mobilization.

There is little doubt that NRA mobilization and communication strategies are responsive in large part to media bias, perceived or real, with media bias themes constituting an important segment of the official communications as manifested in its journals. Communications by NRA officials in other contexts such as speeches and annual reports also refer regularly, in great detail, to media bias. It also appears to be a fundamental assumption of NRA press relations according to interviews I have conducted with NRA officials.

The major lesson here is that NRA has institutionalized around negative media coverage, re-interpreting and redirecting it for its own ends. This *anti-media theory* functions a unifying epistemic foundation to the NRA world. By pointing out and sensitizing members (and potential members) to negative coverage as evidence of class-cultural conflict, NRA is able to more effectively promote an aggrieved sense of identity that in turn sustains the action-in-solidarity that is the structural core of effective group action.

No conflict equals no solidarity in social movement mobilization. NRA is effective precisely because it trades on the winds of journalistic intolerance, though sometimes generating a bit of wind on its own, as will be seen in the examples given below.

NRA Official Publications

NRA currently publishes eleven issues annually of each of its three official journals in magazine format. Members receive a subscription to their choice of one of the magazines as a benefit of belonging, so altogether the combined circulation approximates the number of NRA members, about four million. Foremost in subscription numbers is *The American Rifleman* (1.62 million in 2000) followed by *The American Hunter* (1.24 million) and, the most recent addition to the journals, *America's 1st Freedom* (710,000).

All carry identical political and official NRA positions, identified by articles bylined by NRA officials or otherwise, e.g. monthly columns or departments. Other content varies by magazine to serve the hobby or technical informational needs of a few major subclasses of NRA members, although the overlap is considerable. Some, a number that NRA officials would not provide when asked, receive two or all three magazines, depending on their interests, although such additional subscriptions are available only at additional cost. NRA officials also say that some members receive no magazine at all, but would not provide further details. One doubts though whether this category is considerable in size, for it seems unlikely that a large number of persons would join an organization in order not to benefit by its informational resources.

The reader will have noticed that the circulation numbers provided above do not total 4.3 million, the membership claimed by NRA. When asked for an explanation, NRA officials said that that some members receive no magazine by request; this seems unlikely, in that a major reason to join any voluntary association is to acquire specialized information. Junior members receive their own publication, *Insights*, which goes out to about 35,000 members monthly. Spouse-type memberships do not receive a separate magazine and account for an uncertain proportion of total membership. NRA has not been cooperative in releasing breakdowns of its membership, at least not to me.

It should be added here that the NRA is not the only group examined in this book that apparently carries some degree of phantom membership above the number suggested by its publication subscriptions. HCI promotional letterheads have for a number of years boasted of being "one million strong," yet there is very little evidence of such mass membership. HCI newsletter circulation suggests a more realistic number of about 250,000.

The American Rifleman, NRA's foremost publication in terms of numbers, speaks mainly to gun enthusiasts and collectors, providing hobby and technical information on shooting equipment and technique involving rifles, shotguns and handguns, historic and current technological development, new products and firearms, firearm-related collecting and biographies of men (mainly) and women (some, but an increasing number over time) who have contributed to the broad field of firearm use or development. Many articles are deeply nostalgic in tone, harking back to romanticized eras, values, and bygone craftsmanship or equipment of yore, e.g., the fabled 94 Winchester Rifle.

The American Hunter, as the name indicates, provides information more suited to the needs of hunters; and it should be noted that judging by circulation numbers alone out of all the magazines, hunting is not the interest of the majority of NRA members, despite common misconceptions on this point, e.g., former president William Clinton often made public remarks apparently addressed to voter-hunters assuring them that gun control would not affect weapons used for deer and duck hunting. *The Hunter's* hobby and technical articles describe hunts, locations, game species and their behaviors, appropriate or ideal calibers for different applications, equipment, history, conservation efforts, and biography-adventure.

Then there is *America's First Freedom,* not only the most recent journal in the NRA line of official publications, but also growing at an impressive rate. *First Freedom* is intended for members who are primarily interested in the social issues related to firearms ownership, self- and home-defense. Published since 1997 as *The American Guardian,* the name of the magazine was changed to *America's First Freedom* in June of 2000. According to the editor's introductory column announcing the name change and a sharpening of focus, the magazine exists because:

> It is no longer reasonable to believe that the national media will fairly report the gun debate. In fact, we have to acknowledge that the majority of the mainstream media is complicit in the effort to strip Americans of the constitutionally guaranteed right to keep and bear arms. If the national media won't carry our message of truth and liberty, we'll spread the word ourselves—hence the magazine you are now reading. (Mehall, 2000)

First Freedom's circulation was approximately 710,000 in 2000, an increase of more than 300 percent from only two years before; so apparently NRA is speaking clearly to those who have ears for this message.

NRA publishes two other important magazines, both with much lesser circulations. *Insights* is designed to appeal to junior members—i.e., the sons and daughters, nieces, nephews, and grandchildren of adult members. NRA publishes approximately 35,000 copies monthly.

USA Shooting Sports provides information for competitive target shooters. It is the only one of these magazines available to non-members, who must pay more for their subscriptions than do NRA members. Nor does it come automatically as a membership benefit; members must pay to subscribe. *Shooting Sports* circulation numbers provide a valuable statistical indicator of the actual interests of NRA members. Editions run to only about 15,000 copies monthly, so, then, at most only about four-tenths of one percent of NRA members exhibit sufficient interest in formal competitive target shooting so as to subscribe to a magazine dedicated to the subject. While the promotion of formal target shooting—a foremost purpose of NRA as it was constituted in 1871—is important to the NRA to the point where organizational resources are dedicated to this purpose, most clearly the modern NRA is in nowise an organization of serious target shooters.

NRA Official Journal Content

Most official communication articles in *American Rifleman* carry bylines of NRA officials and functionaries, including regular columns by the president, chief executive officer and the director of the Institute for Legislative Action (ILA), the lobbying component of NRA. Another regular feature is the "The Armed Citizen," which reports incidents in which men and women have used guns to defend themselves or others. Articles on political-social topics appear in many issues, written by various scholars or guest authors, and while not always identified as NRA official statements, are obviously distinct from hobby-technical material and consistent in tone and content with official communication articles. While hobby and technical articles are authored by many different hunters, shooters, collectors and historical re-enactors, the list of NRA officials whose names appear on the bylines changes only slightly over the period of this study in accord with changes in NRA administration. A statement that recurs in monthly *Rifleman* mastheads confirms these articles as a valid source for NRA official communications:

> OFFICIAL NRA POSITIONS ARE EXPRESSED ONLY IN STATEMENTS BYLINED BY NRA OFFICERS OR IN ARTICLES IDENTIFIED AS SUCH.

Articles identified as such are usually captioned as "Special Reports" in the table of contents. Issues run to about 70-100 pages and contain approximately 23-25 articles, out of which 10-12 articles (40-50 percent) are political or official communications and the remainder, hobby-technical. Advertising on guns, ammunition, accessories, books, guided hunts, clothing, and myriad other products or services makes up the rest of the magazine, taking up at least 20-25 pages per issue, subsidizing to a large degree printing and distribution costs.

Social Movement Themes

Figure 4.1 depicts the relative proportions of social movement themes in NRA official communications. *Conflict* themes concern threats, opposition, and surveillance of the potentially (or actual) hostile environment. *Solidarity* themes concern in-group actions or events including routine collective membership activities such as fundraising banquets or shooting matches. *Identity* themes are ideological value statements, e.g., the importance of guns for personal or political freedom, guns and independence, passing on gun heritage to children, etc.

As would be expected for a social movement arising in adversity, conflict themes are greatest in number (48.3 percent), followed by solidarity paragraphs (38.2 percent), with identity paragraphs the least (8.0 percent). Only approximately 5 percent of paragraphs of NRA official communications do not fit into these categories, meaning they fall into hobby, technical, or some other non-political category.

Figure 4.1: Social Movement Theme Proportions of NRA Official Political Communication Paragraphs in *The American Rifleman*, 1990-98

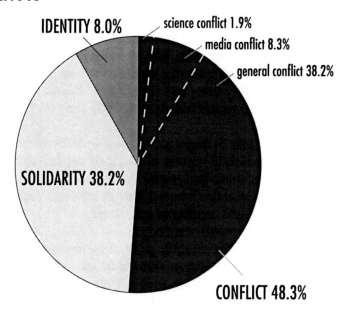

Note: The pie chart includes proportions of paragraphs of social movement themes in official, non-hobby articles. Only about 5 percent of official communication articles contain paragraphs that are coded "other," meaning that they do not fit into one of the categories: conflict, identity, solidarity. For purposes of simplification, "other" paragraphs are not included in this chart and would need to be counted for the graph proportions to total to one hundred percent. N = 23,213 paragraphs of political content.

As the figure shows, conflict themes strongly dominate official NRA communications. Of 23,213 paragraphs of political and official content in *American Rifleman*, 11,223 focus on some form of conflict. Conflict paragraphs can be furthered divided into major sub-categories: *general*, *media*, and *science*, yielding a multi-faceted view of the world as construed by NRA.

Media Conflict Themes

Out of the 23,213 paragraphs of official sociopolitical communications, 1,920 (8.3 percent) explicitly discuss or refer to the subject of media bias. It is a major theme manifested in discussions of media inaccuracy, media sensationalism, bias of individual reporters, bias of news organizations and networks, media favoritism for non-NRA news sources, media hypocrisy, and class-cultural bias as manifested in media content. This proportion remains fairly constant from year to year.

Clearly, media bias is an important premise in NRA official communications to consistently warrant so much consideration. For the sake of comparison, more paragraphs contain mentions of media bias than are dedicated to fundamental identity concerns, such as the meaning of being an NRA member or gun owner.

Media bias mentions often occur *en passant*, almost as if sprinkled gratuitously throughout the monthly political messages of NRA officials who are otherwise speaking on non-media subjects. These seemingly gratuitous mentions, though, tend to treat media as a constant point of reference, a fixed point from which originates many ills.

For an example of a media conflict theme used in this way, the executive vice president's monthly column, "Standing Guard" (LaPierre, 1998) describes, "A generation whose youngsters were not subjected to the kind of anti-gun, anti-hunting enmity that marks mass communication today in the media, education and entertainment." The thrust of the article deals with youth and the inculcation of values, but the media mention squarely anchors blame for contemporary mis-education of youth.

Media are also discussed much more systematically. The same column of a year earlier devotes 30 paragraphs to how media have conducted *active assaults* and *passive assaults* on gun owners and gun culture. *Active assaults* take the form of attacking NRA with "stories designed to dishearten NRA members." The example given is a false news report of NRA "on the verge of financial collapse," that the column attributes to "wishful thinking" by the Associated Press. *Passive assaults* consist of the media ignoring the shooting sports and the positive aspects of gun culture. Given as a passive assault is the example of Ms. Kim Rhodes, who in 1997 at age 17 became the youngest woman shooter ever to win an Olympic gold medal; she was "largely ignored" by media. The column observes, "Had she been a figure skater, or gymnast, she would have been celebrated by the media.... and this is no accident." It then goes on to a discussion of "Those in the media who actively work to divide and conquer."

The reader will certainly note that this dichotomous concept of *active* versus *passive assaults* can be extended to interpret virtually any imaginable circumstance of media omission or commission—either media are ignoring NRA or they are in some way undermining it. The view is total in that it is all-encompassing.

The following examples convey much of the woof and weave of *American Rifleman*'s extensive media criticism:

- One issue decries syndicated advice columnist Ann Landers for her "long on fiction short on fact" writings that it construes as a "nationally syndicated attack on gun owners."

- Over a series of *Rifleman* issues the proposed purchase of the CBS network by NRA members is discussed as a possible way to garner favorable coverage; the proposal is finally set aside as financially unrealistic.

- Repeatedly mentioned is the hypocrisy of anti-gun media executives who produce programming that leads to violence in children. The "Random Shots" column in February 1993 points out the "hypocrisy" of Warner Bros. for releasing an anti-gun Batman comic book, "Batman—The Seduction of the Gun," allegedly spurred by the anti-gun sentiments of a corporate executive, while Warner Bros. simultaneously profits from "gangsta-rap" recordings glorifying the murder of police officers.

- Articles in other issues advise members on techniques for writing publishable letters to newspaper editors and how to most effectively advocate for gun rights on call-in talk radio shows.

- National Public Radio news is criticized in an article for using public money to air anti–Second Amendment views and producing anti-gun, anti-NRA "propaganda which is thinly disguised as news."

- A report of a content analysis of national evening news by the conservative Media Research Center (whose toll-free telephone number is given as 800-243-BIAS) is in the January/February 1995 issue. It examines network objectivity and time allocated to pro- or anti-Brady Bill spokespersons in news broadcasts, concluding that pro-Brady views receive more time. These results are demonstrated with colorful bar graphs. Two other issues contain similar research reports on news coverage that support a conclusion of anti-gun and/or anti-NRA bias.

- Content analysis results from my dissertation (which preceded this book) appear in the September 1999 *American Rifleman*, as "New Study Documents Media Bias Against NRA." The article accurately summarizes research results on many content categories. It also noted my conclusion that NRA benefited from negative coverage, saying, "While that may very well be true, of course it does not absolve the media from its undeniable failure to deal with NRA and Second Amendment issues honestly." The article then denounces a recent *Newsweek* article as a flagrant and unrescinded example of media bias, for even though NRA officials informed *Newsweek* of serious factual errors, the editors only published a short correction of misleading figures on the vertical axis of a mortality table, says the NRA article.

Some of the many terms and phrases used in *American Rifleman* to describe the actions and characteristics of media are:

> *Disinformation campaign. Sow distrust. Media hysteria. Media blitz. Clinton's sentries—the big-city, no-guns, know-it-all media. Media thought police. Media-driven mood swings. Fascist-type propaganda tactics. Concerted effort by media to confuse the public. The anti-gun media. Media-made myth. Manufacture lies. Media misrepresentation. Dominant media culture. Incompetent media. Media elite. TV destruction. Cynical arrogance. Shrill media. Powerful media interests. Media inquisition. Shameless response of media. Propaganda of the popular press. Unsavory and far too often unprofessional. Anti-gun media.*

As can be seen by the unrestrained rhetoric in these examples, NRA gives as good as it gets from the elite dailies whose anti-NRA rhetoric is quoted in chapter 3.

Anti-media themes have come to be officially endorsed by NRA. During the 2000 election contest, NRA president Charlton Heston announced the debut in June of the new NRA magazine *America's First Freedom*, reporting the magazine exists to "bring gun owners hard-edged news from the front lines of this fight, news unavailable from the anti-gun networks and newspapers." He also stated that the magazine "will deliver a journalistic first: News coverage of the political, legislative and cultural conflicts surrounding the Second Amendment told from the point of view of the everyday, mainstream, honest American gun owner" (Heston, June 2000).

After the 2000 elections, which were quite successful from the viewpoint of NRA, *Rifleman* surveys the horizon for new media-borne threats, e.g., "And we face new enemies—with zealots like neo-New Yorker Hillary Clinton bringing unprecedented power to peddle 'spin' through her fawning media following" (LaPierre, February 2001).

But despite their anti-media orientation, *American Rifleman* and all other NRA official publications draw heavily on mass media sources—particularly newspaper accounts—for information on political and social events, in essence having things both ways; for media accounts are not criticized at all when they convey some useful or favorable piece of information. Virtually all of the "Armed Citizen" accounts are taken from local newspapers, for example, with useful political news quoted from elite dailies with regularity.

General Conflict Themes

General conflict themes include surveillance of real or potential threats against gun owners and NRA, cultural war, elite opposition, etc. These comprise the largest sub-category of conflict-theme paragraphs, summing to 8,865 paragraphs, or 38.2 percent of overall political content.

Many hundreds of paragraphs scrutinize proposed legislation and regulatory threats on the local, state and national levels. Entire monthly columns such as the "ILA Report" are typically spent in summarizing bills introduced into Congress or other legislative bodies—the sort of substantive information that the national press fails almost completely in reporting. Chances of bill passage, amendments, and counterproposals are typically assessed. The language and ramifications of proposed bills are scrutinized in great detail. For example, a proposed "American Handgun Standards Act" is criticized because it would ban 54 percent of handguns presently manufactured in the United States, while giving blanket authority to the U.S. Treasury Department's Bureau of Alcohol, Tobacco and Firearms to add more weapons to the list. Policy papers and studies by government agencies are also reviewed in detail.

An important sub-type of the general conflict theme focuses on the world of crime and potential victimization. Crime statistics and the effects of anti-crime initiatives are monitored. Also, each issue of *Rifleman, Hunter,* and *First Freedom,* features a column, "The Armed Citizen," that reports between 10 and 13 incidents of gun owners who used guns to defend themselves, families, or others from criminal attack; *American Rifleman* devotes approximately 1,100 paragraphs to this purpose. Curiously, considering the NRA's anti-media bent, virtually all Armed Citizen articles are taken from newspapers across the country, as is the case previously noted for many other items appearing in columns.

General conflict theme paragraphs also monitor events around the world. Gun control and the search-and-seizure laws of Canada, Japan, Australia, United Kingdom, New Zealand, and other countries are reviewed in considerable detail, often framed in the "it-can-happen-here" style. Litigation, legal decisions, and the implications and motivations of such decisions are also reviewed.

Science Conflict Themes

Science conflict theme paragraphs make up only 1.9 percent of *American Rifleman* political content, 447 paragraphs of the 23,000. Science-conflict themes discuss biased science or education directed against NRA, gun owners or the rights of gun ownership.

A common form of a science conflict theme in *Rifleman* is biased public health and medical research by organizations such as Center for Disease Control (CDC) or as it appears in publications such as *The New England Journal of Medicine*. One article denounces the application of epidemiological models to "frame violence as a public health rather than a criminal justice issue" as an abuse of public trust because research institutions have become servants of politicians' anti-gun agendas. To the CDC, the article states, "Guns are germs and gun owners the new 'Typhoid Marys.'" Methodologies of anti-gun studies are also picked apart, e.g., a study claiming that 1,000 fatal firearms accidents occur annually among children counts anyone under 25 years old as a child. Examples of anti-gun and anti-NRA bias are pointed out in history education and textbooks and in academic settings.

Related to science conflict, *American Rifleman* also reviews academic books and research that affect guns and gun culture. Findings that support NRA goals are reviewed favorably and recommended as essential and illuminating reading. Professor Joyce Malcolm's history on the Anglo-American right to keep and bear arms is praised (Malcolm, 1994). Also praised is economist John Lott's book on his extensive multiple regression–based research that shows liberalized concealed weapon laws that benefit the average citizen are related to reductions in violent crime rates in states where such laws have been enacted (Lott, 1998). David Kopel's sociological comparison of gun control policies in western democracies is similarly treated (Kopel, 1992). And sociologist Gary Kleck's thorough reviews of gun-related research and his own research on rates of defensive uses of guns are regarded as authoritative in their scope. But, on the other side of the fence, historian Michael Bellesile's work is denounced as methodologically incompetent and ideologically biased for its conclusion that the gun culture may have been a relatively recent historical development, based on Bellesile's examinations of early American documents such as wills and testaments wherein gun ownership does not seem to be a norm.

Solidarity Themes

Paragraphs dominated by solidarity themes, describing some form of group activity directed either within or without the organization, comprise 38.2 percent of *Rifleman*'s non-hobby content.

Many solidarity paragraphs concern in-group activities such as forthcoming and recent annual conventions, "Friends of NRA" fundraising dinners scheduled in locations across the country, seminar-classes for women interested in self-defense, and hunter/firearm safety training for children and adolescents.

Another common solidarity sub-theme is united action directed outside of the group such as by means of voting, letter writing, boycotting, demonstrating, or telephoning that may be directed at elected representatives, management of businesses (including news broadcasters), and others that are perceived as anti-gun or anti–Second Amendment. For example, NRA urges members who also belong to the AARP to contact AARP executives to voice opposition to an AARP endorsement of proposed anti-gun measures. Issues also carry letters from NRA members who have resigned from AARP because of its anti-gun stance, recommending that other members do the same.

Solidarity communications regarding voting are precisely customized by the congressional district in which the subscribing member resides. Pre-election issues contain NRA ratings (on a scale of A+ to F) of candidates and incumbents, summaries on races and issues in key districts, and specific reminders of when, where, and for whom NRA members and their families should vote. Post-election issues contain results and strategic commentary on wins, losses, and future prospects.

Internal democratic matters account for a good proportion of solidarity paragraphs. Since the so-called Cincinnati Revolt of 1977, life members have nominated and elected the board of directors. Pre-NRA-election issues carry brief biographies of board of director candidates. These issues also carry paid advertisements for blocks of internal NRA candidates espousing particular platforms, although such ads are not included in this analysis as solidarity because they are not official communications.

Membership recruitment is a ubiquitous solidarity sub-theme. New membership recruitment schemes are stressed, the most frequent being variations on a theme of every-member-recruits-a-member, in this way the NRA membership of three million, at that time, would double to six million virtually overnight. This appeal is found in *Rifleman* issues in the early 1990s, reappears in 1998, and continues into 1999. The 1999 campaign awarded a replica "silver bullet" with NRA president Charlton Heston's engraved autograph to NRA members who signed up another member. Unlike past efforts, the 1999 campaign emphasized that NRA members had for too long been carrying the load for non-aligned gun owners, re-stating Mancur Olson's free-rider problem of interest groups in a nutshell. Membership "upgrades" are also discussed at times, e.g., from annual to life, life to benefactor, benefactor to endowed, etc, as a way of contributing to the group effort.

A common formula of the writing in *American Rifleman* is a series of conflict paragraphs followed by a solidarity series, exactly like the classic "problem-solution" structure used in speech writing and proposals. Voting or membership is presented as the solution to any number of conflict-problems. Even though conflict paragraphs generally dominate NRA official communications, in some few issues solidarity theme paragraphs take precedence, particularly around elections, whether internal board elections or national political elections.

Identity Themes

Identity themes dominate 8 percent of *American Rifleman* non-hobby paragraphs. These are credo-like proclamations of belief and values, e.g., the nature of liberty, freedom, individual rights and responsibilities, the inalienable right of self-defense, etc.

The "Readers Write" section, although by no means an official NRA communication, also frequently contains identity-themed testimonials from members. A letter captioned "Ultimate Authority" provides a rather vivid example of the credo-like nature of such statements. Responding to material in earlier issues on the origins of the right to keep and bear arms, the letter states:

> The Saxons were not the first to introduce . . . the right to keep and bear arms. Our right is even more ancient and well established. . . . Before the human species began there already existed a right and duty . . . that's why other creatures which God created were given arms, such as brains, claws, tusks, wings, etc. Moreover, Christ *commanded* [italics in original]: "He that has not arms, let him sell anything and buy arms." Luke 22:36.

Most identity statements are far less absolute and theological in scope, but do often link the past, present, and future in some sort of normative topography. The September 1997 issue features official articles bylined by Marion Hammer, NRA president, Charlton Heston (then first vice president) and Wayne LaPierre, executive vice president. The focus of the issue is the transmission of Second Amendment rights to the children of the new generation: "We will educate a pro-gun generation." Mr. Heston's articles include a primer—e.g., "The Second Amendment: What Every Kid Should Know," that connects constitutional guarantees of basic rights to current controversy on gun rights, laying out a true meaning for gun ownership. It states, "Owning a gun doesn't make you, by association, a part of the criminal element. It just means that you are a free American who made a free choice." The article, marked "Clip and Save," has a dashed cut line to guide the scissors, presumably so members will clip it and pass it on to the child of their choice, but the language is pitched well above primer level, obviously speaking to the concerns of adult members for their children or grandchildren:

> Many modern youths think the right to keep and bear arms, the Second Amendment to the Constitution, seems sinister, even criminal, mostly because television and movies condemn firearms as tools of violence, glamorize them as symbols of status and stigmatize them as a sign of unstable minds.

Note, by the way, the media conflict theme buried in this particular passage. The remainder of the article is dominated by identity themes that historically construct the interrelationship of equality, firearms, and freedom. The article includes a photograph of Mr. Heston in a classroom setting with blackboard and American flag in the background.

Another set of identity-type paragraphs in "The President's Column," June 1995, marks the fiftieth anniversary of the ending of World War II. It intertwines the marksmanship traditions of NRA and the "secret weapons," i.e., "the individual soldier" that are said to have won every war in modern history, thus making freedom possible.

Woman-as-gun-owner appears to be an emerging identity subtheme. Issues in the early 1990s feature occasional articles addressing women NRA members, but by the second half of the 1990's these have coalesced into a regular *Rifleman* column, "NRA Woman's Voice." Identity themes occur frequently, for example, a participant in workshops known by the acronym BOW (Becoming an Outdoor Woman) summarizes benefits accrued to participants as, "Very gratifying, very empowering, very appealing." Another identity-dominated "Woman's Voice" column celebrates notable women shooters and gun rights activists such as Elizabeth Topperwein, an early 1900s exhibition shooter who broke many of Annie Oakley's rifle and shotgun records for thrown targets; and "woman of action" Marion Hammer, first woman president of NRA, a gun rights activist credited as "the driving force" behind the passage of Florida's landmark concealed-carry weapon law for citizens. The same column states:

> From the pioneer woman of the Old West to today's modern female, American history is filled with women who owned firearms for protection, for sport or for myriad other reasons. And while gun ownership among women is on the rise, so too is home ownership, voting, heading a household, pursuing a career and many other activities traditionally considered the activities of men—including criminal victimization.

The woman-as-gun owner and NRA member themes continue in *American's First Freedom*. The editor is an attractive woman, Karen Mehal, whose photograph appears beside her column in each issue, sometimes wearing business clothing and sometimes dressed for hunting. Her columns include discussions of firearms and family values, education, and media bias.

Themes on Journal Covers

Themes that are hobby-technical in nature dominate a majority (75.5 percent) of the covers of *American Rifleman*, e.g., some depict current and antique firearms or "exploded" engineering-style mechanical drawings that function as assembly guides to rifles, shotguns, and handguns. This practice may simply represent editorial tradition, for covers from the 1950s and decades before often used these sorts of themes.

Relatively few covers depict conflict, showing collages of NRA political enemies, including elected or appointed government officials, e.g., First Lady Hillary Clinton, HCI Chair Sarah Brady, President Bill Clinton, and Congressman Charles Schumer. The photographs are often accompanied by select anti-gun quotations.

Possibly the most lurid example of conflict encountered during the past decade is the rape theme cover of the October 1994, pre-November election issue. Captioned "Stop the Rape of Liberty," it shows a blue-suited politician assaulting the Statue of Liberty. Attacking from behind, the politician-rapist silences the cries of the struggling statue with one hand clapped over her mouth. He tears at her robe with the other hand as the torch of liberty falls to the ground in her struggles. Another cover, "Politicians Show Their Stripes," depicts a shirtless politician with a yellow stripe down his back. Yet another, rather clever, conflict cover takes advantage of the NRA's technical ability to custom-address fund-raising appeals and local election endorsements. It shows a dramatized computer screen for a national gun registration act. The screen shows a template with cells to enter households by resident, number, and types of weapons in the house. The name and address being entered on the form by a bureaucratic-looking functionary is of course the individual NRA member to whom the magazine is addressed.

Only three covers (3 percent) depict media conflict, one a photograph of AR-15 rifles with the caption "AR-15 Keeps Gaining Ground Despite Media Attacks." Another is a collage of anti-gun press clippings with the caption "Anti-Gun Frenzy" while one refers to a "Media Disinformation War." Interestingly, conflict covers (both media conflict and general) tend to appear at times of peak NRA membership growth, 1993-94, when membership grew from somewhat less than 3 million to approximately 3.6 million persons. We see the same tendency for timing with a conflict cover of the November/December 2000 pre-election issue; it bears prominently a quotation attributed as the "Official Position of the Clinton-Gore Department of Justice":

THE SECOND AMENDMENT DOES NOT EXTEND AN INDIVIDUAL RIGHT TO KEEP AND BEAR ARMS.

Solidarity theme covers (8.2 percent) typically show scenes of group photographs of NRA officials in the company of friendly congressional representatives standing in front of the Capitol or at legislative functions. The March 1995 issue shows the NRA executive vice president, NRA-ILA director, pro-gun activist Charlton Heston, and U.S. Senator Phil Gramm, at a "well attended" reception welcoming the 104th Congress to Washington, D.C. The caption is "Freedom Fighters." Another is a drawing of stolidly encircled congressmen and congresswomen, arms akimbo, looking out protectively from the Capitol dome. A caricature of a frustrated, gnome-like, scheming President Bill Clinton is outside the ring in the foreground. "Only You Can Elect a Gun-Saving, Clinton-Proof Congress," says the caption; the cover, although dominated by solidarity themes, also employs conflict as a strong sub-theme. Other solidarity covers show in-group activities such as the National Matches held annually at Camp Perry, Ohio.

Identity themes dominate 10.2 percent of the covers. These show role models such as Olympic gold medal winner Kim Rhodes or firearms designer and manufacturer Bill Ruger. A grim Charlton Heston appears "Armed with Pride" on another cover, an apparent reproduction of an oil portrait, or perhaps an extensively airbrushed photograph; he grasps a finely made flintlock muzzle-loading rifle of the sort that would have been familiar to the Founding Fathers.

The symbols used in political communication rarely stand alone. Distinguishing whether identity or hobby-technical themes dominate a cover is often difficult and has to be done on a preponderance-of-the-evidence basis. For example, a cover featuring the text of the Declaration of Independence with an antique dueling pistol is an identity theme because of its political content and use of the pistol as an evocative symbol of beliefs and traditions, while just the pistol alone or with its case and accessories would be hobby-technical in thematic content.

The Ideological Trend

America's First Freedom covers are quite distinct from *Rifleman* covers. *First Freedom* represents the emergence of something new; it is a magazine that is almost completely ideological and social-utilitarian in scope, sans almost all hobby-sporting material, both in trappings and content. Gone here are the old NRA traditional journal covers of technical firearms drawings. *First Freedom* covers lean heavily to political caricatures that are every bit as crude as the anti-NRA caricatures that grace the editorial pages of elite papers such as *The Washington Post* and *Los Angeles Times*.

The cover of the premiere *First Freedom* issue (June, 2000) shows a composite portrait of presidential candidate and former Vice President Albert Gore. Features of then-president William Clinton, the comb of gray hair especially, blend with features of Gore, producing a well-executed and eerie effect of the spirit of the NRA's archenemy, William Clinton, animating the person of candidate Gore. The communication mechanism is classic transference, augmented by the punning caption "He's Clinton to the Gore: The Face of Gun Hatred in America."

The August 2000 issue gets mileage out of the reaction of New York City politicians and media to the NRA proposal to open an "NRASports" center in Times Square. Captioned "The Big Rotten Apple" the cover also announces "Rancid Hypocrisy Infects New York." Worms are pictured as having bored through the apple, their protruding heads cartoon depictions of then–First Lady Hillary Clinton, now a U.S. senator from New York; Mayor Rudy Giuliani; New York's senior U.S. Senator Charles Schumer; Vice President Al Gore; and New York Governor George Pataki.

Another *First Freedom* cover features a rotund caricature of television celebrity Rosie O'Donnell, who is known for her anti-gun opinions, but particularly to NRA members for an incident involving actor and leading man Tom Selleck, NRA member and occasional spokesman. Selleck was "ambushed" in the view of many pro-gun people with affrontive personal questions about his role in the NRA by O'Donnell when he appeared on her entertainment show. What was seen as rudeness to Selleck on the part of O'Donnell may have been a small boon for NRA mobilization, for many felt sorry for the handsome Selleck. In this regard NRA members that I have interviewed seem to have a particular dislike for O'Donnell, some referring to her as "a pig." K-Mart Corporation, an O'Donnell sponsor, in consequence of her remarks was pressured by a pro-gun grassroots telephone and letter writing campaign to withdraw its sponsorship. O'Donnell, who was also a celebrity speaker at the Million Moms March event, remains a pet subject for NRA denunciation. An article in the August 2000 *First Freedom* discusses her "hypocrisy" in having her bodyguards apply for concealed weapon permits while still maintaining that she does not "personally own a gun" (Lott, 2000). This article was originally printed in *Los Angeles Times.*

The pre-election cover of the November-December 2000 issue is identical for *First Freedom, Rifleman,* and *Hunter,* sending a uniform message to subscribers. The formula is pure social movement problem-solution where a solidarity-response follows from a conflict-stimulus. The cover simply attributes a quote that the Second Amendment conveys no individual right to bears arms to the Clinton-Gore administration. The solution, customized by voting district, is to be found in the lower corner that contains recommendations of NRA's choices among candidate for races for U.S. president, U.S. Senate, U.S. House, governo,r or options of relevant state ballot proposals.

First Freedom, both covers and content, combined with the journal's impressive growth over just a few years, bespeaks recognition by NRA officials of a sea change in gun politics. The ideological gun owner is becoming a norm and may at some point replace the traditional sportsman or farmer, for we have been seeing the emergence of an ideological gun culture in past years. Also, *First Freedom* evidences NRA officials' recognition of the need to bypass mainstream media with a purely ideological message and, in part, NRA's waxing ability to accomplish this feat.

Media Bias Communications of NRA Officials

It is revealing to examine the views of NRA officials in other contexts than official publications. Material in this section derives mainly from officers' reports at a recent NRA annual meeting, a 1997 presentation at a student conference on media bias by the NRA executive vice president and personal communications with NRA officials. Also examined is a speech that may be a classic of sorts, what may be, so to speak, the mother of all NRA speeches: Wayne LaPierre's "Mother" theme oration made in reaction to the Million Moms March.

Jack-Booted Journalists

The 1998 annual NRA meeting convened in Philadelphia. The meeting begins with the introduction of the youngest NRA life member, a child of perhaps four years, who is carried on stage in the arms of her father. (Her age is never stated.) The father says, "Yesterday we were interviewed by a Philadelphia reporter . . . a jack-booted journalist, I would say . . . . She asked me, 'Why would you have your kid in the NRA?' I said, 'Because I don't want my child to learn gun violence from NBC, CBS and ABC.'"

From the wave of applause that follows, it would seem this statement resonates with the thousands of NRA members present.

During subsequent annual reports of NRA officers the subject of media bias is brought up repeatedly. Kayne Robinson, second NRA vice president, speaks of being raised up in rural America where, he reports, "No gun jumped off its rack and seduced me to shoot my best friend or most annoying romantic rival... maybe *Sixty Minutes* should come out and do a show about that some time." No other organization "suffers coordinated attacks," as does the NRA, says Kayne. He continues, "Set against us are significant portions of the national media who repeat their anti-gun mantra with little concern for the truth." He points out "the darlings of the media," the anti-gun U.S. Senators Charles Schumer, Edward Kennedy, and Diane Feinstein, whom he likens to "demagogues" who "scream and shriek." Again, applause resonates.

Tanya Metaksa, executive director of NRA-ILA, includes in her annual report an account of the NRA victory in the state of Washington concerning so-called Proposal 676, an anti-gun referendum that was originally favored to pass by pollsters by a comfortable 60 to 30 percent margin. Metaksa asks, referring to the forecast of an NRA defeat, "Why else would Tom Brokaw [news commentator] come to Seattle to broadcast live? He called it 'a full-blown political war.'" Associated Press, she states, called it "A costly setback for the NRA," while *The New York Times* described it as "a crucial test for the NRA's lobbying power."

Metaksa comments that the "speech ban" for interest groups such as NRA that would exist under proposed so-called campaign reform legislation would give "the media elite absolute power." She states, "The press does not own the Bill of Rights. It is not for sale. And we won't give it away."

She remarks also on the social necessity of "not learning gun violence from NBC, but gun safety from NRA." Throughout, her remarks are punctuated with enthusiastic applause.

Executive vice president Wayne LaPierre in his annual message describes "a cultural war" in the United States where "a couple of generations of kids have grown up on glorified gun violence in the media." He denounces the media world of "crime with no consequences."

NRA first vice president Charlton Heston speaks of the role of media in how NRA has become "marginalized" in mainstream politics. "Year after year, lie after lie, the press and the politicians" have allowed this to happen. He pledges to "win back our rightful place in the mainstream, of American political debate."

Again the applause is enthusiastic. Obviously, these messages on media are not merely dry sociological commentary for this audience.

The Moms Speech

The 2000 NRA annual meeting at Charlotte, North Carolina, was the occasion of a speech that bears quoting at some length. Coming after the considerable media attention given to the Million Moms March, and in the midst of the Gore presidential campaign, the speech might be regarded as NRA's response not only media bias but also to what might be called *momism* as a mobilizing tool by anti-gun special interests. Begins LaPierre:

> After the exchange . . . on *Meet the Press*, my mom called me. "Wayne she said, "tell the truth, but don't quarrel over it." I said, "But Mom, I was telling the truth. The other guy was quarreling. He started it."
>
> There was a long pause. Finally she said, "I was proud of you. You sure told him."
>
> Moms have a way of making us all face the truth.
>
> My point is that all of us had moms. So we all understand moms. Moms are on our side. When mom talks, we listen. What mom wants, mom usually gets. Moms taught us right from wrong. Moms know the truth from lies. And you better not lie to mom.
>
> So when I was watching all the hype leading up to the so-called Million Moms March last Sunday, everything sort of crystallized for me. Those are the kinds of lies we're going to hear this year as Mr. Gore runs against your rights by dividing America's women against men, wives against husbands, moms against dads. . . . What we saw was a Misled Moms March.

It wasn't organized by a "housewife and mother of two from New Jersey." It was pulled off by a professional White House insider on leave from CBS News, the sister-in-law of Hillary Clinton's closest friend, lawyer and political strategist. It wasn't a grassroots campaign rally, but a Gore campaign rally—scripted and coached by the White House.

With the media's help he paints a fictional nightmare of a nonexistent world where a reckless population of stupid gun owners cause 13 innocent kids a day to die from guns. An unreal world where guns are jumping off shelves . . . and tumbling out of school lockers.

Well it's all a big, stinking, dangerous Al Gore lie.

ABC, NBC, CBS, Newsweek, Time—are you reporting my words? Because I defy you to argue with the truth.

LaPierre then cites as "truth" a number of statistics on NRA firearm safety education, mortality from firearms and gang killings, including this surprising number:

NRA is growing stronger by the hour—two hundred thousand new members in just the past six weeks. And by Election Day we will be four million members strong.

Again, this number could be measured against comparable interest groups. If it is accurate, NRA's pre-election spurt of growth in itself exceeds or roughly approximates the entire membership of many so-called public interest groups.

University Media Bias Conference

In a different context we are able to examine NRA positions specific to the subject of media bias. LaPierre spoke in July 1996 at a student conference on media bias at George Washington University staged by the Young America's Foundation, a conservative educational group active on many university campuses and the internet (Gun Issues and The Media, 1996).

In introducing his subject, LaPierre lays down the axiom "Our biggest problem in terms of this issue is the media." Mr. LaPierre comments on what he sees as deliberate media misrepresentation in handling coverage on assault weapons:

> If you ask the American public what type of guns we're talking about in this Clinton Gun Bill, most of the American people will tell you "machine guns" or "automatic guns" because that's what they've been told by the media and that's what they believe. I finally got so frustrated with seeing machine guns being shot over and over and over again on ABC, NBC and CBS, that I said, "I'm not going to do another interview until you guys go to the range with me." And I took NBC to the range for three hours and showed them the type of guns we're talking about and that they're not machine guns. I finally expected the next day that we would get legitimate coverage on the air, at least truthful coverage, and I tuned in the *Today Show*. And the *Today Show* opens with a fully automatic machine gun firing right at the viewer and says, "The Clinton gun ban, it's going to be debated today in the Congress and these are the kind of guns we're talking about."
>
> That's what's showing up in the little box in the living room and that's what people believe because it's on ABC, NBC or CBS. It's a huge problem, not only for this issue but, I'm convinced, for all other issues in terms of political debate for this country.

LaPierre also discusses aspects of media coverage that earlier in this chapter NRA called the "passive assaults" of media; in doing so he levels serious charges against major television and print outlets for refusing NRA advertisements. He states:

> I don't think people realize the amount of censorship that goes on when we at the NRA take an ad. . . . For instance a lot of women are buying guns in the United States because they're scared. They feel alone out there and the criminal justice system has collapsed. We take an ad [saying], "We recommend training at the NRA. Women are buying guns. We have safety training available. We strongly recommend it. Here's a number to call." NBC will tell you, "We won't run that ad on the air. We don't want anything involving guns on the air." And as I've said, they have no problem making the millions in terms of gun irresponsibility in their entertainment programs.

Of *Time* magazine LaPierre states:

They even wrote a letter back to us saying the time for balanced coverage on this Second Amendment issue is past, that they were advocates for this issue on the other side, and needed to be thought of as in this light from then on.

In the same presentation LaPierre states that even though "All the facts and all the statistics are on our side in this issue, where we lose is where the media distorts it."

He cites several issues affected by media distortions and passive assaults:

Right-to-Carry Laws. Of the laws enacted in more than thirty states to provide qualified citizens the right to carry personal concealed weapons, LaPierre says, "the media screamed bloody murder," even though, "everybody admits it's working."

Militia Groups. "The media tried to make it look like NRA was somehow involved, but it was just the media trying to do their thing," LaPierre states, adding, "They tried to find some of the kookiest groups they could find in the country and somehow say this was the NRA." He goes on to describe an incident where ILA executive director Tanya Metaksa met in a hotel lobby "for about ten minutes" with Michigan Militia members in at the request of the militia members. The meeting concluded with Metaksa telling the militia people that the NRA would not be associated with the Michigan Militia. LaPierre states, "When ABC did *Nightline* all day long they promo-ed this 'secret meeting' between NRA and the militias to make it sound like there was something going on there."

Assault Weapons. "The whole issue is a fraud on the American public," states LaPierre. He describes it as an example of sound bite or headline politics.

One-Gun-a-Month. "You talk about a sound bite, one-gun-a month is a great sound bite that the media likes," states LaPierre. He also states, "This isn't about stopping crime, it's about headlines."

Second Amendment. On the meaning of the Second Amendment, LaPierre states, "The media wants to put its head in the sand."

The Monolithic Media

A recurring feature of NRA media criticism is the use of the term *media* as if it were in the singular form. Very seldom is correct verb-subject agreement present in any NRA communication that mentions *media*. To NRA the *media is* rather than the *media are*. This apparently trivial point may be more important than it would seem on the surface; it goes beyond mere usage of vernacular in organizational communications that are intended mainly for popular consumption. In the social universe of NRA official doctrine, media exist as a monolithic oppositional force, hence the singular form. This *monolithification process* via language usage would apply equally well to other organizations or groups dominated by the social movement ethos. Plural opposition (or even simple indifference) is perceived as a united front, e.g., *the establishment* was the looming bugaboo that united radicals of the 1960s, while an impossibly imprecise term, *military-industrial complex* served this same function for the anti–Vietnam War movement, and some fight on against *the system*. NRA's monolith is *the media*. The construction of this monolith streamlines perception. The world is explained.

For monolithic entity or not, only a few basic concepts cover virtually all the discussions of media bias so far mentioned in NRA communications. These concepts include bias of journalists and news elites, including their personal limitations, such as being class-bound or enmeshed in cultural beliefs; distortion and other active assaults on perceived truth, such as cheap sensationalism and sound-bite news; passive assaults as with censorship and non-coverage; and self-serving hypocrisy of politicians and media organizations. An example of the latter would be the often-told NRA stories of conspicuously anti–gun politicians and celebrities who use their influence to obtain permits to carry concealed weapons, or who have armed bodyguards, while they would deny the same to their constituencies or fans.

There is also no doubt that NRA tendentiously interprets media coverage in self-serving ways, accentuating the negative and virtually ignoring the positive; or merely making use of positive coverage that furthers its ends without calling undue attention to the fact that the information derives from mass media sources. NRA has it both ways here.

But it would be a mistake to believe that NRA is merely willfully misinterpreting elite media coverage to suggest the existence of bias. They use media bias; the concept is important in their communications; but they do not need to contrive it. Beyond the findings concerning interest group coverage presented earlier, there is supporting information that is difficult to overlook.

I inquired about Wayne LaPierre's statement, quoted above, concerning a letter from *Time* magazine that allegedly says the time for balanced coverage on the Second Amendment issue has passed, and that *Time* should be considered an advocate for the other side. In response NRA provided a copy of a letter, signed by an editor of *Time*. It includes the following statement, which substantively mirrors LaPierre's remarks:

> The July 17 cover story is the most recent in a growing number of attempts on the part of TIME editors to keep the gun-availability issue resolutely in view. Such an editorial closing of ranks represents the exception rather than the rule in the history of the magazine, which has always endeavored to provide a variety of opinion and comment, in addition to straightforward news reporting. . . . But the time for opinions on the dangers of gun availability is long since gone, replaced by overwhelming evidence that it represents a growing threat to public safety. As we see it . . . our responsibility is now to confront indifference about the escalating violence and the unwillingness to do something about it. (*Time*, 1989)

LaPierre's interpretation seems fair. If the letter can be believed, *Time* has designated gun issues the sole exception to the practice of straightforward reporting, and it advocates antigun viewpoints rather than reports the news. Possibly the most remarkable fact concerning this letter is not that it exists; or that an editor of a major news publication would be injudicious enough to sign a statement that appears to exempt gun-issue reporting from journalistic standards of objectivity, balance, or fairness; but the uses to which NRA put this letter. NRA officials report they have used the letter in an advertisement in the *USA Today* newspaper. And seven years after it was written, the letter still makes for good anecdotal material when LaPierre is speaking on media bias at a conservative student conference. NRA relishes the existence of such evidence and shares it whenever possible.

Institutionalization of Media Bias

A few months after the 2000 National Elections, an "Emergency Media Statement" was mailed to NRA members over executive vice president Wayne LaPierre's signature (LaPierre, 2001). Essentially a direct mail fundraising appeal, the four-page letter (not counting inserts) is similar in tone to other appeals that NRA regularly sends to members. Some members that I have interviewed sometimes complain of receiving too many letters of this sort; that NRA is preaching to the converted who are only able to give so much, and that organizational resources might better be otherwise directed. Despite the complaint, letters of this sort provided much of the NRA-ILA funding that went to the 2000 election. Some of these same members also reported sending an occasional $100 or more to NRA when they felt able.

The letter maps the new, post–2000 election political landscape of the U.S. in these terms (excerpts):

> ... in the few weeks since the swearing in of the new Congress and the inauguration of President George W. Bush, gun owners and the NRA have already become the target of relentless attacks in the media. And in the U.S. Senate and House, I hear of new promises from anti-gunners almost every day that they intend to use media pressure in the hope they can <u>enact more gun laws before this session of Congress is out</u>. [Underline in original.]
>
> ... they know that the way to win more gun control is to relentlessly pound their agenda both in the media and Congress.
>
> ... they know this strategy of never ending media and political attacks will give them their best opportunity to grab outright control of both the U.S. Senate and House in 2002.
>
> Gun hating extremists, using the media, would then have the power to lay a political siege. (LaPierre, 2001)

The letter mentions media in some way in most of its more than 40 paragraphs, specifying biased publications, news anchormen, and television networks by name. The solution to the problem is, of course the solution to all threats posed to all social movements—solidarity; for NRA members to "stand shoulder to shoulder" and to conduct "educational efforts" at the grassroots level; but also for NRA to answer, "the gun-ban lobby's incessant lies and propaganda in the media" with its own media campaign. An enclosed invoice-like "media statement" offers three payment options: one will "Help NRA reach 1,784 Americans" for $22.17, and another will reach 4,002 Americans for $49.73.

This large-scale media campaign response represents something relatively new on the part of NRA. Many will remember the "I'm the NRA campaign" of the mid- to late 1980s where billboards and advertisements in magazines featured photographs of wholesome men and women, professionals, blue collar and housewives, who were identified by name as NRA members. The campaign was a good public relations impulse in that it presumably personalized and humanized "the gun lobby" for those people who knew of NRA only as filtered through mainstream media representations, but the campaign's effect is questionable. The message had no goal in terms of tangible action; for making a fleeting impression on a suburbanite in a sports utility vehicle is not social action. NRA communication is most effective when its builds solidarity and ideology in reaction to conflict or threat.

This new media campaign does just that. During 2000 NRA ran nationwide half-hour "infomercials" (continuing into 2001), especially on late-night television when advertising rates are lowest. The main message is threat—immediate and looming, national and international—and the main argument one of analogy. The professionally produced infomercial documents recent, ongoing gun bans in Australia, Canada, Great Britain, and, now, California (i.e., the threat arrives on American shores), with film clips of common sporting firearms being collected by the ton and destroyed with industrial heavy equipment. Dispossessed gun owners, some quite literally aggrieved, are interviewed. The principal theme that emerges is "We all thought it couldn't happen here, so you people in the United States better join the NRA." The infomercials make joining as easy as possible with special offers and a toll-free number. Without cooperation from the NRA, estimating the direct effect of the infomercials on membership is impossible. However, the infomercials ran in major media markets before and after the 2000 election, a period when membership increased to its all-time high to date.

Many would agree that late-night network television is by and large dominated by tawdry promotions for juicers, buttock exercisers and no-money-down real estate schemes. Intelligible ideology is rare, perhaps to be found only in the transmogrified humanism embedded in perpetual reruns of the *Star Trek* serial and its derivatives, with some late night markets worked by televangelists offering various bargains on personal salvation. Into this marketplace comes the NRA with political ideology, a half-hour lesson on history, political science, and current events. This in itself is remarkable. Apparently, obviously, NRA has found a recruiting field here among late-night viewers, a field sufficiently fertile to recompense the considerable outlay for broadcast time (even at late-night rates).

What NRA is doing of course is bypassing mainstream news media with political information, a tactic that all interest groups use to some extent in order to control the purity of their messages. This new campaign represents ideology-building at a social level at which most interest group administrators, who tend themselves to be middle class in both origin and outlook, would scoff. NRA is indeed recruiting among the masses here. And their efforts seem to be paying off.

Because NRA, unlike the other interest groups in this study, has not been able to utilize major mass media to tell their story on their behalf, they do the best they can. This bypassing of national media with infomercials and by other channels (e.g., the Internet, where NRA is a strong presence) is a logical and necessary development. NRA has developed into a unique political informational node since the days when it was essentially a hobby organization. *First Freedom*, the ideological journal for those who have not come by their interests in firearms by the traditional generational means, is another aspect of this recent phase of development; it is a journal that exists as a "truthful alternative" to elite media news, in the words of its publishers. Importantly, as we have seen by the constant reference by NRA officials to a monolithic deceptive national media, NRA has also provided supporters with a decoding key for mainstream media that re-interprets coverage to the benefit of NRA. This latter development represents what I call *anti-media theory*; and it provides a unifying epistemic foundation to the NRA worldview. In substantial part this is how NRA overcomes its informational disadvantage in the national media, explaining in part the paradox of how NRA can apparently be losing the public information war in the national media forum and yet still increase its power. A good anti-media theory—and NRA has a very good one, if not the best—transforms each exposure to salient mass mediated messages into ideological refreshment.

Now that we have examined NRA official communications as a creature of media bias we shall turn to the positive effect that this negative coverage has had on NRA mobilization.

5

THE MOBILIZATION EFFECT

Negative Coverage and NRA Mobilization

NRA membership increases as the result of negative coverage. The more negative coverage NRA receives in the elite newspapers—and the elite press have been very obliging in this regard, as shown in Chapter 3—the more NRA mobilizes.

Figure 5.1: National Rifle Association Membership and Negative Editorials in U.S. Elite Newspapers 1990-99

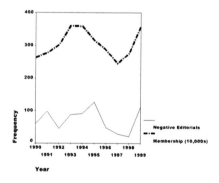

Note: The correlation between NRA membership and negative coverage = .654. The relationship tests for significance, $F(1, 9) = 5.97$) at the $p = .04$ level, $R^2 = .427$, adjusted $R^2 = .356$.

Figure 5.1 illustrates the relationship. Simple bivariate linear regression shows strong correlation, $r = .654$, between the number of negative editorials appearing each year in the five national elite newspapers (independent variable) and the number of NRA members (dependent variable) in the year following. The relationship is significant at the *p* = .04 level. Thus, denunciation is interpreted as an invitation to mobilization.

Membership numbers for the year immediately following the editorials are used for the dependent variable because the effect of negative coverage is not immediately reflected in the circulation statements of the NRA magazines that provided the annual membership figures used for the analysis. A lag time of months is not unusual before a new member's magazine subscription takes effect; and there is also lead time before publication to consider, such that the annual circulation statements always look backward in time.

As might be expected, membership also correlates with the amount of press coverage in general—more attention translates into more membership—but the association is weaker, $r = .509$, nor does it approach statistical significance. Therefore negative editorial coverage, rather than press coverage in general, is a predictor of membership.

A hypothetical scenario aids in explanation. Figure 5.1 should not be interpreted as meaning that the average hog farmer in Iowa happens to read a strident anti-NRA editorial over brunch while browsing the Sunday *New York Times* and the next day, incensed, joins the NRA. The frequency of negative editorials should be regarded as a proxy variable for negative NRA media coverage in general; for *The New York Times* and the other elite papers are known to act as models and sources for many national and local media that disseminate news by radio, television, or newspaper. NRA coverage, additionally, is bound up inextricably with general coverage of gun issues; but it would be fair to summarize much of the elite coverage as a framing discourse on the "gun problem" with NRA presented as obstacle-in-chief to its solution; and it is this model of interpretation that is disseminated.

The more reasonable scenario would be that the hog farmer is exposed to waves of gun-related coverage emanating from national news sources. The hog farmer, unlike most elite journalists, understands mechanical things and thus realizes there is no practical difference between "assault weapons" as described in the news and his Browning shotgun, originally purchased by his father back in the 1930s, since then gathering dust—and now, suddenly, a social issue. If anything the old Browning is a more effective and deadly weapon than the dangerous looking semi-automatic handguns brandished in the news broadcasts. To see an anti-gun president such as William

Clinton, who appeared in many gun-related pseudo-events covered by media in the past decade—a person who obviously knows next to nothing about guns and who has been quoted as saying that ducks are hunted with rifles—to see such a person patronizing "sportsmen" by pretending to hunt ducks for the camera can only play as a transparent manipulation attempt (e.g., Ifill, 1993; Purdham, 1995); even though that which is transparent to an Iowa hog farmer is not necessarily so to a native New Yorker or to an editor at an elite newspaper. Interwoven throughout this news coverage are themes of the extremist NRA, a lobby of psychopathological fanatics opposed to democracy, public safety, scientific expertise and common sense. Our farmer knows better, for this same NRA has not only taught his son and daughter how to shoot a .22 rifle and conducted their hunter safety classes, but also stands for the idea that his old Browning is not a legitimate concern of government. He perceives forces in motion against him and his. He sees what by all appearances is a massive and coordinated propaganda agenda being forwarded via media. Moreover, he has just been reminded quite pointedly by these same media sources that NRA exists. Given the opportunity he joins or, possibly, rejoins NRA, an act of counter-force and solidarity, and maybe he even signs up his son or daughter or wife under a spouse membership.

All this should not be understood as a model of conversion: it is rather a model of mobilization. Our hypothetical farmer well illustrates some of the well-established social cleavages established by survey research on gun issues and ownership: rural versus urban, regional differences, gender, and the generational transmission of values in hunting and gun-owning families (see Kleck, 199, pp. 21-25; Wright, Rossi, & Daly, 1983).

The interpretation aligns with a reality that communication research, too, has long since documented: the existence of selective communication effects among different audiences. Possibly the most well-known proponent of the selective effects of mass media content is Klapper (1960), but the phenomenon has been well understood since Aristotle urged persuaders to tailor messages to fit audience characteristics. A message that has one effect in an urban New York market will likely be interpreted in an entirely different way in rural Iowa. So to some, not a few, negative coverage goads mobilization.

Several historical events seem to affect the relationship depicted in Figure 5.1 and help with its interpretation. The Brady Bill handgun-waiting period, heralded as a first important step by anti-gunners and elite media editorials, receives tremendous amounts of coverage in 1990–93. Its eventual passage in 1993 in a form much modified by NRA lobbying (today's instant background checks) may have been heard as a call for mobilization by pro-gun persons. In the 1993-95 period several events occur: the Crime Bill, with its assault weapon provisions; the so-called Republican Revolution of the off-year Congressional election in 1994, for which President Clinton named NRA as the reason why the Republicans gained control the House; the Branch Davidian tragedy in Waco, Texas; the Ruby Ridge killings involving federal agents in Idaho; and the Oklahoma City Federal Building bombing and the rise of militias. The resignation of former President George Bush (the elder) from NRA, a life member, is the subject of numerous news articles and editorials; the resignation was prompted by an NRA fund-raising letter calling federal law enforcement agents "jack-booted thugs." This letter is said to be one of the most successful NRA fund-raising appeals ever (Eckholm), while NRA officials that I interviewed also say that they received four-to-one comments pro-NRA and anti-Bush from their members. Presidential election years, 1992 and 1996, seem also to affect coverage, displacing NRA coverage somewhat with news of other events.

Still referring to Figure 5.1, sensitive to the issue of numbers, NRA was not willing to release official annual membership numbers when I asked for them. Membership numbers therefore had to be calculated from circulation numbers that are required by law to be published annually in the official journals of the NRA, as is the case for other magazines that sell advertising. Using annual circulation statements from *The American Rifleman, The American Hunter* and *The American Guardian* (or *America's First Freedom*), it is possible to calculate a maximum possible NRA membership for each year. These are maximum possible figures because they assume no overlapping magazine subscriptions; some members pay extra money to receive more than one magazine so they could be counted more than once. Over the decade these estimates range from about 3.6 million in 1994-95 to a low of about 2.45 million in 1998, back to about 3.6 million by 2000. The low point 2.45 million figure is less than the 3 million often referred to by NRA officials around that time. The more recent estimate of 3.7 million is also lower than the number currently cited by NRA officials. Owing to a well-known propensity for officials of interest groups (not just NRA) to inflate membership numbers or public support, these figures are possibly the best available. Spouse members receive no separate magazine and would not be counted in these estimates. I have no way of estimating the number of spouse memberships without NRA cooperation, but these could easily make up for the difference between membership claims and the circulation estimates.

NRA officials will only confirm that these membership calculations agree reasonably well with membership numbers they have published at various times over past years (personal communications, 1999–2000). They also note that some members receive no magazines, citing as an example NRA staffers who are also members and forgo their subscriptions; for any such members would not be included in the circulation-based figures. I generally discount this explanation on the grounds that a magazine subscription comes with membership, an experience that for many NRA members is probably limited to paying dues, carrying a membership card, and receiving the magazine. The magazine would likely be their most tangible link to the organization, coming as it does every month and providing information that is unfiltered by mass media. Still, the "no magazine explanation" provides NRA with a comfortable amount of wiggle room if they wish to be optimistically obscure about membership numbers.

In this matter of membership numbers, as shown the content analysis measures in chapter 3, journalists are much more likely to dwell upon membership decline and/or defeats for NRA than for the other interest groups; recall that NRA stories tend to be framed in this "defeat" fashion and setbacks are celebrated whether they are real or imagined. The NRA reluctance to release exact membership numbers is interpretable as a defensive posture well founded on past experience with journalists and more scholarly investigators who have written exposé treatments of NRA. This reason may also be why NRA also refuses to release fund-raising statistics. Even though NRA has nothing to be ashamed of in the matter of numbers when compared to the other groups examined in this study, they can fairly well count on negative short term fluctuations being "distorted" or "sensationalized," to use the words of NRA officials. A game that could be called *numbership* is important to special interests, to judge by the burgeoning number of polls and survey data reported from such groups via the national news stream over the years. The appearance of mass public support is an objective of this game, with membership one of its most directly tangible indicators.

NRA membership indeed fluctuates over the short-term but is definitely trending upward when looked at over the past 30 years. In 1998-99 it was reported at 2.8 million (Gale Group), although my 1998 estimate based on circulation figures is, again, only about 2.45 million. Membership was certainly down from almost 3.6 million in 1994-95. But by June of 2000 an NRA official told me that membership was at 3.7 million; and by the beginning of 2001 NRA was reporting a number of 4.2 million.

Looked at over a 30-year period. NRA first reached 1 million in 1968, soon after the federal Gun Control Act of 1968; 2 million shortly after 1977, the Cincinnati Revolt; and 3 million for the first time in 1993, after the Brady Bill and the election of the anti-gun Clinton administration (National Rifle Association, 1995).

Looking back even further, NRA numbered 84,000 in 1945; 262,000 in 1955; and 726,000 in 1965, just before the 1968 Gun Control Act (From the Staff Officers, 1971). So NRA has grown quite steadily over the years.

Of the current four million or so, approximately 500,000 were signed up as life members by the time of the 1990-94 period (NRA, 1994), and this number may reach as high as 565,000 by 1998-99, although NRA officials, regarding membership numbers as "proprietary," are also unwilling to release exact numbers on life membership. Higher levels of membership such as benefactor and patron appear to be folded into the life membership numbers.

Mobilization of Comparable Groups

To put this matter of NRA membership in perspective, however, the number of NRA life members in itself either exceeds or equals the overall membership numbers for NAACP (500,000), ACLU (275,000) or HCI (400,000). If we accept as reasonable a base estimate of four million NRA members, NRA ranks among the larger interest groups, including the subcategory of citizens groups. Influential as they may be, groups such as Mothers Against Drunk Driving, National Organization of Women, Common Cause, Greenpeace, and Sierra Club cumulatively do not equal NRA in terms of membership. They all claim considerable mass public support, of course, but this is less tangible than actual membership. In many ways they well fit the model of *advocacy groups,* in that their actions are warranted by the existence of some public, or by an unorganized public sentiment, that does not appear to be able to speak effectively on its own behalf (see Jackal & Hirota, 2000).

Of course, none of these organizations even approaches the magnitude of AARP, with its 30 million-plus members; but AARP membership costs only a relatively painless $8 annually and may also be regarded a function of the changing demographics of the U.S. population and the insurance and social services demanded by senior citizens. AARP membership is well explained by Mancur Olson's member-service incentives theory. A general unwillingness of the so-called Boomer Generation to join associations has been blamed for stagnation or slight losses of AARP membership at various times in recent years (Morris), but despite any such criticism it remains a huge organization that shows no signs of ill health.

Not only does annual membership in the other organizations cost considerably more—approximately three to four times more than AARP membership—the services offered are often not so immediately tangible; the membership impulse in organizations such as NAACP, ACLU, NRA, and HCI is certainly more ideological and social in its scope as opposed to an intentional striving toward material advantage and security that Aristotle thought to be the defining trait of senior citizens.

Time is on the side of AARP, however. In this sense its membership is indeed bound together in the social movement style, for AARP draws upon a profound and inescapable sense of identity that increases over time—Age—that greatly augments AARP's capability for action-in-solidarity.

NAACP has, during approximately the past 30 years, decreased from approximately 1 million during the peak of the civil rights movement in the 1960s to 600,000 in 1984 (Finch, p. 250), with its current membership reported at about 500,000 (National Association for the Advancement of Colored People, 1999; although Gale Group publishes in 1999 a figure of 400,000). Despite the apparent intensity of the civil rights movement, at no time did more than at most about 2 percent of the African American population in the United States belong to the NAACP (Morris, 1984, p. 15). An interesting comparison can be made on this point between NRA and NAACP. Estimates vary tremendously, but if we accept the existence of 60–90 million U.S. gun owners, then NRA mobilizes presently approximately 4-7 percent of them.

ACLU reports that 50,000 new members signed up in response to former president George Bush's direct and well-publicized verbal attacks on ACLU in 1989 (American Civil Liberties Union, 1999), but, again, it has no more than about 275,000 members currently. ACLU has used the recent election of President George W. Bush as a call to mobilization, citing the challenge poised by conservative policies and judicial appointments to civil rights, but it is too soon yet to tell if this tactic will be successful regarding membership increase or fundraising.

HCI proclaims itself "one million strong" in the banners on its press releases, but its reported 400,000 membership (Gale Group) does not match the 275,000 circulation of its newsletter (Handgun Control, Inc.). Despite the large numbers of Americans who say they support gun control measures when asked by pollsters, HCI has not been able to tangibly mobilize millions of members. Their major mobilization difficulties appear to consist of: (1) transcending the gap between talk and action, which survey researchers refer to as the difference between attitude and behavior; and (2) issues related to gun control do not seem to function as well as a kernel for identity crystallization as do issues on the pro-gun side of things. Gun control advocates have attempted to compensate for this identity difficulty by piggybacking on an identity sense that would be complementary, e.g., the Million Moms March, where 300,000 or so mothers were transported to Washington D.C. on buses for anti-gun demonstrations. All this is perhaps best considered as a top-down attempt at mobilization, i.e., professionally managed advocacy, in large part a mobilization that took place with the assistance of patronage, i.e., political party machinery involved in the 2000 presidential campaign. The Million Moms March organization, now lacking the political patronage that nourished it for a time, seems to have lost its head of steam.

The Universe of NRA Mobilization

It would be difficult on the basis of available membership information for all of these groups to support a conclusion that NRA is, or has been at any time in the past decade, a stagnant or declining organization in the ecology of interest groups; quite the reverse appears to be true. How elite newspapers have been able to maintain the fiction of NRA decline in their coverage of recent years is a mystery, explainable more perhaps by groupthink on the part of editorial and reporting staff rather than by substantive events.

It appears that NRA has at present a solid ideological core of approximately 500-600,000 life members, a core that remains relatively constant over the past decade, with perhaps slow growth or slight fluctuation. If life membership is regarded as a constant, it does not, then, contribute to the strong correlation reported earlier in this chapter for the relationship between NRA membership and negative press coverage. The correlation instead would apply strictly to the strength of the relationship between *annual membership* and negative coverage. The correlation, then, must be understood to describe an expansion and contraction of annual membership in accord with high levels of negative press coverage; annual, here, meaning one-year, three-year, and five-year commitments, with one-year members comprising, roughly estimating, three-fifths or more of total membership over the years of this study.

Thus it appears that negative coverage (or the threat conveyed by it) mobilizes a large and varying contingency of persons who come and go in response to threat levels, what could be called a *contingent membership*, while the *ideological core* of life members remains relatively stable over time, developing in size perhaps at a pace too slow to be noticed by this study (without the cooperation of NRA officials).

The evolution over time of an expanding-contracting contingency of threat-sensitive annual NRA members is a quite reasonable development considering that NRA life membership is a fairly expensive commitment. The rate for life membership is $500-750, compared to the $25-35 fee for annual membership. These rates have varied over the past decade, rising to a high point a few years ago, and since returning to the lower level (certainly to stimulate membership). Even when the higher rates were in effect, memberships were still available at the "special" discount of the lower rate through NRA field representatives at gun shows and other public events. Also, like other interest groups, NRA occasionally offers "specials" on upgrades in membership levels. NRA also offers an "easy pay" life membership where members can pay in quarterly installments of $25.

Conversations with NRA officials indicate that many annual members are known to join, lapse, and rejoin a number of times over a period of years (personal communications, 1999-2000). Economic factors doubtless play some part; as one NRA official phrases it, "For some members $35 may mean not being able to buy new shoes for their kids" (personal communication, June 2000). But as suggested by the regression results, this variable membership contingency is spurred by negative media coverage, more so than those whose beliefs would place them at the more stable core. So negative media coverage also functions as a reminder to some persons that their NRA membership has lapsed.

An NRA official referred to this variable contingency as "matriculating members who come an go as the spirit moves them." The NRA estimates—and the official would not say exactly how, but alluded to the existence of proprietary internal survey studies of membership—that there may be approximately 5 million additional such matriculating members. Added to the known four million membership base and what the official described as "a non-member donor file" of approximately 200,000 persons, the official estimated that "the universe of NRA active supporters is almost 9 million" (personal communication, June 2000).

This expanding-contracting membership contingent fits well with observations made by social movement theorists. Oberschall observes:

> Who precisely are members of a movement and how many there are is uncertain. They are frequently part-timers and adherents at the outer edges who fade into the . . . constituency, and sympathizers who participate only episodically in movement collective action. . . . Anyone who wants can quite anytime. Looseness of structure is a byproduct of voluntary membership in a social movement. . . (Oberschall, 1993, p. 25-26).

Some NRA officials interviewed attributed the rise in NRA membership over the period of 1992-95 to the result of a direct threat posed to gun owners by the Clinton presidential administration, which they describe as the first presidential administration that included gun control in its political platform. NRA officials are not alone in the pro-gun world in crediting the Clinton administration with powerfully motivating gun owners. In 1994-95, firearms-related publications were facetiously naming President Clinton as the gun salesman of the year because of the tremendous upsurge in sales of semi-automatic rifles, handguns, and ammunition of all sorts prompted by the anti-gun provisions of the Crime Bill, a key policy item of the Clinton administration. From personal observation, during that period at gun shows in Michigan, supply and demand were such that prices increased by 50 percent or more in some cases of rifles such as the Colt Sporter (AR-15 functional equivalent) and Ruger Mini-14s, both 5.56 mm. military-caliber semi-automatic rifles commonly used with 20- and 30-shot magazines. The Colt Sporter went up in price from approximately $800 to $1,200, becoming scarce for a time. Ammunition in 5.56 mm. caliber increased in price from about $170 per thousand-round case to $250 and more before becoming generally unavailable. The same happened to ammunition in other common calibers. Prices and availability have since returned more or less to the pre–Crime Bill levels except for rifle variants manufactured before the law with banned cosmetic features of interest mainly to collectors.

So it is quite possible that NRA membership and negative media coverage are both stimulated by this third variable, an anti-gun political agenda to which gun owners are so responsive. This is a classic "third variable" explanation, the outside causative variable that undermines claims of causality that are based solely on associational measures. In fact the probable explanation here is that negative coverage is a conditional variable; its presence mobilizes more members than would be the case if coverage were more balanced or reasonable (i.e., less alarming and threat-conveying) from the perspective of potential NRA sympathizers. This accounts for the difference in magnitude between the differing correlations discussed above, i.e., the weaker association for the relationship between membership with editorials in general and the stronger, significant association for the relationship between membership and the frequency of negative editorials. Negative coverage alarms more and thus augments mobilization.

I predicted at an earlier date that in light of intense negative coverage received by NRA as the result of school shootings in the states of Colorado (Columbine) and Georgia, that NRA membership would increase markedly for a time, and that this increase would continue to trend upward as it has in the past 30 years (Patrick, 1999). All this did come to pass.

An interesting parallel to NRA mobilization can be found in Gitlin's analysis of the national media's role in the transformation and mobilization of the Students for a Democratic Society (SDS) organization in the 1960s. Gitlin sees SDS mass mobilization as a product of widespread, simplistic, and inaccurate media framing:

> Media coverage treated SDS as an antiwar organization and nothing more. Especially in the outlying areas, where no other information about SDS was accessible, this sort of image of SDS as an antiwar, single-issue group was then passed from hand to hand, face to face. Among the letters that poured into the National Office by the thousands during the summer, many sounded these notes: "I saw an article on you and wondered of you'd send me more information." (1980, p. 130)

Gitlin underscores how this media-inspired influx radicalized the SDS, which until then had been a comparatively sedate group of East Coast intellectuals, into a "natively radical" group. This transformation resounds with the complaints of elite newspaper editorial writers who denounce the NRA for its transformation from sporting group to an "extremist, monomaniacal group." Gitlin concludes that such "media treatments shape movements" (p. 128).

American Egalitarianism and Gun Culture

What about this population mobilizing in response to negative coverage? Is this what has been called *gun culture*? If so, has America always had a gun culture that has now been successfully mobilized or is the gun culture of more recent origins?

At this point we must visit for a time one of the more deeply cut rivers of American thought — a stream that flows directly out of the Reformation's rejection of centralized administrative control — and which might best be described as egalitarianism suffused with antielitism. This particularly American egalitarianism has long been celebrated and remains still a powerful theme of populist political rhetoric and mass entertainment. Joel Barlow, for example, wrote a mock epic poem in three cantos in the closing years of the eighteenth century in praise of the American staple, corn meal mush. He attributed to a leveling diet of mush the healthy, democratic, and vigorous lifestyle of American citizenry as compared to the enervated aristocrats of the Old World (Barlow, 1969).

Two centuries later lawyer/media personalities such as Gerry Spence are continually able to make the bestseller list, find employment on talk shows, and sway juries with homilies on the homespun virtues of the common man. One of Spence's recent writing efforts, for example, provides a blueprint for a revolution of individual liberty that will free Americans from corporate masters, turning them into servants (Spence, 1998).

The success of NRA in using media bias to mobilize its membership is partly due to the existence of this widespread American antielitist egalitarianism. It provides a comfortable base for social movement mobilization.

Edward Leddy (1987), credited earlier for having first described NRA in terms of social movement, sees a gun culture mobilizing in response to an expanding managerial culture. Nevertheless, *gun culture* is not easy to define with descriptive accuracy, at least not to my satisfaction. In matters of guns and the various people who use or own them, NRA seems to be composed of several rather disjoint constituencies: hunters, sportsmen in general, police, military, collectors of modern or historical guns, people who buy guns for defense against criminals or against farm or suburban pests, historical re-enactors, yuppie trap shooters, urban women, cowboy-style shooting enthusiasts, junior members, Olympic-style competitive target shooters, and political ideologues. Some people appear to own a gun as an insurance policy, just in case they ever need it. Others seem to buy guns merely because they can. Some of these people live and breathe guns, some simply use them occasionally or rarely as tools of work, defense, or pleasure. Do these people comprise sub-cultures of a single culture, new cultures, traditional cultures, adjacent cultures, or separate cultures? The matter is unclear in many ways. Even though conflict might provoke solidarity between these groupings, the mere act of having a gun does not mean someone is a member of a gun culture. Schuman and Presser (1977) failed to find attitude measures in general social survey data that suggested any special kind of ideological fervor on the part of gun owners that might help explain their political effectiveness. In this, though, they were limited by the measures used in the survey research in which they found their data. These measures were by current standards no more than crude indicators of ideology on a liberal–conservative response continuum. Perhaps new survey research data would reveal something telling about gun owners as a cultural group. Ethnographers have only recently begun to examine the subject (e.g., Kohn, 2001).

In American egalitarianism, however, a gun is a symbol of personal autonomy. The gun here becomes an instrument of social leveling, and it was considered so both before and after Sam Colt's advertising claim of the revolver remedying the natural inequalities of men.

There is probably something distinctly American at work here. Kopel (1992) has suggested that the settlement patterns of Canada and the United States account for the huge difference in gun control laws between the countries. In the Canadian pattern the police outpost was established first, then settlement followed. In the United States settlers arrived, fended for themselves, and police were established later, often much later. The attitudes toward higher authority are distinctly different.

I suggest that NRA mobilization can be understood in large part as the excitation of American egalitarianism, rather than as a pure manifestation of something called gun culture. The social movement character of NRA mobilization aligns well with the anti-elite traditions of egalitarianism. Dialectical social philosophy posits the existence of a class that begets its own opposition. Social movements do not create the social tectonics from which they spring, even though they must eventually adapt to, or even learn somewhat to manage the tectonics if they are to be successful in the long term. In the case of NRA mobilization, what are seen as elite management/control efforts have once again revived and re-focused the egalitarian tradition. In the case of NRA mobilization, what was merely a diffuse set of traditions has now been provided with a solid organizational infrastructure that will carry it into the future.

The notion of an American *gun culture* should not, however, be abandoned; the concept merely needs some adjustment—rather than traditional it should be seen as emergent and solidifying. Signs of coalescence can be discerned in many areas.

It matters little that some have denounced gun culture and its tenants as contemporary fabrication or revisionist history. Anti-gunners have welcomed a recent controversial work by historian Michael Bellesiles, who argues well that gun ownership was not prevalent among colonial

Americans, thereby discrediting "the myths" promulgated by NRA of gun ownership being a quintessential American attribute. Bellesiles fixes gun culture's origins much later, in the nineteenth century, a creation of gun industry boosterism. Some anti-gun advocates have acclaimed this a crushing blow to pro-gun ideologues. The quality of this research has been seriously questioned, however. But as interesting as this line of research may be, though, it is largely irrelevant to the existence of a current gun culture. If anything, such denunciations, as they are represented by Bellesiles' work, fuel solidarity by attacking cherished assumptions and beliefs; and even if this research should be discredited—this in turn will be interpreted as evidence of the lengths to which anti-gunners will go to attack gun ownership. Social movements decode events with predictable regularity.

Social movements regularly, if not invariably, romanticize the past, by reviewing it through these lenses of ideology. Beside, all historical interpretation is tendentious to some degree or another; to be otherwise is to be unfocused. Movement-inspired histories, e.g., Women's History, Black History, Gay History, Labor History, all construct and reconstruct according to the needs of the aggrieved sense of identity that lies at their ideological cores, each in its particular way. The politicization involved in no way detracts from the meaning or validity of these histories to the individuals and groups who use them to make sense of their worlds and their places within it. No one performs statistical significance tests on historical interpretation. They are as much mythology as they are history; their function is the clarity of purpose gained through disambiguating the past as the origin of the present conflict.

A gun culture has been in the process of assembling itself beneath the threshold of media and general social perception for a least the past few decades. Is it disjoint from past gun traditions? Does it amplify and minimize features of the past? Is it tendentious in how it justifies its existence and purposes? Probably. Yes. And so what? None of these things makes gun culture any less real or legitimate. NRA speaks both for and to the gun culture and while by no means its sole voice or organizational actor, acts as its figurehead.

Ignoring the signs of emergent gun culture would be difficult. Leddy and others have documented the inner transformation of the NRA from 1970 onward, and this change in purpose has been accompanied by steady increase in membership over subsequent years. A social movement conflict-based ideology, including especially NRA's anti-media theory, reinforces ongoing mobilization. One now sees gun culture referring to *itself* as "gun culture," certainly a sign of the arrival of a collective identity.

Like other successful movements, gun culture constructs its own history. A good example of this construction underway is a massively thick book *Unintended Consequences* (Ross, 1996) available at gun shows and on Internet. Writing in the genre of historical-current fiction, flashing back and forth from past to present, the author follows the evolution of gun culture as personified by a number of renowned shooting personalities of the past and by a fictive current protagonist. The protagonist abundantly possess qualities that might be viewed as a constellation of the principal values of gun culture, as interpreted by the author: independence, expertise, the ability to successfully outwit the ogres of oppression, chivalry, the ability to suffer and recover from ill fortune, quiet bravery, and—above all else—an ongoing sense of conflict accompanied by certain knowledge of who is the enemy. Barring its particular subject matter, the book reads much like novels that came out of the black power movement in the 1960s and 1970s— the struggle of the bravely virtuous against an organized oppression conducted by decidedly non-virtuous characters.

There are other even more tangible signs of emergent gun culture. The meaning of the "shall-issue" concealed weapons movement across the country has gone virtually unnoticed by elite journalist and scholars. More than 30 states now have such legislation. Shall-issue states license ordinary non-police citizens to carry concealed weapons. The usual pattern of this legislation is that licenses are issued to citizens who have no criminal backgrounds after they have completed a training-certification program. The laws are called "shall-issue" because police or licensing boards have no discretion in issuing a license providing the citizen meets the requirements of the law. One of the most recent is Michigan, where shall-issue became law after the state legislature voted it in. The law has survived a petition drive by anti-CCW activists to delay its implementation until a statewide referendum could be held, and controversy continues over it. Immediately to the south, Ohio gun rights activists are currently attempting to engineer a shall-issue law of their own.

Shall-issue laws would have been unthinkable twenty or thirty years ago in most states. The general practice has been to issue concealed carry permits only after convincing a licensing board of need, e.g., the carrying of large sums of cash. Political influence was necessary in many places. The idea was to seriously restrict the number of people carrying weapons. Now many citizens carry weapons at will, so to speak, without having to justify themselves to anyone. Hundreds of thousands of people are licensed nationally. Shall issue laws have been successful. "Road rage" type killings and other lurid incidents predicted by opponents have not materialized. The training and permitting processes filter out the intemperate and impulsive. Claims have been supported that shall issue laws lower violent crime (Lott 1998; Lott & Mustard, 1997). The argument is rationally economic: criminals do not know who is armed and hence turn to crimes against property. Statistics appear to bear out this claim. In any case, though, crime does not increase (Fact Sheet, Right to Carry 2001).

Well-organized gun activists have pushed through these laws, often against public opinion as measured by polls, by persistently lobbying at the grassroots level. In Michigan some counties became "shall issue" before the rest of the state, largely due to pressure on county gun boards from gun activists. These laws are the result of efforts at the state level, with little if any official assistance from NRA—although virtually all of the activists are NRA members (at least this is true in Michigan, based on personal observations.)

I argue that this shall-issue right to carry has been almost totally constructed in recent years. State legislatures of the early part of the twentieth century were only too happy to mandate restrictions to control gangsterism and dangerous vagabonds. NRA in its socio-prehistoric role as a sportsmen's club and the defunct United States Revolver Association helped draft much of this legislation (Kates, 1983). Obviously, many state legislatures and the people they represented agreed to some large extent on the need for the restrictive legislation at the time it was passed. No native gun culture rose up in protest. These concealed weapon laws have been in effect a long time, since the 1920s or before. Some few states had virtually no restrictions whatsoever, e.g., Vermont, while others that are commonly thought of as belonging to the supposedly gun toting "Wild West" did, e.g., Montana, has recently joined the shall-issue states. For years, though, more than half a century, complacency reigned nationwide. (Shall-issue laws emerged in the 1980s, especially, beginning in the early 1990s. Florida served as the prototype in 1987 and—tellingly—Marion Hammer, a leader in that state's effort, later became NRA president.)

Antigun activists have rightly identified shall-issue efforts as the flagship of gun activism. A proposed shall-issue law was defeated in a Missouri referendum. Handgun Control Inc. press relations officials were so busy with this campaign that they did not have time to be interviewed when I contacted them in 1999. Michigan continued for a time, even after passage of the legislation, to be contested terrain, with out-of-state foundations and organizations funding much of the anti-gun effort. Shall-issue activists were able to marshal sufficient logical arguments to convince the Michigan state legislature and the governor to pass and sign the bill. They wrote, telephoned and emailed politicians and media in coordinated campaigns. Antigun activists attempted to use emotional arguments to sway a relatively uniformed electorate to overturn the legislation by referendum. The anti-shall-issue group, is called, emotionally enough, People Who Care About Kids, while the most prominent organizations of gun activists is the 26,000 member Michigan Coalition of Responsible Gun Owners (Boatman, 2001). The state's most prominent newspapers, *The Detroit News* and *The Detroit Free Press* have denounced the legislation (e.g., Gun Battle State Doesn't Need Looser Concealed Weapon Rule, 2000). The Michigan battle continued into 2001, but anti-gun forces appeared to have largely disappeared after their foundation patronage was exhausted. However the fact that this battle was even fought, with the winners so far the shall-issue activists, must be counted a very strong sign that a new social force has emerged. At any rate the law is now in effect and thousands of citizens are undergoing training and filling out their application packages at local county clerk offices. Such a liberalization of the concealed carry laws would not even have been considered by the legislature in years past. There was no group to introduce it or demand it: now there is.

Lastly, indicators of emergent gun cultures turn up in the course research and personal experience. In interviews and discussions with gun owners and NRA members over the past decade, I have seen what I can only describe as a growing awareness of conflict and a sense of solidarity. What is more, a number of first-time gun owners I have encountered acquire guns for apparently ideological reasons. These persons do not immediately descend from gun owners or hunters. Being neither sportsmen nor target shooters, they do not resemble in attitudes or demeanor the sportsmen or target shooters that I have known over the years. They are converts to gun ownership, and as neophytes, tend to carry on at length about the merits of their newly found worldview. Many of these people proudly discuss having joined NRA as life members.

The sense of commitment seems profound at times. One such NRA member states that the NRA was the "only organization out there" working for him. By that he meant social and political representation, for he believes that his congressional representatives do not care about him, nor does any other elected official or government agency. NRA is his only representative that will fight for him, no one else. Mindful of this fact, he sends NRA a hundred dollars a few times each year, a considerable sum for a working-class person. This man who hates his job; who attends no church, social club or university; and who believes strongly that news media "tell lies," willingly belongs to but one organization—the NRA—because he says it speaks for him. Perhaps it does.

6

MEDIA RELATIONS: THE NATIONAL RIFLE ASSOCIATION VERSUS THE JOURNALISTS

NRA Press Relations

An NRA official uses this metaphor to illustrate NRA's situation in dealing with the national press:

> When anti-gun groups hold a press conference or send out a press release, it's [media response] like a bigmouth bass biting on a lure. The other side is able to get stories at will, very often. (personal communication, March 1999)

Accepting elite media bias as a condition of their existence, NRA officials involved with press relations appear to have adapted a limited definition of success in their dealings with elite journalists.

NRA conducts what seems on the surface a fairly standard organizational press relations operation, employing 10-12 full-time staff members. They maintain a web site and send out press releases electronically as well as by more traditional methods. They also provide, or at least did until recently, a handbook on firearms intended for journalists in recognition of many media professionals' limited knowledge in this area. This is a very real need. NRA spokespersons have attributed much media sensationalism regarding firearms such as assault weapons to simple ignorance. Along this vein, independent of NRA, Newton (1990) provides a writers' guide to firearms, a book the author says is designed to avoid embarrassing blunders that he describes as common to professional writers of all sorts. Gest (1992) also reviews a number of incidents in which elite journalists have demonstrated an embarrassing lack of knowledge and fact-checking, a situation which has prompted some media organizations to compile their own style guides on firearms-related matters.

NRA press people monitor various media sources, including the wire services. They perceive themselves as getting along well with most media professionals. They perceive also that, as opposed to national prestige media, "In general local reporters are more likely to be fair and to report on the issues in a balanced manner," to quote one NRA official. They do not feel so well disposed toward the elite media, of whom an official states:

> A lot of the national press is out of places like New York City or the West Coast, and when you live a good part of your life in a place like New York City where you have very strict gun control, that's going to affect your viewpoints. (personal communication, March 1999)

The official cites lack of direct contact with firearms and gun owners as a factor in elite press coverage: legitimate owners of firearms appear as a strange breed to the urban journalist. Consequently, the NRA official observes:

> When a journalist contacts us looking for information, we don't have any expectation of convincing the journalist of our viewpoint, because any individual, and journalists particularly, comes to an issue with their own viewpoint which they've developed throughout their whole lives. It's impossible to think that, from a ten-minute conversation on the phone, that you're going to be able to change their viewpoint. So we don't try. What we do try is to carefully address whatever issue is at hand; to make sure that we can get our core messages and points across, and if these are conveyed in the story, we generally feel that we've been as successful as possible, with the understanding that the journalist is going to put whatever else they think is appropriate in that story.

> Generally, the degree in which you have control [over a story] comes in two forms: what you were directly quoted as saying, and information that you provide to the journalist that is later reflected in the story,

even if it isn't given attribution to you. (personal communication, March 1999)

The above remarks convey a very provisional definition of successful press relations; at least it would be considered so under the pluralistic model of press relations, where success is the overall framing of stories or issues in ways beneficial to the group. It fits well, however, with the challenger message idea of social movement press relations, where if complaints or presence are registered then the story can be considered a success.

The personalization factor in gun issue coverage remains an acknowledged problem for NRA. States the official:

> The press and the public latch onto the sensational and the emotional, and the logical and the empirical argument just don't get a rise out of anyone.
>
> We are learning to adapt, and one of the things we have tried to do is to help make our logical arguments with stories that put those logical arguments in an emotional context for people.
>
> Their [anti-gun organizations] whole paradigm is that they are seeking a social solution to a problem, and they simply want to save lives, protect children, and so on. The whole approach fits well into the developing media market in this country. They focus on tragedy. And we focus on the fact that there are millions of guns in this country that were not misused today: that's not news. (personal communication, March 1999)

From a pluralistic view, NRA's elite press relations seem to be, on this basis, little more than a holding action.

Failed Informational Tactics

NRA officials, then, are well aware of the divide between themselves and national media. From the vantage of accommodative press relations practices, an obvious tactic would to try to close this divide—garnering good coverage in the process—by working closely with journalists in some sort of informational symbiosis. This is how media relations on the part of public and private organizations have worked out for nearly a century and it is a staple of public relations in training and practice. The media relations practitioner works with journalists and provides well-written copy in the form of press or video releases, story angles, background information, access to officials and locations, photographic opportunities, and whatever else it may take to make the journalist's job easier.

Accommodation does not work for NRA, at least not on the national level, and often not at the local level in the cases of which I am aware. Close-up encounters for NRA with reporters turn out like a tribal culture that has been visited by an anthropologist; human *actions* somehow are transmuted to clinical manifestations, i.e., *behaviors*; except the modern fashion is to treat the tribal culture with some degree of respect, according at least some internal validity to their worldview. Reporters do not tend to accord this same respect to NRA, as was shown in the content analysis sections dealing with media treatment of pseudo-events and personalization themes. Unlike the spokespersons for other interest groups, who benefit by such close relations, at times being depicted even as heroic, NRA spokespersons are clinically dissected along psychological lines as manifestations of personality disorders; and unlike events put on by other organizations, NRA events are pointed out as attempts at spin and manipulation. The use of "bloody minded" by a reporter to describe NRA press relations personnel could be considered such a psychological-clinical assessment. While the application of a term such as "patter" to an NRA executive's opinions is an attempt to point out not only their persuasive intent and flimsiness, but also coveys a personality assessment.

NRA officials are well aware of this propensity of reporters. From their point of view, reporters sometimes willfully misunderstand "the facts" preferring a good emotional story to "the truth." One commented on a tendency of reporters to interview outlandish persons found in the parking lots outside of NRA events in preference to NRA officials.

NRA officials are also familiar with some of the news stories used for the content analysis, even though some of these stories were a few years old when the officials were interviewed. An official who was mentioned in one such up-close story guffawed when asked about the circumstances surrounding the story and told of how several NRA officials had spent considerable time, including a dinner outing, with the reporter whom the official eventually referred to as "a little weasel." The official reminded me at this point in the interview that this opinion was not to be attributed in any way that would identify the official or the reporter. Continuing, NRA officials had arranged for this reporter to visit a shooting range to help provide accurate background material. The outcome of the interviews was the more or less standard dark psychological profile, to which the official was, he said, well accustomed. The official reported being surprised, however, at a comment the reporter made in print about how seeing the guns on the range led to the reporter envisioning that he had the power of killing everyone on the range. Admitting this may have been no more than an attempt at a sensationalistic sort of drama, the official regarded this reaction as "sick," wondering what kind of person would have such a response (personal communication, March 1999).

At the state level, an NRA-affiliated member of a shooting association told of inviting a local reporter out to their range for the purpose of "showing" the reporter that the sort of assault-style weapons discussed in the news were not machine guns, a fact that the reporter seemed to grasp. The resulting news story was a first-person account of how the reporter had learned new ways to kill that day at the range. "She knew better," said the association member, rather bitterly, who had not had occasion to develop the thicker skin of the NRA media professionals (personal communication, February 1998).

More often than not, NRA officials attribute bias to impersonal structural or environmental factors that influence a reporter's work, e.g., the reporter was raised in a urban environment, and writes formulaic stories to accommodate media markets, therefore does wrong because he knows no better. NRA members and gun owners interviewed are not so forgiving and tend to interpret and attribute bias at the personal level.

Bypassing Mass Media

Most of what NRA does in the way of communication tactics arises inevitably, as it were, out of its situation. This is what is meant when I stated earlier that social movements arise naturally out of social tectonics. The political situation, and opportunities it offers, predetermines tactics and strategies. Faced with a bulwark of media bias, a virtual geological social formation separating it from the forum for political debate offered (in theory) by the elite national news, NRA does what it must by other means.

First, NRA bypasses national media to they extent it can with infomercials and publications (online and hard copy) that appear to be growing more self-consciously ideological over time. Second, NRA has institutionalized around the concept of media bias; it has become a unifying principle for the interpretation of political social reality, interwoven throughout its official communications and shared by its membership and supporters. Third, NRA press relations assume the existence of an insurmountable bias and their general goal, then, is to register NRA presence—a protest message—rather than set or further issue-agendas, as is the case with most interest groups.

We now turn to see what journalists have to say about the NRA and its relationship with the national press.

Journalists on the NRA

Although I had accurately anticipated the reluctance of NRA officials in releasing information about the activities of their organization, I did not anticipate a general reluctance and the outright refusal of some journalists to explain their activities. Most of the journalists would not return calls when they were contacted and asked to participate in the study. Callbacks did not help. Neither did assurances of anonymity help to reverse the refusals. The non-response rate, thus defined, is almost 95 percent.

Nevertheless, some journalists were willing to talk and in so doing not only supported the patterns inferred from the content analysis of newspaper coverage, but also provided additional insights on their actions and viewpoints. Interviews are discussed below according to how they cluster along several well-known dimensions for potential media bias: *cultural/ideological indicators* concern who journalists are as a product of personal beliefs or cultural background, e.g., middle-class origins; *professional standards indicators* concern matters such as how they are expected or pressured to do their jobs correctly and well, e.g., the normative model for "good" journalism, job routines, practices, etc; and *organizational/structural indicators* include economic and physical factors that affect story choices and treatments such as relative availability of news sources, media market needs, etc.

Unanticipated Results

There were yet other surprises in the interview process. The journalists contacted had no tolerance whatsoever with a survey research–style questionnaire, however short and to the point. Based on their reactions, my impressions are, first that the subject of the survey—journalists and interest group coverage—is a sensitive area for journalists, as well it should be considering the inevitable tension that must exist between journalistic professional standards (and pretensions) and the journalistic dependence for material on interest group pseudo-events and news sources. To use an old but apt idiom, in this case asking specific questions concerning their attitudes on the groups they covered seemed to hit them where they lived; they became very cagey very quickly. At this point almost all withdrew their consent, though they had to this point seemed comfortable with the general idea of the survey.

Second, they seemed hypersensitive to what ends the survey might be directed, and did not like the fact that they were not being told everything up front. In the words of one journalist, "Where are you going with all of this? I need to know this before I can continue." They wanted to know how or in what context their remarks would be framed; in other words, the *angle* of the "story" in which their responses would be used. As is well known, journalists are partial to writing from *angles*, framing the facts in accord with the angle and not necessarily the angle in terms of the facts. David Altheide (1976) has ably documented this reality-creating aspect of journalism. Recollect that the content-analysis findings in chapter 3 showed that many interest group stories are framed in only a few characteristic ways for each of the different groups. It appears here, though, that the framers may be sensitive to the prospect of being themselves the subject of social science framing. This sensitivity suggests a parallel between hypothesis-driven social science conducted by the method of survey research and the methods of journalism: scientific hypotheses are very much like journalistic angles. And I believe that the reporters sensed this immediately and wanted nothing to do with a frame they could not control or predict, or that might not depict them favorably; a frame that might even cause them trouble or embarrassment.

Third, they found disconcerting the fact that they were approached based on specific articles they had written on a specific group; there was here perhaps too much potential accountability. NRA seemed a particular sore point in this regard, so perhaps they had been sensitized by previous criticisms or complaints of their NRA reporting.

Fourth, they seemed sensitive to revealing any personal or background information that might explain why they might tend to frame stories in one way or another. Said one journalist, "I think I can't do this. We're getting into an area that I need to leave quite hazy. I don't know that I want to talk about what goes on inside my head when I write a story about an interest group." Another, despite apparently being intrigued by the content analysis findings, said, "I don't feel like that's really an area that I want to wade into" (personal communications, March 1999).

My fifth observation is that the journalists reacted much like the Roman Catholic priests and nuns whom, as a schoolboy and an adolescent, I would challenge with questions about faith and religion, questions that they found inconvenient, impertinent, or too personal. They would resort often to mystification—the haziness that surpasses understanding—and then would refuse to talk further with me regarding the substance of my questions; but they were often quite willing to speak at length on the ramifications of faith and religious organization as these things unfolded from within their chosen vocational premises. In other words, they were creatures of a legitimating orthodoxy and would not venture out from beneath its wings, for they gloried in this role. So too with almost all of the reporters. With a single exception, those who spoke were willing to do so only from within the shelter of the professional or organizational viewpoint: they were the ones interpreting the world and no others.

The survey questionnaire approach had to be dropped. Cooperation, what little there was to be had, was gained by improvising an utterly straightforward approach. Journalists were asked for their feedback on the basic findings of this study. Specifically they were told that content analysis revealed systematic differences in coverage of interest groups on a number of areas such as proportions of quotes, rates of coverage of media events, etc., where NRA coverage was negative compared to the other groups on these measures. They were also told of the correlation between negative editorial coverage and NRA membership, indicating that NRA benefits from negative press coverage. They were then asked if there was anything about NRA press relations that might make for bad press, in essence an inquiry along *organizational* or *structural* lines, but which also opened the door for discussions of their professional approach to coverage. They were prompted when necessary with open-ended questions along organizational dimensions, e.g., questions on accommodative media relations practices of different interest groups; in short, questions that seemed non-threatening on either the personal or professional level because the questions inquired about actions the journalists observed originating at an organizational site other than their own.

This less direct approach worked better than the original survey questionnaire, and through their explanations and elaborations they revealed additionally some things about themselves and their professional outlooks that will be discussed under the appropriate *cultural/ideological* or *professional standards* dimensions below.

But based on the experience of attempting to interview the journalists with these less-than-satisfactory results, it is likely that for further research on the subject of journalists and interest group coverage, ethnomethodological techniques might be more effective, leaving survey research for more innocuous research questions or to matters where a socially desirable opinion can be expressed at no personal cost or risk whatsoever to the respondent.

It is likely too that the journalists simply did not trust me. One said as much, saying persons claiming to be researchers had approached him in the past. What is usually called a snowball-type sample of the sort used to research deviant-type sub-cultures might overcome this distrust and produce a better response rate with journalists; where one respondent (or initial source who has access to the group) refers the researcher to another respondent, and so forth. This method of being "vouched for" is the technique to which Robert Jackall (1988) resorted to gain access, after many failed attempts, to the organizational elites who were the subjects of his observational studies on corporate management culture of executives who were hypersensitive to the public relations ramifications of their every move. Journalism, in my impression, certainly comprises a culture of sorts and might best be studied by anthropological methods. Such methods have also worked out well in studying religion.

In a last unanticipated problem, while still attempting to conduct interviews, a horrible event occurred in Littleton, Colorado, that has since been codified in media coverage with the label "Columbine." A group of teenagers murdered a number of their schoolmates using common firearms. They also attempted unsuccessfully to blow up the school with crude homemade explosives. This event marked a divide in the interviews, where the few journalists interviewed (or attempted) before the event discussed NRA coverage from the organizational-structural perspective, while immediately afterward coverage was discussed as flowing directly from events as in Littleton, i.e., that NRA coverage mirrored reality and journalists were simply reporting the facts. The journalists directly and immediately linked NRA with the event without any questions to prompt them in this direction; this linkage in itself indicates much regarding their views on NRA.

The original plan was to interview 10 journalists who had bylined content-analyzed coverage, some had been selected because they had bylined a series of articles; but even this modest undertaking did not prove feasible. Out of 15 journalists who were contacted, only one agreed to an interview; two others were "partially" interviewed before withdrawing. In order to acquire some sort of information I interviewed an additional two journalists who were not authors of content-analyzed coverage, but who had both done work on gun issues and NRA. Both are national-level elite journalists, each having more than 20 years of experience. One is a senior editor at a major news magazine, the other a television broadcast journalist.

Also included is relevant material on NRA and guns taken from *Editor & Publisher*, a well-respected publication serving the needs of newspaper editors.

Wholesale generalizing based on the results of three complete interviews is questionable at best and certainly not advisable. Despite this caution, the journalists who provided this information have authored stories that have been read or viewed by millions of people. They are central and elevated figures in their profession. Although a thorough study of journalists and their interactions with interest groups, perhaps by other methods, must be left for the future, the results here may prove useful in shaping further inquiry.

Social Location of Journalism

Further, the subject of journalist–interest group interaction may be so terribly sensitive precisely because it lies near the nexus site at which journalism ultimately operates. In all three theories discussed in chapter 1 concerning social action modes and their corresponding role for media, the site at which journalist–interest group interaction takes place is of utmost strategic and social importance. In the *mass-democracy* formulation, the site is where the journalistic priesthood performs what amounts to a sacrament of transubstantiation; the changing of the raw elements of myriad, discordant information into *the news* required for the citizenry to carry on in a state of democratic grace; we call this process *interpretation,* and it is essentially religious in its scope and totality, for it delineates and explains the social universe. In the *pluralistic* model, it is this intersection where vital interest group transmissions must be collected and relayed to other publics and groups; it is the link-up site between the information nodes called interest groups and the systems of information relays called media. And in the *social movement* conceptualization, it is the site at which ideological filtration and injection takes place, where elites exude their cultural dominance into the system of "correct" thinking and interpretation.

Interview Findings

Cultural and Ideological Indicators

No journalist discusses personal group membership or allegiances, but sentiments are expressed. One who later withdrew expresses some horror at NRA activities, saying, "They're an amazing group," and explained that he meant it was amazing that anybody could think like they did. The interviews reveal general unfamiliarity with guns or gun-culture nomenclature. One repeatedly mentions "gun fairs" for "gun shows." The journalists also seem to speak almost exclusively in terms of agendas popularized by recent media accounts; it is obvious they have been reading and watching the news, e.g., *gun liability,* also referring to related issues such as *loopholes* in gun laws at gun shows.

States one, "Why are there loopholes? It's because of the NRA." The most blanket statement on professional ideology is this third-person observation:

> I've been a reporter for 25 years and I'm familiar with the opinions of other people in the field. Elite reporters sympathize with gun control positions, not with NRA. (personal communication, March 1999)

A reporter makes several remarks that suggest a personal resonance with certain anti-gun as opposed to pro-gun figures, "Sarah Brady is just like us. You can talk to her like a regular person." He goes on to say, "NRA people are bloody-minded" and "want to argue," a comment specifically directed to NRA press relations personnel. The preference for sources "just like us" evokes the Lippmann/Mertz (1920) finding about supposedly objective news reflecting more the hopes and dreams of the people who write it.

Two reporters seemed very fuzzy in their understanding of what NRA does as an organization, appearing to have no knowledge of the extensive informational, training, and safety programs, one saying that NRA stood for the "right to carry arms," adding, "Most people don't want to hear this."

The political nature of the NRA seems to bother some journalists. They see NRA as legitimate primarily as a hobby-sporting group and appear disconcerted when NRA steps into the political area. Many such references were found in the content analysis, e.g., where a sporting group has turned into a lobby, so NRA is fine as long as it minds its own business. Osha Gray Davidson, a popular writer of investigative journalism whose "declining NRA" analysis of the early 1990s, appears to have influenced later journalistic analyses. Writing on the relationship of NRA and the media, Davidson's judgment is:

> As long as NRA dealt primarily with hunters education and training, the modern gun group enjoyed good relations with the press. As calls for gun control grew and the NRA entered the political arena in force, however, these relations grew strained. (Davidson, 1993, p. 165)

Professional Standards Indicators

One journalist described NRA coverage as a function of events, a mirror model of journalism, going on to observe that the nature of real-world events solely dictated the coverage of NRA. He said:

> It's the weight of the issues. There's not much they [NRA] can do to turn this around. . . . It's awfully hard when people are getting shot. Johnny Smith is killed with a handgun. He had plans of going to college: "But we've [NRA] got the right to carry arms." They argue constitutional points, but most people don't want to hear that. (personal communication, March 1999)

Note the assurance with which the reporter seems to know what the audience needs to hear. Likewise, the judgments expressed seem pat concerning how NRA coverage plays along the dimensions of the personalization issue. Correspondingly as was substantiated in the content analysis, on the personalization angle in stories, there seem to be only one way to cast NRA: negatively. NRA is in no wise a sympathetic entity to any of these journalists.

Another comment, well supported by the patterns observed in the content analysis, suggests that media professionals frequently look to other media (or previous work by their own news organization) for models for their stories, giving credence to a cyclical feedback explanation for coverage patterns wherein media professionals copy one another. Said the journalist:

> My reading is relatively parochial. I look at *New York Times, Wall Street Journal* and like anybody else working on a story, at LEXIS-NEXIS to see what other news organizations have written about the topic. (personal communication, March 1999)

Precedence may outpace accurate description; or at least precedence may replace analysis, certainly an understandable practice among those who work under deadline.

Organizational/Structural Indicators

One journalist voices an apparently unexamined preference for Bureau of Alcohol, Tobacco and Firearms sources over NRA sources for expertise on matters of guns, an apparent matter of organizational credibility—governmental sources versus interest group sources (although why any one source should be more credible than the another is always moot). He mentions speaking to the BATF director, "who was trying not to be political," and then seems surprised that NRA should disagree with the director or would want to have some voice: "Here's the director of BATF saying there's a loophole, and NRA is saying, 'Don't shut us out.'" This sort of preference is congruent with the content analysis findings showing journalists as more willing to quote non-NRA sources in articles. It is debatable whether this preference is more a structural factor, i.e., other sources are more accessible or better at accommodating journalists; or whether it is an ideological-cultural factor where reporters prefer sources "just like us." Both combined are likely, for even though these bias dimensions are conceptually distinct, things are not often so distinctly mono-causal in life; to an ideologue or an enculturated person such as a professional, persons of like suasion are likely to be not only more accessible but also more credible.

Some disagreement exists between the journalists on the effectiveness of NRA press relations. One finds NRA, "relatively agile... they're pretty good at getting back to you. They have a clipping service and know what you write." This journalist also has the impression that the NRA press relations office is essentially a "high volume operation," and not as attentive as the press relations offices of organizations such as ACLU:

> ACLU is more responsive. They determine what you need and put you in touch with some of their specialists. The NRA is more inclined to have the press people try to answer the questions, rather than refer you on to the higher senior officials. (personal communication, February 1999)

Another journalist regards NRA press relations as sporadic and "not proactive," citing a number of new hires, firings, and shakeups over time as a serious problem for the organization. Terms he used to describe NRA press relations are "generally none too cooperative" and "head in the sand." The journalist is personally familiar with media bias against NRA and admits to its existence (but not in his own work, which he describes in terms of scrupulous balance, with each "side" receiving the exact same amount of space). He describes also a "vicious cycle" of NRA press relations, where "the press comes to hate them more than ever" while NRA in turn increasingly hates the press for the coverage it receives. This same journalist regarded HCI press relations personnel as more helpful than NRA personnel. "They [HCI] just give you the information you need," he said, referring to what he had earlier described as an NRA penchant for argument (personal communication, February 1999).

A reporter cited the NRA's 1993 move to Fairfax, Virginia, from Washington, D.C., as a factor in gun issue coverage. HCI, he said, is located right in Washington D.C., while to interview NRA officials he and his crew had to drive out to Fairfax, a 45-minute remove from their production facilities. No watershed, though, appears in NRA coverage around the time of the move, where coverage along any dimension suddenly shifts, so this explanation may be mere rationalization.

Journalistic Trade Publications

A useful alternate perspective on journalistic practices regarding NRA may be gained from an influential trade publication. In 1993 *Editor & Publisher*, a journal that describes itself as "the oldest publishers and advertisers newspaper in America," urged editors to "step up the war against guns," announcing, "It is time to square off against guns. We are talking a sustained newspaper crusade." The article in which these quotes appears suggests a number of approaches along which editors may pilot their publications: concentration on manufacturing levels of firearms; tracing the flow of guns; and highlighting youth killings on the first page; all themes encountered many times during the content analysis of NRA media coverage. Also recommended is:

> Investigate the NRA with renewed vigor. It may be on the run, but its spokesman claims membership ($25 annual dues) is up 600,000 over 10 years ago. Print names of elected officials who take NRA funds. Interview them. Support all forms of gun licensing, in fact all causes NRA opposes. (Winship, 1993, p. 24)

It is impossible to judge exactly what effects such an exhortation might have on journalists and editors, but it reads as a declaration of war, a "sustained newspaper crusade." To an uncanny extent, it mirrors and prefigures thematic content of the NRA coverage of prestige U.S. newspapers during the past decade. While it certainly sums up the approach taken by elite journalists toward NRA, once again the article does not mark any divide in the qualities of coverage. It should perhaps be regarded as a particularly pure expression of journalistic bias rather than its cause.

7

ADMINISTRATIVE DEMOCRACY

A General Theory of Media Bias

Throughout the analysis of media coverage constituting the third chapter, the interest groups almost always seem to fall into in the same negative to positive order on the different content measures. The overall ranking ascends in this order: NRA, ACLU, AARP, NAACP, and HCI.

Why should this be so? It happens far too many times to be coincidental. Slight variation occurs—e.g., NAACP and HCI exchange places at the top a few times and AARP enjoys a slight ascendancy in pseudo-event coverage rates—but for the most part the order remains as stated.

Some measures are obviously related, thus partly explaining the consistency between them. In illustration, the rate of pseudo-event coverage of a group directly affects its opportunities for quotes and photographs, thus because NRA pseudo-events are least covered, NRA receives less in terms of quotes and photographs. But for most of the measures no such obvious relationship appears to exist. What possibly could be common to the measures for personalization, satire-mockery, democracy themes, joke headlines and pseudo-events?

The rankings have another unusual aspect. Recalling that many of the measures assess valences for differing thematic treatments, the mean scores for NRA and often ACLU fall on the negative side of the neutral point, while the other groups cluster on the positive side. Or else NRA and ACLU cluster conspicuously low compared to other groups on the proportional measures. For example, in the use of photographs of group actors or events in articles, NRA averages only six percent, but ACLU has only 11.8 percent, compared to a range of 21-41 percent for HCI, AARP, and NAACP. Again, why?

I suggest that a larger concept lies behind all of these measures of interest group coverage. Certainly the measures all indicate, each in its own way, media bias in some discrete aspect of coverage. Bias does not stand alone, for bias in small, seemingly discrete things exists as a manifestation of something larger. Or put in another way, bias exists for or against some particular thing, person, group, idea, or constellation of ideas but this bias must arise from within a frame of reference. Thus, mainstream physicians tend to despise homeopathic and "natural" medical treatments, not because physicians harbor some innate dislike of herbs or treatment through visualization, but because physicians have been trained and thoroughly enculturated in a scientific clinical positivism. Their bias is a manifestation of this deeply inculcated way of seeing (which they call *examination*) and interpreting the world.

So do the rankings reveal about whatever may be inculcated in the interpretive heart of journalism? For one thing, it leads to the dismissal of some common explanations of elite media bias. Certainly, it is by now evident from the content analysis results alone that elite journalists who wrote the articles considered in this study do not on the whole care for the NRA or guns: there is too much evidence in the form of their own words, works and statistical significance tests to ignore. Many would therefore ascribe these reportorial tendencies to that venerable bugaboo, *liberal bias* or to simple anti-gun bias, as NRA officials and many political conservatives often in fact do. Why, then, should ACLU, a "leading liberal champion" according to some of the content-analyzed articles, also find itself so often shaded by negative coverage? ACLU remains and has been since its origin, very much a left-leaning organization, with "ultra-liberal" often a term applied to it. While on the matter of guns, despite ACLU being denounced at times as constitutional rights absolutists, ACLU explicitly does not support the individual right to bear arms interpretation of the Second Amendment; they are anti-gun by proclamation. If the predominant bias of the elite press were liberal or simply anti-gun, ACLU would be highly revered. So the liberal and anti-gun bias concepts illuminate nothing here.

It is not that liberal-conservative bias does not affect coverage at times. Or that other forms of bias do not exist. One would have to be naïve to the point of addle-headedness to believe otherwise. Elite journalists tend to identify themselves with politically liberal causes, and personal idealism cannot possibly be segregated from the interpretation of events. Doubtless, too, old-fashioned economic concerns have killed many a news story. Many discern in the national media, some on the basis of good evidence, a conservative bias supporting economic imperialism and mindless consumerism.

Additionally, the powerful forces of personal psychological projection interact with the amorphous nature of external events that media professionals must daily interpret, in ways that allow just about everyone to see what they need or want to see in the media. The Left sees bias for the Right; Right sees Left; schizophrenics and the devoutly religious see the Hand of God, devils, or aliens at work; we could also list racism, sexism, internationalism, and the exploitation of women and girls, men, animals, and classes. There are bugs and bugaboos in the media appropriate to nearly every orientation or fixation. So bias is often not just about what affects coverage, but also what affects perceptions of coverage. Both credible and incredible evidence exists supporting the existence of bias in one direction or another along many dimensions.

Few have conducted rigid comparative studies of the sort presented in this book, however. That elite media may be biased for or against a particular issue or topic is interesting, and this knowledge may help an interest group rally indignation or manage its public relations; however it tells but little about the overall functioning of media in society. This latter concern is the broader and more important idea, with larger implications. The overall ranking results provide such an explanation.

The larger concept that lies behind the consistent ranking is a broad cultural level phenomenon that I will label an *administrative control bias*. It has profound implications. Administrative control in this usage means rational, scientific, objective social management by elite, symbol-manipulating classes, and subclasses, i.e., professionalized administrators or bureaucratic functionaries. The thing administered is often democracy itself, or a version of it at least. Here and throughout this chapter terms such as "rational," "objective," "professional," and "scientific" should be read in the sense of the belief systems that they represent, i.e., *rationalism, objectivism, professionalism,* and *scientism*. Scientism is not the same as being scientific; the first is a matter of faith and ritualistic observance, the other is difficult creative work. William

James made a similar distinction between institutional religion and being religious, the first being a smug and thoughtless undertaking on the part of most people, the second, a difficult undertaking affecting every aspect of a life (James, 1902). The term *scientific administration* would pertain here. Note that we move here well beyond the notion of mere gun control and into the realm of general social control, management and regulation.

This administrative control bias is the manifestation of a hermeneutic that could be termed "the administrative gaze," honoring the style of Michel Foucault. This interpretive view organizes, manages, objectifies, implements, and looks downward toward a subject world that has been defined in such a way as to beg administration or clinical-style intervention. Too, it is a basic power relationship, or an attempt at one, for such is the nature of all management. Some theorists regard this sort of approach to the world as the defining epistemic view and encroaching organizational form (i.e., bureaucracy, which is by definition a scientific form of organization) of the modern era (see Foucault, 1965, 1973, 1979; Mills, 1959; Weber, 1948). Jacques Ellul (1965) describes the hermeneutic, its equivalent that is, in terms of a general social propaganda toward centralization that cannot be resisted lest the resister appear to oppose the notion of progress.

In illustration of how the administrative control bias plays out in the national news coverage of interest groups and social action, imagine a valence scale with a neutral midpoint, anchored at one end by a pro-administrative control position, and at the other by an anti-administrative control position. The interest groups figuring in this study can be situated along this scale in exactly the same order as they embody or align with the idea of administrative control; and this ranking precisely matches the ranking of their respective average scores on the content analysis measures.

Of the five groups, NRA necessarily anchors the negative end. The very existence of the potential for uncoordinated violence represented by guns is a threat to an administrative control hermeneutic. Guns simply invite administration. Correspondingly, it can be seen that the underlying messages of NRA coverage is that NRA defies regulation, rational democratic administration, common sense, and scientific progress. NRA organizational actors require clinical, psychological interpretation. NRA finds itself an object of a discourse conducted by administrative bodies, hence a relatively small proportion of NRA pseudo-events coverage and NRA quotes are complemented by a much larger proportion of discussions of the NRA as problem in the context of other pro-administrative organizations' pseudo-events and proceedings.

Next up the administrative control scale is ACLU, which because of its mission must often position itself "athwart the road" chosen by administrative ambition. While not flaunting the administrative control hermeneutic to the same extent as NRA with its inherently dangerous firearms, ACLU often confounds administrative attempts to implement efficiently rational, scientific policies in educational settings, workplaces, law enforcement interactions, prison environments, and other social institutions. Accordingly, the underlying theme of much of its coverage is ACLU frustrating rational democratic administration by its pursuit of absolutist visions of constitutional rights of individuals and groups. That ACLU is also a well-known champion of the First Amendment—which embodies a principle that is in the self-interest of journalists to endorse and understand—is doubtlessly helpful in ACLU receiving more favorable treatment than NRA.

AARP is not at all controversial in regard to administrative control, hence its position at the neutral midpoint of the scale. In fact, AARP demands a high level of administration and regulation, an orderly world with health care, law enforcement, no surprises and bank drafts that are direct-deposited the same day of each month, now and continuing into the foreseeable future. AARP sometimes wants more for its members than some non-members might see as a proportionate share, thus explaining much of the negative AARP coverage in the elite news, but AARP is essentially a coordinator and mass consumer of administrative services.

Higher yet on the administrative control scale, very clearly on the positive side, NAACP has since its beginnings been dedicated to integration, to lowering and removing social barriers of racial injustice. Despite, however, the epic nature of the struggle for civil rights, NAACP has been and is in no sense whatsoever a revolutionary or controversial organization, at least not from the administrative control perspective. The ultimate goal is essentially to join through participation—i.e., integrate rather than combat, replace or dominate—the administrative classes. NAACP coverage reflects this alignment perfectly. On occasion NAACP opposes some excess of law enforcement or other regulatory attempts, but for the most part the themes of coverage are a celebration of NAACP progress (or concern over its lack) in various administrative fields and professions. Integration equates here with administrative assimilation.

At the top of the scale, HCI represents the essence of the administrative hermeneutic. It stands for scientific management or rational control and regulation of a problem quite often framed as a general public health concern. Working with its scientific sister organization, the Center for the Prevention of Handgun Violence, it issues studies, publishes findings, and conducts other activities expected of a research institute. Press coverage conveys this image. Absolutely antipathetic to NRA (which is disassociated in coverage from science), HCI is associated in coverage with science, progress, common sense, rational progressive democracy, public safety, and all good things administrative.

Although this study deals with five interest groups, this result generalizes to elite news coverage of other interest groups. In the form of a proposition, then: *an interest group will in the long term receive negative, neutral, or positive coverage in elite media in accord with how well the group aligns with the administrative control hermeneutic.*

This proposition could be put to a larger test, but it applies to any number of interest groups or interest group-generated issues common to elite news. A number of cases virtually suggest themselves.

Environmental groups receive generally favorable coverage, at least when these groups tend to be advocates of regulation and administration. Such groups employ scientific-style studies to advance their viewpoints or highlight a perceived problem. And the solution to the problem—all environmental problems it seems—calls for setting up or enlarging an administrative regulatory agency to monitor the problem. The hugely powerful Environmental Protection Agency is the natural outgrowth of this line of thought. Environmental groups might show scenes of whales and mountains in their newsletters, but in terms of social functioning they stand for careful, detailed management by professionals. Anti-environmental regulation groups in both the United States and Canada have the difficult task, from the perspective of obtaining favorable media coverage, of opposing scientific administration, although they often attempt the technique of opposing science with more science.

Regarding the *anti-smoking, anti-drug,* and *anti-drunk driving* and *anti-alcohol movements,* it is debatable to what extent these issues are "movements" in the sense of being mass movements involving many thousands of mobilized people. Some are perhaps more or less so than others. The interest groups cultivating these issues fare well in terms of support as measured by public opinion polls, but this is not at all the same thing as mass group membership or mass social mobilization. These issues are, however, quite understandable if looked at as standardized post–World War II, top-down communication campaign conducted by administrative professionals. Groups advancing such issues receive favorable coverage generally. Themes of this coverage concern on the whole regulation, control, and administration, always ostensibly for the social good, but control and regulation nonetheless. The alcohol, tobacco, and public safety issues form a busy intersection where the machinery of public health and law enforcement merges with the big engines of socialization, K–12 and university education, on the journey to a more administratively perfect world.

The Priestly Function of Elite Journalists

All this begs questions. Why would journalists be so compelled to color their interpretations with this administrative control hermeneutic? For do not journalists pride themselves on their freedom from interpretive restraints? They remind us ad nauseam of their vital role in independently illuminating the U.S. political process. Plus, having talked with a number of journalists over the years—socially, professionally, and for research purposes—not one of them has ever confessed to being in the grips of an administrative control hermeneutic.

The "why" in this case reveals itself by looking at their preferred interpretations of events, their professional origins, and their social role in mass democracy.

Preferred Interpretations

"Advocacy group" is a euphemistic label often applied in journalism to interest groups located on the higher end of the administrative control scale; these are the groups consistently receiving the more favorable coverage. What these groups may lack in mass membership is made up for by their claim of representing persons, groups, creatures, or ecosystems that for some reason do not speak clearly for themselves.

When journalists represent an interest group as being antidemocratic, they tend to be saying one of several, but closely interrelated things. The group opposes ideas supported by public opinion polls; or it opposes some advocacy group that claims to be warranted by public opinion; or it opposes some administrative agency that claims to be warranted by a mass democracy mandate or opinion polls; or that the interest group has bypassed public opinion polling, advocacy groups, and administrative bodies altogether and has appealed directly (often successfully) to elected representatives or the judicial branch of government; or the group opposes some idea that journalists support, acting in their role as socially responsible public guardians. Tellingly, editorial denunciations of NRA and other groups are most frequently warranted on public opinion. Editors can thunder on as they do only because they speak for "the public," for if they spoke with such immoderation on their own behalf we would think them asses.

Not only is a seriously limited understanding of the complex, pluralistic nature of American representative democracy evidenced by these reportorial and editorial tendencies, they confirm rather clearly that national journalists operate from comfortably within the perceptual framework of the mass democracy mode of social action. You will recollect that the mass democracy mode envisions social action as a rational accretive process of gathering individual opinion and compiling it through the constitutional apparatus of government. The system is legitimated only by rational mass participation and therefore the social importance of journalists becomes magnified, because for mass democracy journalists provide illumination, therefore informing rational participation. They are indispensable social guardians and interpreters. They work by the combined means of objective and interpretive reporting; the former justified on the merit of their training, the latter on their status as political experts.

No other modern mode of social action other than mass democracy accords any such solemn importance or prestige to journalists. Pluralism regards them as hacks, quite often, although they can and do at times rise to respected professional status; but this is a far less elevated role than the guardian interpreter. Social movement theory regards elite journalists as mere lackeys for their being on the wrong side of the ideological fence (unless they are practicing social activists), so there is no glorious role for the journalist here, either.

Judging by their works as analyzed for this study, journalists seem entirely amenable to just those kinds of story frames and interpretations of political events that one would expect under the mass democracy formulation of social action. This is curious in itself for a profession that takes pride in its ability to question seems to have little or no critical ability in its dealings with administrative-organizational claims that are warranted on the basis of polling results and formulated in mass democracy terms. It seems merely to repackage them in the form of objective-style news. Mass democracy formulations flatter journalists, though, by according them a vitally important place in the social order—one of interpretive responsibility. There are few if any other ways for a professional-technical writer, for we must admit this is largely what a journalist is by trade, to garner such prestige. This may be the reason why journalists are suckers for administrative democratic story frames; these frames socially legitimate not only the organizations that produce them, but also the journalists that convey them.

Profession Origins

The mass democracy conceptualization of social action — especially its vision of the role of mass media professionals — is consonant with the administrative control hermeneutic that has suffused throughout modern mass democracy. I will go even further and suggest that the objective, scientific model of mass media journalism that accompanies mass democracy theory is itself in large part, or perhaps in its entirety, a manifestation of the administrative control hermeneutic.

If one examines the historical rise of objective journalism in the nineteenth century (Schudson, 1978), one sees the practice arising in response to the decision-making and informational needs of far-flung elites, both political and commercial. The mass communication system itself was a hardware triumph of scientific, progressive administration. Objective journalism developed as its software and accordingly spread around the world.

Previous to objective journalism, baldly partisan news media were the norm; under *objectivity* news became a scientific tool of social progress and management. The elite press continues also to serve this function, connecting administrators and managers not only to the world they seek to administer but also to other managers with whom they must coordinate their efforts. So in this sense social movement-based critiques have been correct in identifying a sort of pseudo-pluralism operating in the public forum, a pluralism that is in reality no more than an exclusive conversation between elite class subcomponents— but this over-class is administrative in outlook and purpose.

We should not think of this way of thinking and interpreting reality as an entirely deliberate process. We are dealing here with the diffusion of a hermeneutic that accompanies an organizational and cultural style, a scientific management method of proven effectiveness, with wonderful social benefits and also terrible side effects. Journalists, like everyone else, steep in this hermeneutic throughout their education and upbringing; moreover they work in and serve organizations that arose in response to administrative needs. High-level journalists especially have survived a rigorous selection process that favors those who are most suitable and effective for this environment. Journalists are probably no more conscious of the hermeneutic than fish are conscious of the water around them.

The middle-class origins of many elite journalists likely augment this situation, as the middle classes are the world's managers. Research by Gans (1980), Johnstone, Slawski, & Bowman (1976), Wilhoit & Weaver (1986), and others shows also that journalists have over time become less working class and more urban and middle-class in origins and outlook. This social distance might in itself be sufficient to explain bias against NRA, which still in some large part consists of people whose interests in firearms tend to have been transmitted to them through families whose origins tend more toward working class and rural (Kleck, 1991, p. 22), and whose experiences and values might be so far removed from those of an urban middle-class journalist as to approach incomprehensibility.

It is also established that journalists tend to be politically liberal compared to the general population. Elite journalists often identify themselves and colleagues as leaning to the left (Rothman & Lichter, 1982). Social movement researcher Sara Diamond (1995) notes the defining characteristic of the Left as the favoring of a distributive idea of government power wherein the state is not a protector-enforcer of individual rights, but an interventionist distributor, i.e., the administrator, of social progress and goods. This idea is, of course, congruent with the administrative hermeneutic.

Social Role

Journalists acquire importance in the mass democratic system precisely because they gather, convey, and interpret the data that inform individual choices. Mere raw, inaccessible data transforms to political information that is piped to where it will do the most good. Objective, balanced coverage becomes essential, at least in pretense, lest this vital flow of information be thought compromised, thus affecting not only the quality of rational individual decision-making, but also the legitimacy of the system.

Working from within the perspective of the mass democracy model for social action it is difficult to specify an ideal role model of journalistic coverage other than a "scientific objectivism" at work. An event (i.e., reality) causes coverage, or so the objective journalist would and often does say. Virtually all of the journalists that I have ever talked with regard coverage as mirroring reality. They truly seem to believe this, that they have access to information to which philosophers and scientists have been denied. I spoke once to a journalist who worried out loud about "compromising" her objectivity when covering a story. The claim being advanced here, by assumption, is that journalists can truly convey or interpret the nature of reality as opposed to the various organizational versions of events in which journalists must daily traffic. The claim is incredible and amounts to a Gnostic pretension of being "in the know" about the nature of reality, or at least the reality that matters most politically.

An ecclesiastical model most appropriately describes this elite journalistic function under mass democracy. Information is the vital substance that makes the good democracy possible. It allows, as it were, for the existence of the good society, a democratic state of grace. *Information* is in this sense analogous to the concept of *divine grace* under the pre-Reformation Roman Catholic Church. Divine grace was essential for the good spiritual life, the life that mattered. The clergy dispensed divine grace to the masses in the form of sacraments. They were its intermediaries, who established over time a monopoly, becoming the exclusive legitimate channel of divine grace. In mass democracy, objective-interpretive journalists act as the intermediaries, the legitimate channel, of the vital information needed for correct democratic functioning.

Recollect that the interposition of intermediaries, the clergy, along a vital spiritual-psychological supply route was the rub of the Reformation. The clergy cloaked themselves in the mantle of spiritual authority rather than acting as its facilitators. Many elite newspapers have apparently done much the same thing, speaking and interpreting authoritatively for democracy, warranting these actions on the basis of social responsibility. Of course, then and now, many people do not take the intermediaries seriously.

It is no accident, then, that the pluralistic model of social action largely discounts journalists as an important class. In the same way the decentralized religious pluralism generically known as Protestantism discounts the role of clergy. This should be expected. Pluralism and Protestantism share common historical origins (Adams, 1986). American pluralism particularly is deeply rooted in the Reformation's reaction to interpretive monopoly.

Journalists, particularly elite journalists, occupy under mass democracy this ecclesiastical social role, a functional near-monopoly whose duty becomes disseminating and interpreting the administrative word and its symbols unto the public. Democratic communication in this sense is sacramental, drawing its participants together into one body. We should not overlook the common root of the words *communication, community,* and *communion.* What might be termed as the process of *demo-communication* has aspects of *transubstantiation,* an interpretive process by which journalists use their arts to change the bread and wine of raw data into democratically sustaining information. Democracy is a kind of communion. *Objectivity* and *social responsibility* become social necessities, legitimating doctrines much like the concept of *papal infallibility,* which had to emerge to lend weight to interpretive pronouncements.

In this light, even the laudable professional value of *objectivity* can appear as a nearly incredible claim. Both claims, *objectivity* and *infallibility,* function to lend credence, authority, and an impeachment-resistant moral/scientific base to organizational or professional products. Both are absolute in nature. Both also serve the quite necessary social function of ultimately absolving from personal responsibility or accountability the reporter, whether ecclesiastical or secular, who is, after all, merely duty-bound to report on the facts. As it is in heaven so it will be on earth; and as it is on earth, so shall it appear in *The New York Times.*

In the matter of to whom journalists are accountable, Gans (1980) reports that the elite journalists he observed were accountable for their stories only to each other, an audience of peers, except in cases where a major advertiser took offense. They dismissed complaints from the public as coming from cranks or frustrated interest groups. This sort of behavior suggests a possibility of a professional elite grown pharisaical; an elite cloaked in values and traditions; holding itself above and apart; ostensibly looking outward, but whose perceptions are molded by group pressure; a profession that occupies a well developed, albeit self-serving, moral/scientific position. Of course many other professionals beside journalists justify their behavior by means of similar moral-scientific schemes (including, of course, academics).

Even the relatively recently emerged style of interpretive journalism is justified in the same way as the interpretive words of priests—guiding pronouncements made in the name of the greater good—e.g., social responsibility journalism. Journalists shepherd the democratic flock. They glory in this role, to judge by their voluminous, semi-autobiographical writings, and their reciprocating interviews of one another concerning their roles in and perspectives on world and national events. The dimensions of the role explain some of their legendary arrogance of which public relations professionals and others often complain.

Journalism's social import is also recognized when *Journalism*, as profession and art, is enshrined, studied, often with the help of handsome endowments, at special programs in major universities, rather than merely taught as an applied set of skills (which it essentially reduces to under pluralism).

We might consider also the interconnected set of ideals that seem to constitute a journalistic ethos. These are the traditions and models of journalism as it is fundamental to democratic social action, such as the investigative journalist, who selflessly exposes corruption, waste, and evil for the benefit of society; or the reforming, muckraking, and Progressive-era styles of journalism; and the commonly encountered adversarial style of reporting summarized under the metaphor of the "watchdog of democracy." Here, arguably, are near-mythic vocational underpinnings that provide a strong, presumably easy-to-learn-and-transmit, moral-ethical foundation upon which professional self-esteem can rest secure.

This professional self-esteem seems quite intact and survives the years well. Lippmann and Mertz, in analyzing news coverage of the Russian Revolution from 1917 to 1920, concluded, "The news as a whole is dominated by the hopes of the men who composed the news organizations" (cited in Sproule, 1996, p. 20). Later events showed that coverage of the revolution was more wishful than accurate. Judging by recent journalistic tendencies, as demonstrated in the content analysis earlier in this study, elite journalists are still partial to interpret organizations such as NRA in accord with their own visions for the mass democratic City of God.

Journalists, elite journalists especially, comprise the informational priesthood of the administrated democratic order, without which the mass democratic system would shrivel away and its administrators would lose their warrant of informed consent.

Mass Administrative Democracy

Journalism, elite journalism especially, though, is the creature of modern *mass administrative democracy*. Mass administrative democracy is what happens when mass democracy meets the administrative control hermeneutic. The result is scientifically managed democracy. Its apparatus is that of the modern rational management system — an assembly line form of democracy — where in accord to Tayloristic principles of scientific management, the work of the citizen, after having read the newspapers to learn about "the issues," has been simplified to that most elemental possible democratic act of pulling a lever. In some cases, participation may be taking part in a poll, literally a response to a survey research question formulated by an administrative agency. It is infinitely better to be able to vote than not, but few would argue that the mere act of voting, or answering a survey question on an issue that one may likely know nothing about, is in itself a highly meaningful form of political participation. Nor is it a good way of offering meaningful input to the formulation of policy. Meaningful policy input becomes therefore the province of administrative elites.

Lippmann (1922) pointed this out as a problem in mass democracy as it existed nearly eighty years ago and it is still true today. The citizen-customer in the mass democracy generally has not the time, resources, access, nor often the inclination to become substantively involved in distant political events and therefore must rely on interpretive experts to inform and simplify the available choices. Elite mass journalists are the group most responsible in the mass democratic system for conveying and generating expert interpretations.

Leaving journalists behind for the moment, the simplification of political participation to the individual's vote or item-response on a survey questionnaire, or forming an attitude in regarding to something heard on the news, is a great boon to administrators, who in the spirit of the age must rule in accord with democratic ideology. Administration in the name of democracy becomes the highest calling.

Sproule discusses the contribution made to modern political administration by social science in the form of survey research polling (i.e., attitudinal data):

> Attitude type data of the type gathered by Thurstone and Likert offered, in the view of Erwin Esper, " a disembodied statistical abstraction characterizing a group." Such data permitted the unwieldy notion of a whole discursive public to be replaced with a more manageable construct presenting a "public" as the sum of individual responses recorded on questionnaires." (Sproule, 1996, p. 63)

Administrative elites provide alternatives, frame questions, and justify complicated policy on the basis of "agree/disagree/don't know" and "Smith versus Jones" response options. Administrative publics are defined and constructed by rational management techniques based on responses. Highly manageable, the responses can be added, subtracted, and the results are a *public opinion* used to justify policy, for policy is what administrators do.

Of course the pluralistic theorist balks at these constructed publics, saying these "publics" are not anything of the sort, e.g., a person does not become an environmentalist merely by strongly agreeing with a question upon which he or she had no opinion whatsoever the second before it was asked. The pluralist would opine that a person becomes an environmentalist only because of some active interest followed by socially directed action such as conversing, seeking out information and finding like-minded persons, i.e., aligning with a group. This is the *discursive public* as discussed by pluralistic theorists; it is tangibly behavioral in its attributes and active in its approach to the world. The *administrative public* is a more diffuse thing entirely, for it is largely attitudinal in its attributes, in many cases existing merely as a response to some projection of administrative interest, in a word, passive, e.g., consider the "diffuse constituencies" of so-called "public interest" groups (Daniellian & Page, 1994, p. 1057).

Truly discursive publics, i.e., mass membership interest groups, can impede the smooth administration of administrative democracy if they are not aligned with current administrative policy formulations and if they are powerful enough so that they must be reckoned with. They are neither diffuse nor manageable and become anti-democratic by administrative definition. This is exactly the variety of anti-democracy theme that appeared so often in the content-analyzed coverage earlier in this book. If a discursive public or interest group advances the cause of administration, it becomes by this definition pro-democracy. In other words, pluralism appears to be acceptable in elite media coverage as long as it is administrative pluralism, i.e., a complementary pluralism among administratively minded groups.

In the case of the NRA, the conceptual discrepancy between the administrative and discursive public lies behind the *paradox of extremism*. Harking back to the introduction, the paradox arises from the incompatibility of NRA, an "extremist" organization according to the dominant media gloss, surviving and prospering as it does in a U.S. political culture that eschews extremism.

How does such an incongruity exist? The NRA is a discursive public, meaning that behavioral components are present that are largely lacking in the passive administrative public. To administrative democracy, uncoordinated opinion that is not cultivated and gathered through normal channels is irksome, even threatening. The truly discursive public propagates its own views independently, with little heed to mass democratic administrators. Independent discursive publics do not fit into the administrative worldview. They are lumps in the batter. They will not be ministered to, except on their own terms, and do not accept on faith the pronouncements of those who speak in the name of mass democracy. In the elite media, i.e., the mass interpreters of administrative democracy, discursive publics risk being designated as heretical voices. This is what is conveyed by the designation of *extreme* applied to an interest group, meaning it is outside the pall of civil society as it unfolds under the administrative hermeneutic. Interest groups do not fit into rational democracy, for it is a jealously absolutist system in that either a social system is rationally democratized or it is not: interest groups that are not of the "public interest" sort are regarded as civic irregularities should they step out of the bounds of the pursuit of harmless pastimes.

Trends to Suppress Heresy

Two related social trends appear confluent in the national media. First, is the trend of *the perception of the interest group as a social problem*. News and editorial articles on campaign and special interest reform often call for the elimination of interest group influences from the political process. Some legislative proposals under the guise of campaign reform would make it illegal for interest groups to publish and distribute to their membership the voting records of congressional representatives: political information would instead come by default from "objective" mass media sources. This proposal represents a pure form of mass democracy theory in which it is believed that democracy would be so much more rational, in the administrative sense, if only the political influence of irksome special interest groups could be neutralized. Interest groups are acceptable providing they confine their activities to the realm of hobbies or to administrative causes, often called *the public interest*. In the content-analyzed articles, for example, journalists and editors were annoyed that NRA does not confine its activities to duck marshes. Journalists seemingly are never annoyed with Common Cause, an interest group often depicted in news media accounts in the apparently oxymoronic state of opposing political influence by interest groups, and a group that is a champion of rationally administered mass democracy. This is because it is perceived as a public interest group, and called so by its officials and journalists, and accordingly receives much favorable coverage. So we see calls for the neutralization of non–public interest group influence in order to more effectively rationalize the mass democratic political process.

A second trend is an appeal for *a more politically effective mass media* in the mass democratic sense, a trend already suggested by reform proposals mentioned in the above paragraph. A great deal of political communication research focuses on how much the *electorate* learns from election coverage in mass media. The *electorate* when it is referred to in this fashion is a disembodied statistical abstraction that administrative political science and communication researchers apply to people who might vote. It is considered a serious problem, a crisis of legitimation, when the electorate does not learn enough to participate meaningfully in the system. A fashionable problem along this same vein is called *political cynicism*. This happens when some substantial portion of the electorate stops believing in or caring about the administrative solutions conveyed by mass media and either stops voting altogether or does not believe in the benevolence of political administrators or media. This non-belief is evidenced by responses to a standardized survey question that asks how much government officials are out for themselves as opposed to being out for the good of society. In other words there is a crisis of democratic faith. Media sensationalism, feeding frenzies, and the quirky vagaries of the interpretive versus the more substantive style of news reporting and other abuses of the clergy have also been blamed for the lack of an informed or motivated electorate. There can be little doubt that a widespread unwillingness to vote or to evince belief in the system is a serious problem to administrative mass democracy because it questions the validity of its administrative warrant. So prescriptions are written, formulated on the normative basis of mass democratic theory, regarding the preferred content and style of mass media coverage of the political process, i.e., it must be made more representative of administrative interests by more accurately conveying the choices to be made. What many political communication researchers are saying is that if we could just somehow improve the quality of the clergy and the liturgy, the system would be better.

So we see attempts to diminish interest groups in the mass democratic political process, especially interest groups that are on the anti-administrative control side of the continuum, while simultaneously augmenting the role of journalists, who appear to most favor those groups that are most deeply committed to the principles of administrative control. The promise is that scientific administration will combine with socially responsible mass media coverage to form and inform a better mass democracy.

On the whole, in my considered opinion, these trends represent a return to an Age of Faith; to Faith in administrative science to serve the best interests of its client-citizens; to Faith in administratively sympathetic journalists to convey essential truths; and to Faith in administrative elites to exercise power without independent checks, balances, or the interference of well-organized oppositions. Journalists become more and more like the pre-Reformation clergy in this system, connecting the common person to the sources of higher truth that guide daily existence. Without the socially responsible journalist this system cannot function.

Social Applications

It is possible to apply the lessons learned in the course of this study to some matters of current interest.

Education

A good point of beginning might be to scrutinize exactly how journalists are trained regarding interest groups and mass democracy. Based on a number of conversations with journalism graduate and undergraduate students (and their professors), it appears that proto-journalists may be inculcated with a naïve suspicion of interest groups, little understanding for pluralism, and a reverence for the mass democracy glorification of the social role of journalism. These combine to lead them to an unreasonably high opinion of the place of themselves and their chosen profession in the social order. Professional self-esteem is wonderful, but has its limits. Educators might consider how to start training rather than ordaining journalists.

Undergraduate students, in my experience, also appear in thrall to the ethos of administrative mass democracy. To the point of cognitive deprivation, they have little or no notion of pluralism, nor of interest groups, nor of the informational specializations and social contributions of interest groups. They understand social action as either administrated mass democracy or, in some cases, along the cruder formulations of social movement theory, as protest demonstration, i.e., "taking it to the streets." As such they have been cut off from one of the most powerful forms of political participation and representation available to the individual—membership and participation in an interest group.

Social Stratification

That elite journalism is an extension of an administrative control hermeneutic and that interest groups must be aligned with this viewpoint to receive equitable treatment in coverage amount to a serious problem for a truly participatory democracy. Both pluralism and social movement theory offer more meaningful, behavioral forms of political participation for an individual than does pure mass democracy alone. They also offer individuals efficacious ways to resist administrative power or elites, or even to become a member of a counter-elite. The apparent direction, if not the reality of mass democracy, is toward social stratification: the administrators and the administrated. Agreeing at least in spirit with Foucault (1979, 1973, 1965), Ellul (1965), and C. Wright Mills (1959), I suggest this administrative route is not the road toward human freedom or creativity. As a trend, I believe that it represents a continuation of Western society's colonial habits. Except energy that was once directed outward, often under the justification of bringing order to the heathen, is now sublimated into making the more perfect democracy, at home and abroad. So the administrative control hermeneutic, in its untrammeled form, can be regarded as an inward-directed, interior type of colonialization by elite managerial classes over client underclasses.

C. Wright Mills (1959) felt strongly about this trend and recommended pluralism and "a liberating education" as a solution. Writing primarily to an audience consisting of professors of social science, he states:

> [The social science professor's] aim is to help the individual become a self-educating man, who only then would be reasonable and free. What he ought to do for the society is to combat all those forces which are destroying genuine publics and creating a mass society—or put as a positive goal, his aim is to help build and strengthen self-cultivating publics. Only then might society be reasonable and free. (p. 186)

We might doubt the capabilities of social science professors and researchers to carry out this charge, but if they merely enlarged their own views on social action, the results might spill over to their students. At some point the pretenses of administrative democracy fall down of their own weight and people begin to see the all-too-human being beneath the vestments. If professors examined the ramifications of their assumptions on social action, at least they might not unintentionally abet the democratic posturing of self-interested administrators.

Hybridism of Social Action Modes

Administrative democracy is also bureaucratic democracy, and as such, the laws pertaining to bureaucracies apply. When sociologist Max Weber (1948) definitively cataloged the attributes of bureaucracy, he noted its power and long-term effectiveness over all that had gone before it in the way of organizational forms. Bureaucracy equates with a sort of inexorability. When enshrined under the label of mass democracy it becomes perhaps even more difficult to counter. The only effective long-term antidote is of course another bureaucracy. Unaligned individuals have no chance against it.

Spontaneous social movements cannot prevail against bureaucratic forms (in the long run) unless they too bureaucratize, but once institutionalization sets in, the result is no longer a social movement. Pluralistic style interest groups bureaucratize readily, perhaps too readily, institutionally solving the problem of effective action over time, but they come to lack the mobilization intensity of social movements.

However, combining the pragmatic style of the pluralistic interest group with the identity-based social movement makes for an effective organization that is capable of sustained action. Adding a true participatory democratic dimension improves group hardiness even more. A lesson of this study is that this *hybrid vigor* effectively stands against powerful administrative control efforts. This combination explains why NRA succeeds and endures in the face of administrative action, an important point for those who are interested in social activism.

A solution to the problem of forming an effective citizens group—as distinguished from the public interest group that merely claims to speak for citizens—is a hybridism in social action. The truly successful groups in this study have all achieved this hybridism in varying blends.

NRA combines the social movement mobilization intensity of an emerging gun culture with traditional pluralistic mechanisms of influence. These mechanisms, institutionalized long ago, were hijacked by the membership back in the 1970s when the organization ceased being a hobby group. NRA responds to and represents its members through their active democratic participation in selecting leadership. It is dynamic in this regard, despite an inherited institutional component that has many "Byzantine" qualities, in the words of one NRA observer. Through these combined means, it withstands the relatively diffuse public opinion (compared to that of NRA members) managed by the essentially administrative democratic groups that seek gun control. Schuman and Presser (1977), with their gun control paradox, were on the right track in hypothesizing that pro-gun people held their opinions with some special intensity, but it is behavioral "opinion" a kind that would not show up on a simplistic survey measure of political ideology. Plus this gun culture has had many years to coalesce since.

ACLU combines a social movement sense of aggrieved identity (probably an aggregation of identity subsets, considering the number of identity issues on which they work) with a vital, energetically democratic organization. Yet they work legalistically and pragmatically within the system, for as a group dominated by attorneys they are well prepared to protect individual or collective interest. Also, compared to NRA, they are very much a middle-class group, which helps considerably in negotiating pluralistically with middle-class administrators.

AARP is a very classical pluralistic incentive group, essentially non-democratic in its structure. Politically powerful, it would probably be more powerful yet if its membership could better dictate its agenda, and thus be more well represented. Its hybrid effectiveness springs in large part from incentives and in part from serving the acute sense of identity of senior citizens, who mobilize fiercely to protect their own interests. In this sense AARP has a captive, growing audience for mobilization.

NAACP, also a very middle-class organization compared to NRA, draws upon an acute sense of aggrieved identity in African Americans. To this it melds an excellent pluralistic influence network of middle-class supporters. NAACP conducts itself democratically, and hence, well represents the interests of its members locally and nationally.

HCI, although a darling of national mass media, has not been able to advance its agenda except on "feel good" matters of largely symbolic importance. Although it is well established as a pluralistic public interest group, plugged firmly into the administrative middle classes, and funded handsomely by foundation patronage, HCI lacks essential mobilization components. The pro-control approach does not lend itself to mobilization of an aggrieved sense of identity specific to the issue. Few people identify themselves, in the social movement sense, as non-gun owners.

There is no emerging antigun culture. Antigun public opinion compared to pro-gun opinion is a relatively diffuse thing, largely attitudinal, without significant behavioral dimensions. Recent HCI attempts to piggyback on existing social identities, e.g., the Million Moms March, have garnered favorable national media coverage, but have not mobilized enduring mass support. The recent merging with the Million Moms March is more HCI acquiring the symbolic assets, i.e., the name and slogan, of a bankrupt concern, rather than any true alliance, for the march appears at this time a defunct organization. Neither have HCI efforts sufficiently impressed politicians, a thoroughly pragmatic group as a whole, who are well acquainted with the difference between behavior and attitude. Further, HCI is not truly democratic in its organization, and thus lacks the energizing accountability of the direct representation of a large group of members. Unless they can overcome these lacks, a feat requiring more than their recent name change to Brady Campaign to Prevent Gun Violence, they will not better NRA at the national level under the extant political system. Gun culture is the more viable and tangible of the two positions, and NRA the more effective example of social action hybridism.

Appendix A

THE INTEREST GROUPS

To aid in making comparisons between the interest groups discussed throughout this study, short descriptions are provided below. The groups are alike in many ways, but also differ in many ways. For purposes of this study the important features are several.

Mass Membership. Although the groups vary considerably in size and purpose, they are open to interested citizens generally, rather than being trade associations, professional associations, or other narrow economic-interest groups.

Ongoing Cost of Belonging. Although membership dues vary considerably, members spend money to join and maintain their association with the groups.

Democratic Structure. To a greater or lesser extent, the groups are responsive to their individual members, as opposed to predominantly staff run or patronage type groups.

Political-Social Involvement. The groups pursue active social agendas and exert political influence directed outside of the organization at all levels of government. This social dimension distinguishes them from hobby groups.

Interior and Exterior-Directed Communications. The groups act as nodal centers for collecting, interpreting and distributing specialized information for members, media, policy makers, and others.

Interior and Exterior-Directed Programs. All provide or broker services and programs to members (even if they are only in the form of specialized information) and to the community.

Voluntary Association. Members initiate, continue or discontinue their association on their own terms.

Political Representation. A major function is to represent their members at the local, state, national, and even international level (e.g., NRA's involvement in recent United Nations small arms–control talks). This representation may be extra-constitutional in terms of the U.S. political system, but it is perhaps more direct, tangible, and broadly effective than are so-called duly elected representatives. These groups matter.

National Rifle Association of America

Founded in 1871 by a group of former Union Army officers, the original purpose of NRA was the promotion of marksmanship, a need suggested by the abysmal shooting skills demonstrated by federal soldiers during the Civil War (NRA, 1995). A core function of NRA continues to be the training of civilians and law enforcement officers. NRA officials report that 50,000 NRA-certified instructors taught gun safety and marksmanship to approximately 1 million persons in 1997 (Sandler, 1998). However, since 1968 NRA has increased fourfold in size, and has developed from essentially a hobby-sporting organization into a social-political organization. After passage of the Gun Control Act of 1968, the NRA established its Institute for Legislative Action, which has worked to oppose what it sees as unreasonable efforts at gun regulation at both the state and federal levels. Sporting use of firearms, however, remains an organizational concern, e.g., NRA sponsorship and regulation of target shooting competitions.

The NRA provides a number of services to its members and to society at large. Member services include a subscription to one of its three monthly magazines (in addition it publishes number of highly specialized periodicals for target shooters and books on firearms, firearms safety and related topics), and basic accidental death and dismemberment insurance, as well as group rates on firearms insurance. NRA law enforcement officer members (approximately 200,000) are automatically insured for $25,000 in the event of being "feloniously killed" in the line of duty. NRA sells jackets, hats, coffee cups, decals, and other paraphernalia to its members.

Membership for 2001 was reported at 4.2 million by NRA officials, although their three basic magazine subscriptions, one of which is included with all membership levels, totaled to a monthly average of about 3.7 million in circulation in 2000. Annual dues are $25, with life memberships available for $500-750. Higher membership levels such as Benefactor and Patron cost considerably more.

A 76-member board of directors elected by its 500,000 life members runs the NRA. Its current president is actor Charlton Heston, an effective public speaker and figurehead. Wayne LaPierre is Executive Vice President in charge of daily operations.

National Association for the Advancement of Colored People

NAACP was founded in 1909 by a multiracial group of concerned citizens with the support of *The New York Evening Post*. Their stated objective is the achievement of "political, educational, social, and economic equality of minority group citizens of the United States." The NAACP pursues this goal through a wide variety of initiatives across all aspects of American society, although the courtroom and lobbying have always been principal sites of this activity (Finch, 1981; National Association for the Advancement of Colored People, 2001). The NAACP has achieved or been involved in a number of significant legal victories during the period of its existence. Its Legal Defense and Educational Fund, for example, was party to the famous *Brown vs. Board of Education* desegregation decision of 1954. It is currently involved in a suit against the paint industry concerning lead-based paints.

Programs/services include ACT-SO, which aligns young people with mentors, and a long-standing health initiative for minorities (NAACP, 1999).

The Gale Group (1999) reports 400,000 members, but NAACP reports that its 1999 membership exceeds 500,000, a figure that appears to include junior members. Regular membership dues are $30 annually. Membership levels range from Bronze Life ($400) to Diamond Life ($2,500) to Corporate ($5,000). Describing itself as the "oldest, largest and strongest Civil Rights Organization in the United States," the organization has 2,200 branches in the United States, as well as in Germany and Japan (NAACP, 1999). It offers a subscription to its publication, *The Crisis*, to members above the junior level. Current circulation is 250,000. A national board governs NAACP, a true citizens group, with board members representing local NAACP branches from across the U.S. The current chair is civil rights activist Julian Bond, and the president–executive director, Kweisi Mfume, former U.S. representative from Maryland.

American Civil Liberties Union

ACLU describes itself as "The nation's foremost advocate of individual rights" and "a non-profit, nonpartisan, 275,000-member public interest organization devoted exclusively to protecting the basic civil liberties of all Americans, and extending them to groups that have traditionally been denied them" (ACLU, 1999, p. 1). ACLU was founded in 1920 in response to the First World War–era amended Sedition Act, which allowed for the imprisonment of thousands of people for "crimes" such as anti-war views and trade union organizing.

Known mainly for its legal challenges, ACLU was party to the censorship cases such as the Scopes trial and the U.S. Customs office attempt to ban the importation of James Joyce's *Ulysses*. It was also party to *Brown vs. Board of Education*. It currently is involved in a number of individual rights issues: privacy, censorship, freedom of expression and religion, and discrimination of various sorts.

The basic membership contribution is $35. A higher level of membership, Guardians of Liberty, can be achieved by means of monthly gifts, while the Liberty Council (285 members) is open to those who give annual gifts of $5,000 to $9,999. ACLU reports that 50,000 new members signed up in response to former president George Bush's attacks on ACLU (ACLU, 1999).

Also very much a citizens organization, ACLU is governed by a national board of 84 directors elected by autonomous state affiliates. The executive director is Ira Glasser, and the president is Nadine Strossen, a New York University Professor of Law.

American Association of Retired Persons

Ethel P. Andrus, a former teacher who also founded the National Retired Teachers Association in 1947, founded AARP in 1958. AARP has grown over the years into an organization with more than 1,700 paid staff members at least 30 million members. NRTA and AARP eventually merged. Among AARP's many activities are the dissemination of information to its members, funding for gerontological research, legislative and consumer advocacy, and a wide variety of member services (see below). Membership is available for an annual fee of $8, which includes a subscription to its publications (*Modern Maturity* and *AARP Bulletin*). AARP is renowned for its ability to direct mail membership invitations to persons at the time of their fiftieth birthdays.

AARP members appear to be largely mobilized through incentives (Olson, 1965). The considerable number of services offered to members is certainly an attractive feature. In this vein, AARP continues in its original mission of making available health insurance to retirees at attractive group rates, an unheard-of thing before Andrus. AARP's success in this field was aided in part by its association with businessman Leonard Davis, who has been called "a direct marketing genius" and who is said to have virtually invented direct mail order sales of insurance (Morris, 1996). Membership includes guaranteed discounts through the AARP Purchase Privilege Program, including airlines, auto rentals, hotels, and vacation packages. They also offer several different types of insurance, legal services, credit cards, health care, and investment opportunities. This list is far from complete. They are also a powerful lobbying force.

AARP has a volunteer board of directors, but appears to be essentially a staff-run group (Morris, 1996).

Handgun Control, Inc./Brady Campaign to Prevent Gun Violence

Dr. Mark Borinsky, a mugging victim, founded Handgun Control, Inc., in 1974 in an effort to push for tighter gun laws and regulation at both the state and federal levels. Pete Shields, a business executive whose son had been the last victim of the so-called Zebra Killer, joined him soon after. The non-profit organization has promoted a variety of gun-related regulations and bans. Handgun Control perceives itself as being the voice of reason in the debate over gun control, using the terms "rational" and "common sense" to describe the policies it endorses. There is also a subsidiary unit of the organization, the Center to Prevent Handgun Violence (CPHV), which is primarily responsible for disseminating their viewpoint to the public as well as for providing legal counsel. They report a staff of 60 and an annual budget of $7.5 million.

The Gale Group reports Handgun Control, Inc.'s 1999 membership as 400,000, although their newsletter, included with membership dues, has a circulation of 250,000. Basic membership is $15. HCI does not offer incentive type services to its members apart from their publications. It does offer a variety of public services. These include the Legal Action Project, offering pro bono legal assistance to attorneys working on lawsuits against gun manufacturers, also to persons who are victims of gun violence who may be contemplating such action. The Legal Action Project has also been a force behind so-called gun industry lawsuits by municipalities.

The current President is Michael D. Barnes. Since 1985, Sarah Brady has been the chair of Handgun Control, Inc. Sarah Brady is the wife of James Brady, the presidential press secretary who was wounded in the assassination attempt on President Ronald Reagan in 1981. The Bradys have since become Handgun Control's most important and visible spokespersons, with the Brady Bill the outstanding example of this partnership. In 2001 HCI changed its name to the Brady Campaign to Prevent Gun Violence, with CPHV correspondingly becoming the Brady Center to Prevent Gun Violence. The organization also announced an "alliance" with the Million Moms March (Brady Campaign, 2001). The "one-million strong" banner that graced the HCI web site in the past has been replaced with "Leading the Fight for a Safer America."

HCI has an elected board of directors, but members may not nominate candidates for the board.

Appendix B

METHODOLOGY

Content Analysis of Interest Group Coverage

The Sample

A total of 1,474 newspaper articles are content-analyzed concerning five interest groups, NRA, NAACP, ACLU, AARP, and HCI. The articles represent coverage in five newspapers, *NYT, WSJ, WP, CSM,* and *LAT,* from January 1, 1990 to July 15, 1998. Additionally, approximately 150 NRA editorials from the same papers, appearing between July 16, 1998 and December 31, 1999, were also content-analyzed.

Rather than a sample, all of the NRA coverage found in the five elite dailies is content analyzed, subject to certain necessary exclusions discussed below. The reason for not using a sample—a random sample of sufficient size has been proven adequate for estimating parameters—is an interest in identifying possible variations in frequencies, patterns, and effects of events on coverage over time. For the sake of feasibility in conducting the study, the coverage of non-NRA groups is merely sampled, subject to the same exclusionary rules of course, mainly because this coverage is used for comparison across content categories, with less interest in identifying trends over time. HCI articles include those on the Center to Prevent Handgun Violence (CPHV) because they are sister organizations. In the same way NRA articles also include those on the Institute for Legislative Action (ILA).

Articles are drawn from a master sampling frame compiled from three smaller sampling frames, as no single source satisfactorily represents all five of the newspapers over the time frame of the study. For example, the popular data base NEXIS does not index *WSJ* or other Dow-Jones publications, while the Dow Jones News Retrieval Service, an apparently exhaustive source of *WSJ, CSM* and *LAT* coverage, has only the most rudimentary index of *NYT* coverage. The National Newspaper Index (NNID), while an excellent source for *NYT*, dates back three only years and, even though it indexes coverage that is also included in some of the other databases, has listings that are at times not found in the other sources. Also, there is no comprehensive listing of political cartoons, even though such cartoons are regularly found on editorial pages.

The sampling frames, then, used to compile the master sampling frame are the (1) National Newspaper Index (NNID), a computerized index that lists articles by headings and subheadings; (2) NEXIS and the (3) Dow Jones News Retrieval System, the latter two sources being capable of full text, headline, or headline/lead searches for the mention of a key word or phrase. Duplication is eliminated on the master list. Attempts to narrow the scope of the sampling frame by restricting searches to mentions of the interest group in headlines-only or in leads-only of articles proved unsatisfactory because in many cases a group not mentioned in either headline or lead received considerable attention later in the body of the article. Hence full-text cites are relied upon. Samples for the non-NRA groups are drawn using a random number table to select from a numbered master list of articles for each of the interest groups.

The unit for analysis is the entire item, article, editorial, or cartoon, including any headline, photograph, drawing or caption that applies to the item.

The inclusionary decision rule for articles requires the interest group or its agent(s) to be a meaningful portion of the "story." This requirement eliminates obituaries or personality profiles where interest group membership is mentioned *en passant*, however the rare obituary or profile of group executives are included when membership-relevant activities are discussed. Examples of other articles thus excluded are detailed architectural reviews of the cornices and fascia on a new AARP headquarters building in Washington, D.C., and articles on a hotel chain that moved into quarters vacated by NRA when it removed itself to Fairfax, Virginia, from Washington D.C. AARP mutual fund offerings are also eliminated although, rightly, these could be considered AARP pseudo-events.

Measures

Articles are classified into commonly understood categories: Op-ed (which includes editorials and columns), Straight News, Feature Article, Letter to Editor, and Other. The Other category includes book reviews, entertainment announcements, and obituaries, and makes up only 1.7 percent of the sample. Most (92 percent) of the sample is made up of articles categorized as Straight News (59.5 percent), Op-ed (20 percent), or Letter to Editor (12.7 percent).

Some researchers, who have relied on content analysis to substantiate claims about mass media tendencies, often fail to allow sufficiently for the possibility of neutral, objective coverage. This use of relatively crude measures can force analysis of ambiguous coverage into misleading clear, dichotomies of good/bad, negative/positive, etc. Social statistician Blalock warns of such heedless dichotomizing merely for the purpose of simplifying measurement, calling it, "one of the worst practices still prevalent in both sociology and political science" (Blalock, 1979, p. 444). Such polarizations can magnify an otherwise ambiguous effect. Sometimes, though, dichotomies are appropriate, e.g., an article either has a photograph or does not. Media researchers should, though, sufficiently take into account that perhaps foremost among the professional standards of the modern journalist is the idea of *objectivity* (See Schudson, pp. 121-159, for an extensive discussion of the objectivity doctrine and its historical origins). Objectivity is generally understood as at least the appearance of fairness, impartiality and neutrality in presenting "the facts." So in this study many of the content categories are sensitive to the neutral style required of straight news by journalistic standards of objectivity to avoid the amplifying error. In other words, content categorizations that force coders to place coverage into absolute either/or category are avoided whenever feasible because such categorizations tend to disambiguate at the expense of accuracy.

Since this study deals with journalism and journalists from the most professional of U.S. newspapers, the papers that set journalistic standards, it would only be reasonable to expect straight news coverage to at least appear neutral. Bias would probably take subtle forms in order to avoid violating the objectivity standard. It would be more likely to be manifested through the preference of certain sources over others; in matters such as the number lines of quotations typically used from each source or the preferential placement of quotes within stories; and in the selection of "frames" (Goffman, 1974) or journalistic "angles" (Altheide, 1976) that would depict group actions in a favorable or unfavorable light. Bias would be more obviously manifested in editorial page content that is not expected to conform to the professional objectivity standard.

As Berelson (1952) wrote, "Content analysis stands or falls by its content categories," so a few words will be spent in justifying these categories. Many of the categories are derived or inspired by Lasswell's (1927, 1936) discussions of the symbol manipulation techniques common to communications and propagandas. In particular, the personalization measure descends directly from the techniques of caricature, stereotypes, and the atrocity stories that were the mainstays of early propaganda as discussed in the theoretical literature on that propaganda. Compelling personal stories rather than impersonal accounts of events, i.e., "just the facts," can be used in ways that are positive, neutral, or negative toward the group being covered. Similarly, a group can be shown as pro- or anti- democracy, progress, education, or any of a number of values that define, in some large part, American society. For example, in a contemporary positivistic American culture that highly values scientific progress and education, whether an organization is represented as being for or against science/progress is no light matter.

Systematic bias in coverage can be described in a number of other ways. Bosmajian (1974) catalogs a number of reporting techniques and rhetorical practices that he collectively calls the "language of oppression." He includes rhetorical techniques such as *dehumanization*, where individuals or groups are portrayed as disease organisms or as cogs in some infernal machine. By representing, for example, one mass membership group as a "lobbying juggernaut" and a second group as a "citizen advocacy group," the first group is dehumanized. In like vein, Bosmajian points to the importance of "mere" labeling, using examples of derisive or slighting labels and names attached to racial groups by their colonizers or would-be oppressors as contrasted to labels and names used by and of groups able to determine their own fates. An analogous labeling/naming device in journalism is the use or potential misuse of titles of organizational actors and spokespersons. Biased coverage would be likely to strip unfriendly or suspect organizational actors of their titular dignity by some substitution, e.g., consider the statement "The Chief and his Henchmen" versus "The President and his Cabinet Ministers." Hence, a category concerns the use of appropriate titles of organizational actors.

Some categories derive from or are inspired by Holsti's (1969) classic review of a number of content analysis–based investigations of journalistic bias. Professional, objective, journalistic standards require the use of neutral *verbs of attribution* such as *said*, *reported*, or *released* when attributing information. By "loading" these verbs of attribution—e.g., using terms like "claims" or "contends" instead of neutral terms like "said" or "says," journalists can subtly or not-so-subtly marginalize or discredit a source. Examples of positive verbs of attribution are *shown, demonstrated, proved*, etc.

Similarly, pejoratives, euphemisms, and other devices of semantic shading can color a story or a source just about any hue that could possibly be desired. Semantically loaded adjectives, verbs, and other descriptives do the same. Although professional standards for objective, straight news journalism eschew editorializing through adjectives and other embellishing devices, standards for editorial page content obviously do not. It would be reasonable to expect op-ed writers to employ these techniques either for or against particular groups. Indeed, how else could opinion be expressed via newspaper editorials?

Humor, satire, and mockery are also traditional tools of journalism that can be directed on behalf of or against a group. Or an article can simply be neutral in this aspect regarding any particular group. In exactly the same way, group intensity can be described negatively, neutrally, or positively according to whether or not the article frames group members as fanatical extremists or dedicated idealists. Any number of similar valence measures can be constructed, anchored at the negative end by a dysphemism and at the positive end, by a euphemism. Or measures can be anchored by simple antonyms; e.g., the treatment of group unity can be conceptualized along a cohesion-dissension scale, while a dwindle-growth scale can be used to measure whether group action is framed in terms of defeat or victory. It is also reasonable to expect a group subjected to media bias to complain of this treatment. Fairness standards would require that at least some of these objections be published and these are measured nominally.

Levels of measurement of content categories vary from nominal to interval-level. Some are nominal, e.g., an article either is or is not headed by a joke headline; it either is or is not a media event staged by an organization. Others are categorical variables that allow for classification into item type, e.g., editorial, article, cartoon, etc. Interval level categories measure negative-neutral-positive valences such as verbs of attribution, democracy or science-progress themes by use of five-point (1–5), interval-level semantic differential scales covering the range: very negative, negative, neutral, positive, very positive. A group average of 3.0 for all coverage on such a scale would be interpretable not that there is no negative or positive coverage for that particular group, but rather that negative and positive coverage have balanced out in the long run.

The content analysis is the work of two coders, conducted over a period of approximately two months. A preliminary series of reliability checks and refinements of the coding protocols were conducted prior to the coding, during which definitions of content were refined and protocol agreements arrived at between the coders. A number of content categories were eliminated entirely or conditionally from the final analysis for lack of reliability. For example, a measure of the general tone of articles, while reliable on op-ed type articles, was virtually impossible to apply consistently to straight news articles. A measure of semantic tone of articles was also inconsistent on straight news, but reliable on op-ed articles. Reliability tests are based on a random sample of ten articles analyzed independently by the coders. Averaged for all measures using the Holsti method, the intercoder reliability coefficient equals .89, out of a possible range of 0.0-1.0, with no individual measure less than .75.

Statistical Significance Tests

Two sorts of difference-of-means tests are applied to the measures. Valence differences for interest group comparisons are tested with standard Analysis of Variance methods (ANOVA), with Bonferroni multiple comparisons tests used for examining differences between individual interest groups. Bonferroni tests are preferred because they are conservative in their significance calculations. Differences of proportions on nominal and categorical variables are calculated with standard Chi Square tests. Probability levels in almost all comparisons, difference of means, or proportions are less than 0.01, meaning the probability of such results not being the result of chance is greater than 99.9 percent.

Those who are not familiar with statistical significance tests should note here that *significance* does not mean the same thing as *magnitude*. Often journalists report social science results as "significant" when the results are really very small in magnitude. Significance refers to how much confidence we can place in an estimate. It is to a large extent a function of sample size, so if the sample is large enough, significant differences may exist, even when there really is little practical difference between scores or proportions on a measures, e.g. 51 percent "agree" versus 49 percent "disagree." The results of this study, however, are both large in magnitude *and* they are significant at high levels of probability.

Additional details can be found in Patrick, 1999, which reports the results of all comparison tests, sub-sample sizes, and the actual measures themselves as they were used in coding the articles.

NRA Communication Analyses

The content analysis of the NRA official journal, *The American Rifleman* quantifies the relative proportions of the conflict, solidarity, and identity themes that define social movements. The time frame for analysis is identical to the media coverage analysis, with all issues are analyzed from January 1990 through July 1998, exactly 99 issues. The unit of the analysis is the entire issue. Additionally, some recent examples are drawn from issues in 2000 and 2001 but not included in the quantitative analysis itself. Each political and official article is coded for the number of paragraphs dominated by themes of conflict, solidarity, identity, and other. Conflict is further parsed into three subtypes: media conflict, science conflict, and general conflict. The numbers of paragraphs for each content category per issue are tabulated.

Paragraphs assigned to the general conflict category are dominated by themes of opposition and external threat, e.g., cultural war or opposition, hostile powers, regulation, out-of-control bureaucracy, conspiracy, unfriendly or self-interested elites, hostile social environments such as victimization by crime, and hostile political situations. Conflict themes monitor the environment for threats, actual or potential.

Media conflict paragraphs contain specific mentions of mass media bias. They include discussions of journalistic tendencies, media as lapdogs of political elites, inaccuracy and distortions in reporting, or suggested methods for interacting with mass media representatives.

Science conflict specifically mentions biased science or education themes including public health models, government-funded medical research, and "revisionist" history taught in schools.

Group action motifs dominate solidarity paragraphs, either directed within or without the group. These include grassroots action, voting in local and national elections, nominating or voting in elections of the NRA board of directors, fund raising, calling or writing in order to pressure elected political representatives, group activities and membership increase.

Identity paragraphs establish the individual at a fixed point of reference, so to speak, in relationship to the universe. Identity is couched in credo-like statements, i.e., normative beliefs, values, or definitions of the nature of existence that sets a member apart from those who are otherwise. The term "politics of identity" applies, so depending on the particular movement, identity consists of existing a member of a class or group, a group rather than individual construal. Identity themes include pride, tradition, patriotism, heritage, individualism, gun culture, and romanticized or social-historical conceptualizations of what it means to be a gun owner or citizen. Paragraphs not fitting any of the above categories are coded as "other."

The analysis is also the work two of coders, after an initial series of reliability checks, consultations, and refinements of definitions and decision rules for applying coding categories. Reliability for agreement between coders is calculated from a random sample of ten articles, also using the Holsti method. The averaged intercoder reliability coefficient for all the category measures is .85, with no measure less than .75.

Interviews with Journalists, NRA Officials, and NRA Members

Journalist and NRA official interviews are conducted via telephone and tape-recorded, with an assurance that information provided will not be used in any way that could identify the journalist or the news organization. Journalists are asked for explanations of coverage patterns, both from the perspective of their news organizations and from their experiences with interest groups as observed in the course of their work. Other sources for NRA information are official documents and recorded presentations by NRA officials before various audiences. NRA members are interviewed in a variety of places, including gun shows and shooting events, sometimes quite literally out in the field while hunting. They represent a convenience sample. No formal interview is conducted—the method is observation and neutral encouragement, e.g., "I see."

Study Limitations

Content analyses can provide descriptive, correlational, and comparative data over time. Causal inferences based on the results of content analysis can be seriously overextended. The tendency has been to demonstrate manifest content and infer the presence of some causative agent. For example, Herman and Chomsky (1988) show content patterns wherein friendly and unfriendly groups are treated differently. They largely infer the presence of hegemonic capitalist-controlled mass media that operate through a widely applied set of *propaganda filters*, a leap that requires some faith without the presence of adequate supporting evidence. This study, however, attempts to provide evidence on both sides of the causal equation.

A study such as this is vulnerable to outside variable-type alternate explanations. Even though negative press coverage is demonstrated and, further, correlates highly with mobilization, a third, outside factor might be the cause of both. The interviews with journalists and interest group officials and members help to eliminate alternative explanations that might otherwise erode the confidence in inferences made just on the basis of the content analysis.

But even though content analysis ultimately can only show manifest content of documents, its results are not exempt from probabilistic applications of common sense. If content analysis is performed in a systematic, reliable fashion using valid measures on representative samples or populations of documents concerning comparable groups, any clear results must be reckoned with in some way. The results that have been presented here are quite clear.

REFERENCES

Adams, J. L. (1986). In J. R. Engel (Ed.), *Voluntary associations: Socio-cultural analyses and theological interpretation*. Chicago: Exploration Press.

Altheide, D. (1976). *Creating reality: How TV news distorts events*. Beverly Hills, CA: Sage Publications.

Altheide, D.L., & Johnson, J. M. (1980). *Bureaucratic propaganda*. Boston: Allyn and Bacon.

American Civil Liberties Union (1999). ACLU Briefing Paper. In *American Civil Liberties Union Freedom Network* [On-line]. Available: http://www.aclu.org

Anderson, J. (1996). *Inside the NRA: Armed and dangerous: An expose*. Beverly Hills, CA: Dove Books.

Arendt, H. (1948). *The origins of totalitarianism* (second edition). New York: Harcourt Brace Jovanovich.

Aristotle (1984). *Rhetoric* (W. Rhys Roberts, Trans.). New York: Modern Library.

Associated Press (1990, January 17). A Massacre Remembered. [photograph and caption.] *The Washington Post*, A12.

Associated Press (1995, May 16). Mothers protest effort to appeal assault gun ban. *Los Angeles Times*, A12.

Associated Press (1995, June 12). Voter poll: "Good" guns OK. *Ann Arbor News*. Ann Arbor, Michigan.

Auth (1992, February 1). NRA [cartoon]. *Los Angeles Times*, B5.

Babcock, C. R. (1996, March 27). Campaign support from the NRA. *The Washington Post*, A19.

Ban on recruiters. (1993). *Editor & Publisher*, August 21.

Barlow, J. (1969). *The hasty pudding: A poem in three cantos written at Chamberry in Savoy during January MDCCLXXXXIII*. Boston: D. R. Godine.

Bentley, A. F. (1908). *The process of government: A study of social pressures*. Chicago: University of Chicago Press.

Berelson, B. (1952). *Content analysis in communication research*. Glencoe, IL: Free Press.

Bernays. E. L. (1928). *Propaganda*. New York: Horace Liveright.

References

Bernays, E. L. (1929). *Crystallizing public opinion.* New York: Horace Liveright.
Berry, J. M. (1997). *The interest group society.* New York: Longman.
Blalock, H. M., Jr. (1979). *Social statistics* (second edition). New York: McGraw-Hill.
Blumer, H. (1946/1950). The mass, the public and public opinion. In B. Berelson & M. Janowitz (Eds.), *Reader in public opinion and communication* (pp. 43-49). Glencoe. IL: The Free Press.
Boatman, B. (2001). Right to carry war rages in Michigan. Available: http// www.mcrgo.org (Reprint of article appearing in *Frist Freedom*, April 2001).
Boorstin, D. J. (1961). *The image: A guide to pseudo-events in America.* New York: Harper & Row, Publishers.
Bosmajian, H. A. (1974). *The language of oppression.* Lanham, MD: University Press of America.
Bragg, R. (1994, May 23). The NRA's faithful hear a rallying cry after 2 defeats on Capitol Hill. *The New York Times*, B6.
Bragg, R. (1996, April 14). New leader at the NRA is talking a harder line. *The New York Times*, C14.
Bumiller, E. (1997, August 29). Gadfly lands in unlikely place. *The New York Times*, B1.
Canadian Firearms Centre (2002). Canadian firearms manual. Available: http://www.cfc-ccaf.gc.ca/
Cappon, J. (1982). *The Word: An Associated Press guide to good writing.* New York: The Associated Press.
Clark, P. B., & Wilson, J. Q. (1961). Incentive systems: A theory of organizations. *Administrative Sciences Quarterly 6*, 129-166.
Creel, G. (1920). *How we advertised America: The first telling of the amazing story of the Committee on Public Information that carried the gospel of Americanism to every corner of the globe.* New York: Harper and Brothers.
Cummings, J., Davis, B. (2000, December 15). Dance over, Gore faces his Tennessee faults, *The Wall Street Journal*, A18.
Cutlip, S. M. (1994). *The unseen power: Public relations, a history.* Hillsdale, NJ: Lawrence Erlbaum Associates.
Cutlip, S. M., Center, A. H., & Broom, G. M. (2000). *Effective public relations*, (eighth edition). Upper Saddle River, NJ: Prentice-Hall.
Dahl, R. A. (1963). *Modern political analysis.* Englewood Cliffs, NY: Prentice-Hall.
Dahl, R. A. (1982). *Dilemmas of pluralist democracy: Autonomy vs. control.* New Haven: Yale University Press.

Danielian, L. H., & Page, B. I. (1994). The heavenly chorus: Interest group voices on the news. *American Journal of Political Science*, Vol. 38, No. 4, 1056-78.

Dao, J. (2000, September 11). The 2000 Campaign, the endorsements: To help Bush, NRA withholds backing. *The New York Times*, A23.

Dao, J. (2000, May 26). As convention opens, NRA sound defiant note. *The New York Times*, A26.

Davidson, O. G. (1993). *Under fire: The NRA and the battle for gun control*. New York: Henry Holt.

Dean, P. (1994, May 18). The straight shooter. *Los Angeles Times*, B10-11.

Death of a brave deputy. (1992, April 2). *Los Angeles Times*, B6.

Diamond, S. (1995). *Roads to dominion: Right-wing movements and political power in the United States*. New York: The Guilford Press.

Eckholm, E. (1995, May 28). The dark science of fund-raising by mail. *The New York Times*, E6.

Edelman, M. (1977). *Political language: Words that succeed and policies that fail*. New York: Academic Press.

Edsall, T. B. (2000, May 21). NRA aims assets at beating Gore in November. *The Washington Post*, A3.

Ellul, J. (1965). *Propaganda: the formation of men's attitudes*. New York: Knopf.

Etten, T. J. (1991). *Gun control and the press: a content analysis of newspaper bias*. Paper presented to the American Society of Criminology, November 20-23, 1991, San Francisco, CA.

Ewen, S. (1996). *PR! A social history of spin*. New York: Basic Books.

Fact Sheet, Right to Carry 2001 (2001). Available: http//www.nraila.org

Finch, M. (1981). *The NAACP: Its fight for justice*. Metuchen, NJ: The Scarecrow Press, Inc.

Foucault, M. (1965). *Madness and civilization: A history of insanity in the age of reason*. New York: Random House.

Foucault, M. (1973). *The order of things: An archaeology of the human sciences*. New York: Random House.

Foucault, M. (1979). *Discipline and punish: The birth of the prison*. New York: Vintage Books.

Freeman, B., & Gamson, W. A. (1979). Utilitarian logic in the resource mobilization perspective. In M. Zald & J. D. McCarthy (Eds.), *The Dynamics of Social Movements*. Cambridge, MA: Winthrop Publishers, Inc.

From the Staff Officers. (1971, January). *The American Rifleman*, volume 19, Number 1.

Gale Group. (1999). *Associations Unlimited*. http://www.galenet.com

Gallup, G., & Rae, S. F. (1940). *The pulse of democracy*. New York: Simon and Schuster.

Gans, H. J. (1979). *Deciding what's news: A study of CBS Evening News, NBC Nightly News, Newsweek, and Time*. New York: Pantheon.

Gest, T. (1992). Firearms follies: How the news media cover gun control. *Media Studies Journal*, Winter 1992, 138-149.

Gitlin, T. (1980). *The whole world is watching*. Berkeley, CA: University of California Press.

Goffman, E. (1974). *Frame analysis: an essay on the organization of experience*. New York: Harper & Row.

Goodman, W. (1993, Sept. 16). Measuring the lines between religion and politics. *The New York Times*, C16.

Graber, D. (1989). *Mass media and American politics* (third edition). Washington, DC: CQ Press.

Gun Battle State Doesn't Need Looser Concealed Weapon Rule (2000, December 16). *The Detroit Free Press*. Available: http://www.freep.com/newslibrary/

Gun Issues and the Media. (1996, July 25). Student Conference by Young America's Foundation. Purdue University Public Affairs Video Archives.

Guthrie, M. (1994, June 19). President of Carson NAACP unit is ousted. *Los Angeles Times*, A16.

Hall, S. (1980). Encoding and decoding in the television discourse. In S. Hall, et al. (Eds.), *Culture, media, language: working papers in cultural studies, 1972-79*. University of Birmingham, Centre for Contemporary Cultural Studies.

Handgun Control, Inc. (1999, April 22). Statement of Jim and Sarah Brady regarding the Littleton, Colorado school shooting. In *Handgun Control, Inc. Home Page* [On-line]. Available: http://www.handguncontrol.org

Harris, J. F. (1990, February 8). Virginia senate panel votes gun bill. *The Washington Post*, D7.

Herblock. (1991, May 8). Now I see where the "instant check" comes in. *The Washington Post*, A30.

Herman, E. S., & Chomsky, N. (1988). *Manufacturing consent: The political economy of the mass media*. New York: Pantheon.

Holsti, O. R. (1969). *Content analysis for the social sciences and humanities*. Reading, MA:Addison-Wesley.

Horney, K (1950). *Neurosis and human growth: The struggle toward self-realization*. New York: W.W. Norton.

Ifill, G. (1993, December 28). Clinton hunts, making point on guns. *The New York Times*, A8.

Isikoff, M. (1991, May 31). The "Brady Bill": Success and growing pains. *The Washington Post*, A17.

Isikoff, M. (1990, January 17). Assault pistols now being imported in place of banned rifles. *The Washington Post*, A12.

Jackall, R. (1988). *Moral mazes: The world of corporate managers* Oxford: Oxford University Press.

Jackall, R., & Hirota, J. (2000). *Image makers: Advertising, public relations and the ethos of advocacy*. Chicago: The University of Chicago Press.

James, W. (1902). *The varieties of religious experience: a study in human nature*. New York: Longmans, Green.

Johnston, H., Larana, E., & Gusfield, J.R. (1994). Identities, grievances, and new social movement. In E. Larana, H. Johnston, & J. R. Gusfield (Eds.), *New social movements: From ideology to identity*, pp. 3-35. Philadelphia: Temple University Press.

Johnstone, J. W. C., Slawski, E. J., & Bowman, W. W. (1976). *The news people: A sociological portrait of American journalists and their work*. Urbana, IL: University of Illinois Press.

Jung, C. (1956). *Symbols of transformation*. Princeton: Princeton University Press.

Kates, D. B. (1983). Handgun prohibition and the original meaning of the Second Amendment. *Michigan Law Review, 82*, 204-273.

Keirsey, R. D. (1992, April 10). Death of Deputy Yamato. *Los Angeles Times*, B6.

King, W. (1990, December 9). Target the gun lobby. *The New York Times*, Section 6.

King, W. (1993, March 12). Brady speaks out for Florio's gun ban. *The New York Times*, B4.

Kingdon, J. W. (1984). *Agendas, alternatives, and public policies*. Boston: Little, Brown.

Klapper, J. T. (1960). *The effects of mass communication*. New York: Free Press.

Kleck, G. (1991). *Point blank: Guns and violence in America*. New York: Aldine De Gruyter.

Kleck, G. (1997). *Targeting guns: firearms and their control*. New York: Aldine de Gruyter.

Kohn, A. (2001) Their aim is true: Taking stock of America's gun culture. *Reason* (May). Available: http://reason.com

Kopel, D. B. (1992). *The samurai, the mountie and the cowboy: Should America adopt the gun controls of other democracies?* Buffalo, NY: Prometheus Books.

Kopel, D. (1990). The media and gun control: A case study in world-view pushing. In W.R. Tonso (Ed.), *The gun culture and its enemies*. Bellevue, WA: Merril Press.

Kovaleski, S. F. (1996, April 23). New chief aims NRA at Future: First Female leader targets youth for growth of lobby. *The Washington Post*, p. A1.

LaPierre, W. (January, 2001). Standing guard. *American Rifleman*, p. 14.

LaPierre. W. (October, 1998). Standing Guard, *American Rifleman*, p. 14.

LaPierre, W. (1994, March 23). NRA and "Three Strikes." [Letter to the editor] *Los Angeles Times*, B6.

Lasswell, H. D. (1927). *Propaganda technique in the World War*. New York: Alfred A. Knopf.

Lasswell, H. D. (1934). Propaganda. In E. R. A. Seligman (Ed.), *Encyclopaedia of the social sciences, 1st edition, Vol. XII*. London: Macmillan.

Lasswell, H. D. (1936). *Politics: Who gets what, when, how*. Glencoe, Illinois: The Free Press.

Lautman, B., & Henigan, D. (1990, February 20). Aiding and abetting a bad aim. *The Washington Post*, p. A17.

Leddy, E. F. (1987). *Magnum force lobby: The National Rifle Association fights gun control*. Lanham, MD: University Press of America.

Lenin, V. I. (1929/1966). What is to be done? In H. M. Christman (Ed.), *Essential works of Lenin*. New York: Bantam Books, pp. 55–76.

Lippmann, W. (1922). *Public opinion*. London: Allen & Unwin.

Lippmann, W., & Mertz, C. (1920, August 4). A test of the news. *New Republic* (supplement), pp. 1-42.

Lott, J. R. (1998). *More guns, less crime: Understanding crime and gun control laws*. Chicago: University of Chicago Press.

Lott, J. R. (2000). When it comes to firearms, do as I say, not as I do. *America's First Freedom*, August, p. 72.

Lott, J. R., & Mustard, D. B. (1997). Crime, deterrence, and right-to-carry concealed handguns. *Journal of Legal Studies, Vol. XXVI*, January.

Lowi, T. J. (1969). *The end of liberalism: Ideology, policy, and the crises of public authority*. New York: Norton and Company, Inc.

McAdam, D. (1982). *Political process and the development of black insurgency 1930– 1970*. Chicago: University of Chicago Press.

McAdam, D., McCarthy, J. D., & Zald, M. N. (1996). Opportunities, mobilizing structures, and framing processes: Toward a synthetic, comparative *perspective on social movements*. Unpublished manuscript presented at Sawyer Social Movement Seminar, University of Michigan.

McCombs, M. E., & Shaw, D. L. (1972). The agenda-setting function of mass media. *Public Opinion Quarterly*, pp. 176-187.

McLeod, J. M., Kosicki, G. M., & McLeod, D. M. (1994). The expanding boundaries of political communication effects. In J. Bryant & D. Zillmann (Eds.), *Media Effects: Advances in Theory and Research*. Hillsdale, NJ: Erlbaum, pp. 123-162.

Malcolm, J. L. (1994). *To keep and bear arms: The origins of an Anglo-American right*. Cambridge: Harvard University Press.

Marx, G. T. (1979). External efforts to damage or facilitate social movements: some patterns, explanations, outcomes and complications. In M. N. Zald & J. D. McCarthy (Eds.), *The Dynamics of Social Movements*. Cambridge: Winthrop Publishers.

Mehall, K. (June, 2000). Letter from the editor. *America's First Freedom*.

Merrill, J. C. (1990). Global elite: A newspaper community of reason. *Gannnet Center Journal 4* (Fall), p. 93.

Meyer, J., & Feldman, P. (1995, April 28) Lobbyists stymie effort to trace explosives. *The New York Times*, A26.

Michigan Civil Rights Commission. (1996, September 30). *The role and responsibility of the media in the community: final report*. Lansing, MI: Michigan Department of Civil Rights.

Mills, C. W. (1959). *The sociological imagination*. New York: Oxford University Press.

Mintz, J. (1995, May 29). Ideological War Pits NRA Hard-Liners Against More Moderate Staff. *The Washington Post*, A4.

Morris, C. R. (1996) *The AARP: America's most powerful lobby and the clash of generations*. New York: Times Books.

Moving Forward at the NAACP (1998, February 24). *The New York Times*, A20.

NAACP Post Gives Julian Bond New Start (1998, February 28). *The New York Times*, A6.

NAACP's New Hope (1995, December 11). *The New York Times*, B8.

National Association for the Advancement of Colored People (1999). What you should know about the NAACP. In *NAACP Home Page* [On-line]. Available: http:// www.naacp.org/about/factsheet.html

National Rifle Association (1994). The American media's anti-gun agenda. *The American Rifleman*, January.

National Rifle Association. (1994) *NRA '94: Financial Report*. Fairfax, VA: National Rifle Association of America.

National Rifle Association (1995). *Annual Report 1995*. Fairfax, VA: National Rifle Association of America.

National Rifle Association Annual Meeting (1998, June 6). *NRA Annual Convention in Philadelphia, PA*. [Videotape]. Purdue University Public Affairs Archives.

National Rifle Association. (1999, April 21). Letter from the NRA Office of the President to its Colorado members. In *National Rifle Association Home Page* [On-line]. Available: http://www.nra.org

Newton, M. (1990). *Armed and dangerous: a writer's guide to weapons.* Cincinnati: Writer's Digest Books.

Nisbett, R. (1996). *Culture of honor: The psychology of violence in the South.* Boulder, CO: Westview Press.

Oberschall, A. (1993). *Social movements: ideologies, interests and identities.* New Brunswick: Transaction Publishers.

Olson, M. (1965). *The logic of collective action.* Cambridge: Harvard University Press.

Pacer, M. A. (1995, May 17). George Bush. *Los Angeles Times*, B6.

Patrick, B. A. (1999). *Social movement pluralism: Negative media coverage and National Rifle Association Mobilization.* Unpublished doctoral dissertation, University of Michigan, Ann Arbor.

Patrick, B. A. (1999). Oppression as a by-product of administrative hermeneutics and group processes: A case study. *Quarterly Journal of Ideology.* 22, 3-4, pp. 33-62.

Patrick, B. A. (1997). Media bias and the National Rifle Association. Paper presented Central States Communication Association, April 16-17, St. Louis, MO.

Patterson, T. E. (1994). *Out of order.* New York: Vintage Books.

Petty, R. E., & Priestler, J. R. (1994). Mass media attitude change: The implications of the Elaboration Likelihood Model of persuasion. In J. Bryant and D. Zilmann (Eds.), *Media effects: Advances in theory and research,* pp. 91-122.

Pressley, S. A. (1991, September 22). When tragedy lurks an error away. *The Washington Post,* p. A1, A18.

Purdham, T. S. (1995, Jan 4). Clinton's luck takes upturn on duck hunt. *The New York Times,* A1.

Rosenstone, S. J., & Hansen, J. M. (1993). *Mobilization, participation and democracy in America.* New York: Macmillan.

Ross, J. (1996). *Unintended Consequences.* St. Louis, MO: Accurate Press.

Rothman, S., & Lichter, S. R. (1982). Media and business elites: Two classes in conflict. *Public Interest 69*, 111-125.

Ryan, C. (1991). *Prime time activism: Media strategies for grass roots organizing*. Boston: South End Press.

Sandler, C. (speaker) 1998. Annual report of general operation manager. NRA Annual Meeting.

Schattschneider, E. E. (1960). *The semi-sovereign people*. New York: Holt, Rinehart and Winston.

Schudson, M. (1978). *Discovering the news: A social history of American newspapers*. New York: Basic Books.

Schuman, H., & Presser, S. (1977). Attitude measurement and the gun control paradox. *Public Opinion Quarterly, 41*: 427-37.

Schumpeter, J.A. (1943). Marx the prophet. Marx the sociologist. In *Capitalism, socialism and democracy* (pp. 5-20). London: George Allen & Unwin Ltd.

Schwada, J. (1994, April 14). Roberti sees victory as lifting gun foes' fears. *Los Angeles Times*, A1.

Seeyle, K. Q. (1997, September 12). Heston asserts gun ownership is nation's highest right. *The New York Times*, A14.

Shaw, D. L., & McCombs, M. E. (1977). *The emergence of American political issues: The agenda-setting function of the press*. St. Paul, MN: West Publishing Co.

Sisk, R. (2001, January 9). Gun control fear tactic bombed, Clinton says. *Daily News*, p. 6.

Spence, G. (1998). *Give me liberty: Freeing ourselves in the twenty-first century*. New York: St. Martin's Press.

Shils, E. A., & Janowitz, M. (1948). Cohesion and disintegration in the Wehrmacht in World War II. *Public Opinion Quarterly, Vol. XII*: 300-315.

Spitzer, R. J. (1995). *The politics of gun control*. Chatham, NJ: Chatham House Publishers, Inc.

Sproule, J. M. (1989). Progressive propaganda critics and the magic bullet myth. *Critical Studies in Mass Communication, 6*, 225-245.

Sproule, J. M. (1997). *Propaganda and democracy: The American experience of media and mass persuasion*. Cambridge, UK: Cambridge University Press.

Stengel, R., & Pooley, E. (1996, December 6). Masters of the message. *Time*.

Streeter, T. (1978). An alternate approach to television research: Developments in British cultural studies at Birmingham.

Szasz, T. S. (1970). *The manufacture of madness: A comparative study of the Inquisition and the mental health movement*. New York: Harper & Row.

Taming the monster: the guns among us. (1993, December 10). *Los Angeles Times*, p. B6.

Tapscott, R. (1996, March 6). Journalists take their best shots: NRA hopes to prove points on gun bill. *The Washington Post*, D6.

Tarrow, S. (1994). *Power in movement: Social movements, collective action and politics.* Cambridge: Cambridge University Press.

Tartaro, J. P. (1981). *Revolt at Cincinnati.* Buffalo, NY: Hawkeye Publishing, Inc.

Terry, D. (1995, July 13). NAACP audit shows lavish spending, members say. *The New York Times*, A21.

Terry, D. (1995, July 12). NAACP faces squabble about its road to the future. *The New York Times*, A10.

Terry, G. P. (1994, May 8). Charles Schumer: vanquishing the NRA with his assault-weapons ban. *Los Angeles Times*, M3.

Tilly, C. (1978). *From mobilization to revolution.* Reading, MA: Addison-Wesley.

Time (1989, July 17). Letter from editorial offices.

Tonso, W. R. (Ed.) (1989). The media and gun control: a case study in worldview pushing. In W. R. Tonso (Ed.), *The gun culture and its enemies.* Bellevue, WA: Merril.

Violence Policy Center. (1999, April 20). Fact sheet: Colorado gun laws and statistics on teenagers and guns in Colorado. In *Violence Policy Center Online Resource Center* [On-line]. Available: http://www.vpc.org

Violence Policy Center. (1999, April 23). Guns reportedly used in Littleton had combat-style designs. In *Violence Policy Center Online Resource Center* [On-line]. Available: http://www.vpc.org

Walker, J. L. (1983). The origins and maintenance of interest groups in America. *American Political Science Review 77* American (June), pp. 390-406.

Walker, J. L. (1991). *Mobilizing interest groups in America: Patrons, Professions and social movements.* Ann Arbor: The University of Michigan Press.

Weber, M. (1948). Bureaucracy. In H.H. Gerth & C.W. Mills (Eds. & Translators), *From Max Weber: Essays in sociology.* New York: Oxford University Press. pp. 77-128.

Weiss, P. (1994, September 11). A hoplophobe among the gunnies. *The New York Times*, pp. 65, 100.

Wilhoit, G. C., & Weaver, D. H. (1986). *The American journalist: A portrait of U.S. news people and their work.* Bloomington: Indiana University Press.

Winerip, M. (1992, August 23). Gun juggernaut vs. a gentleman named Keen. *The New York Times*, Sec. 1, p. 33.

Winship, T. (1993). The New Curmudgeon: Step up the war against guns. *Editor &Publisher*, April 24, p. 24.

Wright, J. D., Rossi, P. H., & Daly, K. (1983). *Under the gun: weapons, crime and violence in America*. New York: Aldine.

Wright, J. R. (1995). *Interest groups and Congress: Lobbying, contributions, and influence*. Boston: Allyn and Bacon.

Zald, M. N., & Garner, R. A. (1987). Social movements organizations: Growth, decay and change. In M. N. Zald & J. D. McCarthy (Eds.), *Social movement in an organizational society: collected essays*. New Brunswick: Transaction Books.

Zoroya, G. (1995, June 25). On the Defensive. *Los Angeles Times*, B10-11.

INDEX

A

AARP Bulletin 211
ABC 138, 140–142
Adams, J. L. 31–33, 195
administrative control hermeneutic 25, 187–190, 192, 197, 203
administrative democracy 26–29, 184, 197, 199, 203–204
advertising 4, 43, 50, 62, 79, 121, 146, 152, 162
advocacy groups 50, 155, 191
Altheide, David 174, 216
American Association of Retired Persons (AARP) 66–69, 71, 73–74, 78, 80, 82, 86, 89–96, 98–100, 102, 104–107, 110, 112, 115, 130, 155, 184–185, 188, 205, 210–211, 213–214
American Civil Liberties Union 9, 25, 28, 65, 156, 210, 222
ACLU 66, 68–69, 71, 74–75, 77–80, 82, 86–87, 89–100, 102–105, 107, 110, 112, 154–156, 181, 184–185, 188, 205, 210, 213
American Guardian, The 59, 120, 152
see also America's First Freedom
American Hunter, The 59, 118–119, 152
American Rifleman, The 53, 57, 59, 117–119, 121, 123, 125–129, 131, 133, 152, 219

America's First Freedom 59, 120, 127, 152
ammunition, cost of influenced by political situation 11, 17–18, 58, 121, 159
Andrus, Ethel P. 210–211
anti-gun groups, see gun control group
anti-media theory 24, 29, 49, 55, 117–118, 147, 164
see also National Rifle Association
anti-smoking groups 189
Arendt, Hannah 38–39, 49
AR 84, 134, 159
Aristotle 40, 151, 155
Arizona 84
assault weapons, banning of 16, 71, 73, 88, 104, 141–142, 150, 168
Associated Press 16, 76, 81, 124, 138
Attorney General, see United States Attorney General's Office
Australia 128, 146

B

Baker, James 78, 86
Baker, Josephine 78, 86
Barlow, Joel 160–161
Barnes, Michael D. 212
Batman 125
Bellesile, Michael 129
Beltway interest groups 44
Bentley, A. F. 32–33, 222

Berelson, B. 216
Bergen, Candice 83
Bernays, Edward 43
Bethune, Mary 86
Bill of Rights 138
black power groups, as social movement 24, 37–39, 164
Blackman, Paul 71
Blalock, Jr., H. M. 215
Blumer, H. 31–32
Bond, Julian 86, 209
Boomer Generation 155
Boorstin, D. J. 70
Borinsky, Mark 211
Bosmajian, H. A. 216
Boston Globe, The 62
Bowman, W. W. 193
Brady Bill 17, 126, 151, 154, 212
Brady Campaign to Prevent Gun Violence 19, 206, 211–212
Brady Center to Prevent Gun Violence 9, 212
Brady, James 9, 17, 19, 77–78, 82–83, 89, 93, 126, 133, 151, 154, 179, 206, 211–212
Brady, Sarah 9, 17, 19, 77–78, 82–83, 89, 93, 126, 133, 151, 154, 179, 206, 211–212
Branch Davidian standoff 152
Brokaw, Tom 138
Brown vs. Board of Education 209–210
Browning shotgun 150
Buckley, William F. 92
Bureau of Alcohol, Tobacco and Firearms 128, 181
BATF 181
Bush, George H. W. 15, 18–19, 93, 114, 145, 152, 156, 210
Bush, George W. 15, 18–19, 93, 114, 145, 152, 156, 210

C

California 64, 74, 77, 146
Camp Perry, Ohio 135
campaign reform legislation 138
Canada 17, 128, 146, 162, 189
Carbuncle, Fred 90
Carter, Harlon 102
CBS 125, 138, 140–141
Center for Disease Control
  see United States Center for Disease Control
Center to Prevent Handgun Violence 74, 211, 213
CPHV 211–213
Charlotte, North Carolina, NRA annual meeting in 139
Chicago Tribune, The 62
Chomsky, Noam 48, 79, 221
Christ 131
Christian Science Monitor, The (CSM) 9, 16, 63–64, 213
churches, American 50
Cincinnati Revolt 57–58, 102, 130, 154
  see also National Rifle Association
Citizens Against Gun Violence 72
citizens groups 32, 65, 154
civil rights movement 20, 50, 112, 155
Civil War (U.S.) 57, 208
Civilian Marksmanship Program 58
Clark, P. B. 33, 88
clergy, see Pre-Reformation clergy 26–27, 194–195, 201–202
Clinton, Hillary 15, 19, 73, 115, 119, 126–127, 133–137, 140–141, 151–152, 154, 158–159
Clinton, William Jefferson 15, 19, 73, 115, 119, 126–127, 133–137, 140–141, 151–152, 154, 158–159
Coca, Imogene 83

collective identity 38, 164
Colorado 159, 177
Colt, Samuel 159, 162
Colt Sporter 159
Columbine school shooting 159, 177
Common Cause 97, 154, 200
concealed weapons carry laws 19
conflict 23–24, 28, 37–38, 48–51, 55–56, 100, 110, 117–118, 122–124, 127–129, 131–136, 142, 146, 161, 163–164, 166, 219–220 see also National Rifle Association
Connecticut 88
cop-killer bullets 71
Corbin, Bob 84–85
corporations 44
Crime Bill (1994) 17, 159
Crisis, The 201, 209
Crooks, Louise 73
Cutlip, S. M. 43

D

Dahl, R. A. 34, 42
Davidson, Osha Gray 58, 179
Davis, Leonard 19, 211
Declaration of Independence 135
Democratic party 73
Detroit Free Press, The 166
Detroit News, The 166
Diamond, Sara 193, 209
disambiguation 79
Divine Grace 26, 194
Dow Jones News Retrieval Service 213
DuBois, W. E. B. 86
dueling pistol 135

E

Edelman, Murray 17

elections 19–20, 35, 60, 97, 117, 127, 131, 145, 220
elite newspapers, definition of 9–10, 54, 61–64, 66, 82, 88, 91–92, 95–96, 99, 102, 105, 107, 114, 116, 149, 157, 195
Elizabeth, Queen of England 77
Ellul, Jacques 38, 49, 187, 203
environmental activists/groups 37, 39–40, 48, 198
  NRA as 58
Environmental Protection Agency 189
EPIC/MRA 16
Esper, Erwin 198
Etten, T. J. 54
existential informational condition, of democracy 21

F

Fairfax, Virginia 182, 214
Feinstein, Diane 138
felons 17
feminist movement, as social movement 24
firearm dealers 17
First Amendment of the U. S. Constitution 91, 99, 188
flintlock 135
Florida 19, 133, 165
Florio, Jim 77
focus groups 22
Foucault, Michel 187, 203
Founding Fathers 135

G

Gadsen Minutemen 78
Gale Group 154–156, 209, 212
Gallup firm 16
gangsta-rap 125
Gans, Herbert 95, 193, 196

gay rights groups, as social movement 24, 37–38
General Social Survey 16, 161
George Washington University, media bias conference at 140
Georgia 159
Germany 209
Gest, T. 169
Gitlin, T. 160
Giuliani, Rudy 136
Glasser, Ira 74, 210
Gnosticism 194
God 131, 186, 197
Gore, Albert 15, 19, 134–137, 139–140
Graber, D. 63
Gram, Phil 134
Great Britain 146
grievances 37–38, 56
Greenpeace 154
Gun Control Act 154, 208
gun control groups 18, 168
  see also specific groups
gun control legislation 19
gun control paradox 17, 205
gun culture 8–10, 12–13, 38, 57, 124, 129, 137, 160–165, 204–206, 220
Gun Culture and its Enemies, The (Tonso) 57
gun owners 8, 10, 12, 16, 20, 24, 85, 90, 96, 124–125, 127–128, 130, 140, 145–146, 156, 158–159, 161–162, 166, 169, 172, 206
gun rationing 72
gun shows 157, 159, 164, 178, 221

H

Hammer, Marion 84, 131, 133, 166
Handgun Control, Inc. (HCI) 9, 19–20, 28, 65, 93, 111, 156, 166, 211–212
  elite newspaper coverage of 61
handguns, banning of 17, 19, 83, 104, 119, 128, 133, 150, 159
Harvard Law School 97
Hegelian dialectic 39
Herman, E. S. 48, 79, 221
Heston, Charlton 88, 90, 94, 127, 130–132, 134–135, 139, 209
Hitler, Adolf 39
Holsti, O. R. 64, 217–218, 220
Horney, Karen 56
House of Representatives, see United States House of Representatives
hybridism, and interest groups/ social action 24–25, 28–29, 60, 204, 206

I

Idaho 152
identity movements 24, 37–41, 55–57, 117–118, 122–124, 131–132, 204–206, 219–220
ideology 8, 21, 23, 32, 38, 48, 146–147, 162–164, 179, 198, 205
imperialism, U.S. 186
incentives, as driving force of interest groups 32–33, 58, 60, 65, 95, 155, 205, 211
informational model, of interest groups 44, 58
Insights 119–120, 173
instant-check, firearm purchases 17–18
Institute for Legislative Action, see National Rifle Association 19, 78, 102, 121, 208, 213
interest groups, see special interest groups
interpretive journalism 196
Iowa 150–151
issue groups 32

Index

J

Jackall, Robert 44, 176
Jackson, Jesse 77
James, William 23, 77–78, 82, 89, 187, 210, 212
Japan 128, 209
Johnston, H. 37–38
Johnstone, J. W. C. 193
journalists 7, 10–11, 18, 20, 22, 27–29, 42–47, 49, 54, 59, 62, 72–73, 78, 82, 86, 90, 93–96, 101, 107, 109, 112, 137, 143, 150, 153, 168–171, 173–181, 183, 185–186, 188, 190–198, 200–202, 215, 217, 219–221
Joyce, James 129, 210
Jung, C. G. 49
Justice Department, see United States Justice Department

K

Kaiser Wilhelm II 79
Kean, Thomas 83
Kennedy, Edward 138
King, Jr., Martin Luther 77, 83, 86
Klapper, J. T. 151
Kleck, Gary 16, 129, 151, 193
K-Mart 17, 91, 136
Knox, Neal 88
Kopel, David 129, 162

L

labor movements, as social movement 24, 38, 163
Landers, Ann 125
LaPierre, Wayne 15, 71, 78–79, 84, 88, 105, 124, 127, 131, 137–142, 144–145, 209
Lasswell, Harold D. 35, 42, 56, 79, 216
Leddy, Edward 56–58, 161, 163
Lee, Ivy 43
Legal Action, see Center to Prevent Handgun Violence 74, 212
legislation, see gun control legislation 19, 71, 73, 82, 93, 96–97, 104, 127, 138, 164–166
Lenin, Vladimir I. 40
LEXIS-NEXIS 180
Lippmann, W. 21, 46, 63, 100–101, 179, 197
Littleton, Colorado 177
lobbies 32, 100–101, 109, 111
Los Angeles Times (LAT) 9, 16, 63–64, 71–72, 83–84, 103–104, 112, 114, 135–136, 213
Lost Dutchman mines 84
Lott, John 129, 136, 165

M

Madison, James 36
Madisonian factionalism 36
magazines, high-capacity, banning of 17, 60, 62, 65, 118–120, 146, 150, 152–153, 159, 208
Malcolm, Joyce 129
Marxism 13, 24, 33, 37, 48
Maryland 210
mass administrative democracy, see administrative democracy
mass democracy theory/theorists
mass media 15, 18, 20–21, 23, 26, 28, 30, 42–46, 48–49, 51, 67, 114, 117, 127, 143, 147, 151, 153, 172, 192, 200–201, 205, 215, 220–221
see also elite newspapers
mass membership associations 21
material group 33
McAdam, D. 41
McVeigh, Timothy 77, 98
media event 50, 217
Media Research Center 126
Medicare 73

Meet the Press 139
Mehal, Karen 133
Merrill, J. C. 63
Metaksa, Tanya 78, 85, 93, 138, 142
Mertz, C. 100, 179, 197
Mfume, Kweise 85–86, 210
Michigan 7, 11, 19, 142, 159, 164–166
Michigan Coalition of Responsible Gun Owners 166
Michigan Militia 142
Michigan State Legislature 166
militias, see also Gadsen Minutemen, Michigan Militia 142, 152
millennialist religions 39
Million Moms March 19, 136–137, 139, 156, 206, 212
Mills, C. Wright 187, 203
Missouri 166
mobilization effect 10, 15, 24, 29, 49, 55, 149
Modern Maturity 211
Montana 165
Mothers Against Drunk Driving 154

N

National Association for the Advancement of Colored People (NAACP) 9, 20, 28, 66–69, 74–75, 77–80, 82, 85–90, 92–100, 102–107, 109–110, 112, 115, 154–156, 184–185, 188–189, 205, 209, 213
National Newspaper Index (NNID) 214
National Opinion Research Center 16
National Organization of Women 154
National Public Radio 125

National Retired Teachers Association (NRTA) 210
National Rifle Association (NRA) 7–12, 14–25, 28–31, 33, 42, 51, 53–61, 66–173, 175–185, 187–189, 191, 193, 197, 199–200, 204–209, 213–214, 219–221
NBC 138, 140–141
New England Journal of Medicine, The 128
New Jersey 77, 83, 140
New Jersey Governor's Office 77, 83
New Jersey State Attorney General 77
New York 7, 9–10, 16, 20, 22, 62–63, 87, 103, 136, 138, 150–151, 169, 180, 196, 209–210
New York Evening Post, The 209
New York Times, The (*NYT*) 7, 9–10, 16, 20, 22, 62–63, 87, 103, 138, 150, 180, 196
New York University 210
New Zealand 128
newspapers, see elite newspapers 7, 9–10, 16, 20, 22, 28, 43, 54, 61–64, 66–67, 82, 88, 91–92, 95–96, 99, 101–103, 105, 107, 114–116, 127–128, 149, 157, 166, 183, 195, 197, 213, 215
Newsweek 62, 126, 140
Newton, M. 168
NEXIS 180, 213–214
Nightline 142
94 Winchester Rifle 119
Nisbett, R. 57
nodal informational systems 44, 59, 65, 111, 207
nomothetic forces (Hegel) 39
North Carolina 139

O

Oakley, Annie 133

Oberschall, A. 158
O'Donnell, Rosie 136
Ohio 135, 164
Oklahoma City Federal Building bombing 152
oligarchies, mass membership groups as 21
Olson, Mancur 32–33, 58, 130, 155, 211
opinion polls 16, 34, 50, 190–191

P

papal infallibility 27, 195
Pataki, George 136
Patrick, Brian Anse 14, 54, 115, 159, 219
patronage, as force in interest groups 25, 33, 57–58, 60, 156, 166, 205, 207
Patterson, T. E. 46, 100
People 62
People Who Care About Kids 166
Philadelphia, NRA annual meeting in 137
pluralism 28, 31–32, 34–37, 41–43, 47, 191, 193, 195–196, 199, 202–203
see also National Rifle Association, mass media
pluralistic interest groups, see pluralism 41, 67
pluralistic media, see pluralism 42, 45, 53, 61
polis 36
political communication 21, 23, 26, 28, 123, 135, 200–201
political cynicism 26, 201
Pre-Reformation clergy 27, 202
Presser, S. 17, 21, 161, 205
professional associations 32–33, 207

propaganda 7–8, 12–14, 43, 47–49, 64, 79, 105, 125–126, 146, 151, 187, 216, 221
Proposal(Washington)
Protestant-Judaic tradition
Protestantism 195
pseudo-events 66, 70–74, 76–77, 82, 93, 151, 171, 174, 184, 188, 214
public relations theory 43
public interest groups 140
public servant 35
public service 26, 35
purposive group 33

R

Rand, Ayn 85
Reagan, Ronald 212
Reformation, The 26–27, 160, 194–195, 202
Religion 74, 111, 175–176, 187, 210
Republican Party 19
revolver, as instrument of egalitarianism 162, 165
Rhodes, Kim 124, 135
rifle, bolt action 58
rifle, .22 caliber 151
rifle, .22 caliber semiautomatic 18
right-to-carry laws, see concealed weapons carry laws
Robinson, Kayne 138
Roman Catholic Church 26, 194
Ruby Ridge, Idaho 152
Ruger, Bill 135, 159
Ruger Mini 159
Russian Revolution 100, 197
Ryan, C. 48

S

Saxons 131
Schattschneider, E. E. 34
Schools of Choice 112
Schudson, M. 43, 192, 215

Schuman, H. 17, 21, 161, 205
Schumer, Charles 84, 133, 136, 138
Schumpeter, J. A. 39
Scientism 111, 186
Seattle 48, 138
Second Amendment of the U. S. Constitution 8, 53, 71, 98, 114, 125–127, 130–132, 134, 136, 142, 144, 185
Sedition Act 210
Selleck, Tom 136
semi-automatic rifles, banning of 159
senior citizens 22, 97, 106, 155, 205
Shields, Pete 211
shooting matches 122
shotguns, banning of 17, 119, 133
Sierra Club 154
Sixty Minutes 138
Slawski, E. J. 193
social action, see mass media and National Rifle Association
social movement theory 24, 28, 31, 33, 37–38, 41–42, 60, 191, 202–203
solidarity 24, 37–40, 49, 55, 117–118, 122–123, 129–131, 134–136, 145–146, 151, 155, 161, 163, 166, 219–220
see also National Rifle Association
special interest groups 7, 11, 18, 22–23, 25, 27–29, 31–32, 40–44, 54, 56, 61, 64–70, 72, 74–76, 79–80, 87, 91, 95, 103–105, 107, 109, 111, 115, 117, 130, 138, 140, 147, 152–154, 157, 171, 173, 175–178, 184, 187, 189–190, 196, 199–204, 207, 213–214, 218, 221
see also hybridism
Spence, Gerry 161
Sproule, J. M. 43, 197–198

staff groups 58
Stalin, Joseph 39
Star Trek 147
Stockton, California 77
Strossen, Nadine 210
Students for a Democratic Society (SDS) 160
Sugarman, Josh 78

T

Tarrow, S. 38, 48, 50
Tartaro, J. P. 57
Tennessee 15, 19
Texas 19, 152
Time 8, 10–12, 16, 18, 21, 23, 25, 32, 41–42, 45, 56, 58, 60, 62, 77, 85, 90, 94, 100, 102–103, 115, 119, 126, 130, 138, 140–142, 144, 146–147, 150, 152, 154–157, 159–160, 165–166, 168, 171, 173, 181–182, 193–194, 198, 204, 206, 211, 213, 219, 221
Times Square 136
"tobacco" lobby 18
Today Show 141
Topperwein, Elizabeth 133
totalitarianism 39, 49
Truth, Sojourner 86
Tubman, Harriet 86
tyranny of the majority 36

U

Ulysses 210
Uncle Sam 79
undergraduates 59, 202
Unintended Consequences (Ross) 164
United Kingdom 128
United Nations 207
United States, anti-environmental regulation groups in 16–18, 32,

55, 110, 128, 138, 141, 146, 155, 162, 165, 189, 209
United States Attorney General's Office 72, 77, 84
United States Center for Disease Control (CDC) 93, 112, 128
United States Customs office 210
United States House of Representatives 19, 96
United States Justice Department 112
United States Revolver Association 165
United States Senate 90, 137, 145
United States Treasury Department
universities 44, 196
USA Shooting Sports 120
USA Today 62, 144

V

Vermont 165
Violence Policy Center 78
Virginia 72, 91, 182, 214
voluntary associations 7, 21, 31–33, 43–44, 108

W

Waco, Texas 152
waiting period, for firearm purchases 16–17, 152
Walker, J. L. 33–34, 58, 78
Walker, Robert 33–34, 58, 78
Wal-Mart 17
Wall Street Journal, The (WSJ) 9, 16, 62–64, 87, 101, 106, 180, 213
Washington Post, The (WP) 9, 16, 20, 62–64, 72, 76–78, 81, 84, 97, 103, 106, 103, 135, 213
Washington, D. C. 9, 16, 20, 48, 62–63, 100–101, 103, 108, 111, 134–135, 138, 140, 156, 182, 214
see also Beltway

Washington, Thomas L. 84
Weaver, D. H. 62, 193
Weber, Max 187, 204
White House, The 44–45, 73–74, 140
Wilhoit, G. C. 62, 193
Wilson, J. Q. 33
World Trade Organization protests 48
Wright, J. R. 18, 32, 44, 58, 65, 151, 203

Y

Yamamoto, Nelson 83
Young America's Foundation 140

Z

Zebra Killer 211

Other books published by Arktos:

Beyond Human Rights
by Alain de Benoist

Carl Schmitt Today
by Alain de Benoist

Manifesto for a European Renaissance
by Alain de Benoist & Charles Champetier

The Problem of Democracy
by Alain de Benoist

Germany's Third Empire
by Arthur Moeller van den Bruck

The Arctic Home in the Vedas
by Bal Gangadhar Tilak

Revolution from Above
by Kerry Bolton

The Fourth Political Theory
by Alexander Dugin

Hare Krishna in the Modern World
by Graham Dwyer & Richard J. Cole

Fascism Viewed from the Right
by Julius Evola

Metaphysics of War
by Julius Evola

Notes on the Third Reich
by Julius Evola

The Path of Cinnabar
by Julius Evola

Archeofuturism
by Guillaume Faye

Convergence of Catastrophes
by Guillaume Faye

Why We Fight
by Guillaume Faye

The WASP Question
by Andrew Fraser

War and Democracy
by Paul Gottfried

The Saga of the Aryan Race
by Porus Homi Havewala

Homo Maximus
by Lars Holger Holm

The Owls of Afrasiab
by Lars Holger Holm

De Naturae Natura
by Alexander Jacob

Fighting for the Essence
by Pierre Krebs

Can Life Prevail?
by Pentti Linkola

Guillaume Faye and the Battle of Europe
by Michael O'Meara

New Culture, New Right
by Michael O'Meara

The Ten Commandments of Propaganda
by Brian Anse Patrick

Morning Crafts
by Tito Perdue

A Handbook of Traditional Living
by Raido

The Agni and the Ecstasy
by Steven J. Rosen

The Jedi in the Lotus
by Steven J. Rosen

It Cannot Be Stormed
by Ernst von Salomon

The Outlaws
by Ernst von Salomon

Tradition & Revolution
by Troy Southgate

Against Democracy and Equality
by Tomislav Sunic

Nietzsche's Coming God
by Abir Taha

Generation Identity
by Markus Willinger

The Initiate: Journal of Traditional Studies
by David J. Wingfield (ed.)

Lightning Source UK Ltd.
Milton Keynes UK
UKOW05f1445061113

220546UK00001B/22/P